DAVID BUSCH'S

NIKON™ D60 GUIDE TO DIGITAL SLR PHOTOGRAPHY

David D. Busch

Course Technology PTR
A part of Cengage Learning

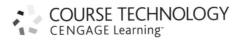
COURSE TECHNOLOGY
CENGAGE Learning™

Australia, Brazil, Japan, Korea, Mexico, Singapore, Spain, United Kingdom, United States

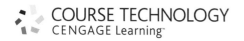
COURSE TECHNOLOGY
CENGAGE Learning™

David Busch's Nikon D60 Guide to Digital SLR Photography
David D. Busch

Publisher and General Manager, Course Technology PTR:
Stacy L. Hiquet

Associate Director of Marketing:
Sarah Panella

Manager of Editorial Services:
Heather Talbot

Marketing Manager:
Jordan Casey

Executive Editor:
Kevin Harreld

Project Editor:
Jenny Davidson

Technical Reviewer:
Michael D. Sullivan

PTR Editorial Services Coordinator:
Erin Johnson

Interior Layout Tech:
Bill Hartman

Cover Designer:
Mike Tanamachi

Indexer:
Larry Sweazy

Proofreader:
Sara Gullion

For product information and technology assistance, contact us at
Cengage Learning Customer & Sales Support Center, 1-800-354-9706

For permission to use material from this text or product, submit all requests online at **cengage.com/permissions**
Further permissions questions can be emailed to
permissionrequest@cengage.com

Nikon is a trademark of Nikon Corporation. All other trademarks are the property of their respective owners.

Library of Congress Control Number: 2008902419

ISBN-13: 978-1-59863-577-5

ISBN-10: 1-59863-577-8

Course Technology
25 Thomson Place
Boston, MA 02210
USA

Cengage Learning is a leading provider of customized learning solutions with office locations around the globe, including Singapore, the United Kingdom, Australia, Mexico, Brazil, and Japan. Locate your local office at:
international.cengage.com/region

Cengage Learning products are represented in Canada by Nelson Education, Ltd.

For your lifelong learning solutions, visit **courseptr.com**

Visit our corporate website at **cengage.com**

Printed in the United States of America
1 2 3 4 5 6 7 11 10 09

For Charlie Cervenak.

Charlie, I didn't know you for very long,
but it was long enough to appreciate how
enthusiasm for photography can energize a soul.

Acknowledgments

Once again thanks to the folks at Course Technology PTR, who recognized that a camera as popular as the Nikon D60 deserves in-depth full-color coverage at a price anyone can afford. Special thanks to executive editor Kevin Harreld, who always gives me the freedom to let my imagination run free with a topic, as well as my veteran production team including project editor Jenny Davidson and technical editor Mike Sullivan. Also thanks to Bill Hartman, layout; Larry Sweazy, indexing; Sara Gullion, proofreading; Mike Tanamachi, cover design; and my agent, Carole McClendon, who has the amazing ability to keep both publishers and authors happy.

About the Author

With more than a million books in print, **David D. Busch** is one of the best-selling authors of books on digital photography and imaging technology, and the originator of popular series like *David Busch's Pro Secrets* and *David Busch's Quick Snap Guides*. He has written six hugely successful guidebooks for Nikon digital SLR models, and five additional user guides for other camera models, as well as many popular books devoted to dSLRs, including *Mastering Digital SLR Photography, Second Edition* and *Digital SLR Pro Secrets*. As a roving photojournalist for more than 20 years, he illustrated his books, magazine articles, and newspaper reports with award-winning images. He's operated his own commercial studio, suffocated in formal dress while shooting weddings-for-hire, and shot sports for a daily newspaper and upstate New York college. His photos have been published in magazines as diverse as *Scientific American* and *Petersen's PhotoGraphic*, and his articles have appeared in *Popular Photography & Imaging, The Rangefinder, The Professional Photographer*, and hundreds of other publications. He's also reviewed dozens of digital cameras for CNet and *Computer Shopper*.

When About.com named its top five books on Beginning Digital Photography, debuting at the #1 and #2 slots were Busch's *Digital Photography All-In-One Desk Reference for Dummies* and *Mastering Digital Photography*. During the past year, he's had as many as five of his books listed in the Top 20 of Amazon.com's Digital Photography Bestseller list—simultaneously! Busch's 100-plus other books published since 1983 include bestsellers like *David Busch's Quick Snap Guide to Digital SLR Lenses*.

Busch earned top category honors in the Computer Press Awards the first two years they were given (for *Sorry About The Explosion* and *Secrets of MacWrite, MacPaint and MacDraw*), and he later served as Master of Ceremonies for the awards. Visit his website at http://www.nikonguides.com.

Contents

Chapter 2
Nikon D60 Roadmap   33

Chapter 3
Setting Up Your Nikon D60   65

Chapter 4
Getting the Right Exposure   149

Chapter 5
Advanced Shooting Tips for Your Nikon D60   171

Chapter 6
Working with Lenses   191

Chapter 7
Making Light Work for You   223

Chapter 8
Useful Software for the Nikon D60   253

Chapter 9
Nikon D60: Troubleshooting and Prevention   269

Glossary   295

Index   307

Preface

The Nikon D60 is Nikon's latest upgrade to its pace-setting super-compact digital SLR camera line launched by the introduction of the Nikon D40 in November 2006. Although easy to use, the D60 is packed with a meager 190-page black-and-white manual that is almost impossible for beginners and more experienced photographers alike to wade through. Everything is in there, but how do you find it? And what does it all *mean?* What you really need is a comprehensive guide that explains the purpose and function of every one of the D60's controls, how you should use them in specific situations, and why.

If you want a quick introduction to the D60's focus controls, flash synchronization options, how to choose lenses, or which exposure modes are best, this book is for you. If you can't decide on what basic settings to use with your camera because you can't figure out how changing ISO or white balance or focus defaults will affect your pictures, you need this guide. I won't talk down to you, either; this book isn't padded with dozens of pages of checklists telling you how to take a travel picture, a sports photo, or how to take a snapshot of your kids in overly simplistic terms. There are no recipes here. I give you all the information you need to cook up great photos on your own!

Introduction

Whether you're a veteran of my previous books or a new convert, I think you'll find this introduction to the D60 quite different from the other books on the market. When Nikon surprised many of us by introducing the D60 in January 2008, I scanned the new camera's list of features and realized that it deserved an entirely different approach than that offered by most so-called "guidebooks." Feedback from readers of my previous books has convinced me that a compact "field guide" doesn't really provide all the information needed to become proficient with a digital single lens reflex (dSLR) camera.

You don't need a book that devotes almost a third of its pages to little sections that provide the rudiments of shooting the most basic types of pictures. Even if you're a rank beginner, does it really help all that much to be told that you ought to use a fast shutter speed when shooting sports—you probably already have figured out that there are many different kinds of action situations when *slower* shutter speeds are superior (such as motor sports with spinning tires). But, don't worry, I provide this kind of information, too. I just don't waste dozens of pages on these basic techniques when they can be covered in the same pages that teach you enough about *photography* that you can apply to taking any kind of pictures you want. Instead of recipes, I'm going to emphasize the exciting things you can do with the Nikon D60 digital SLR. After a couple introductory chapters that help you get your bearings with this innovative camera, we're going to explore dSLR photography using a significant new tool.

Compared to offerings from other companies, the Nikon D60 has some significant advantages. For the broad range of cool features and capabilities it provides, the D60 is, first and foremost, *affordable.* Certainly, the sub-$700 price neighborhood is an important price point if you're in the early throes of passion for digital photography. But, you also need a full complement of features that won't impose serious limitations on your creativity.

In that vein, it's nice to know that the Nikon D60 is also *expandable,* thanks to the huge line of Nikon AF-S lenses, and a full line of close-up attachments and other accessories that have been developed for the D40/D40x and earlier Nikon cameras. You'll find that the Nikon D60 also includes tons of *very cool features,* such as the new sensor self-cleaning mode and the ability to make stop-motion movies right in the camera. There's a Retouch mode that allows you to fix up your pictures in the camera, and even create a "small picture" copy suitable for e-mailing.

I sincerely believe that this book is your best bet for learning how to use your new camera, and for learning how to use it well. If you're a Nikon D60 owner who's looking to learn more about how to use this great camera, you've probably already explored your options. There are DVDs and online tutorials—but who can learn how to use a camera by sitting in front of a television or computer screen? Do you want to watch a movie or click on HTML links, or do you want to go out and take photos with your camera? Videos and web pages are fun, but not the best answer.

Of course, there's always the manual furnished with the camera. It's compact and filled with information, but there's really very little in there about *why* you should use particular settings or features, and its organization may make it difficult to find what you need. Multiple cross-references may send you flipping back and forth between two or three sections of the book to find what you need. The basic manual is also hobbled by black-and-white line drawings and tiny monochrome pictures that aren't very good examples of what you can do.

As I mentioned earlier, I haven't been happy with the third-party guidebooks to Nikon cameras, either—especially those written for entry-level models like the D60. The existing books range from skimpy and illustrated by black-and-white photos to lushly illustrated in full color but too generic to do much good. Photography instruction is useful, but it needs to be related directly to the Nikon D60 as much as possible.

I've tried to make *David Busch's Nikon D60 Guide to Digital SLR Photography* different from your other D60 learn-up options. The roadmap sections use larger, color pictures to show you where all the buttons and dials are, and the explanations of what they do are longer and more comprehensive. Instead of the checklists devoted to general topics like "architectural photography" or "landscape photography," you'll find tips and techniques for using all the features of your Nikon D60 to take *any kind of picture* you want.

Nor is this book a lame rewriting of the manual that came with the camera. Some folks spend five minutes with a book like this one, spot some information that also appears in the original manual, and decide "Rehash!" without really understanding the differences. Yes, you'll find information here that is also in the owner's manual, such as the parameters you can enter when changing your D60's operation in the various menus. Basic descriptions—before I dig in and start providing in-depth tips and information—may also be vaguely similar. There are only so many ways you can say, for example, "Hold the shutter release down halfway to lock in exposure and focus."

But not *everything* in the manual is included in this book. I don't include a table of error messages, for instance, because their appearance is fairly rare to begin with, and I'd expect you to go grab the manual to look one up if an error occurs. Nor do I provide advice on how to store your camera, or a complete list of memory card capacities for various file formats. I want you to *use* your D60, not store it, and you can easily figure out the capacity of any freshly formatted memory card you own from the figure displayed on the top panel LCD. Thinking of buying a card with twice as many gigabytes as your current memory card? Multiply the figure you get with the old card by two; that will be close enough. Not *everything* should be included in a guidebook like this one.

David Busch's Nikon D60 Guide to Digital SLR Photography is aimed at both Nikon and dSLR veterans who want to learn how to use this new camera, as well as newcomers to digital photography and digital SLRs. Both groups can be overwhelmed by the options the D60 offers, while underwhelmed by the explanations they receive in their user's manual. The manuals are great if you already know what you don't know, and you can find an answer somewhere in a booklet arranged by menu listings and written by a camera vendor employee who last threw together instructions on how to operate a point-and-shoot digital camera.

Once you've read this book and are ready to learn more, I hope you pick up one of my other guides to digital SLR photography. If you've jumped right into the pool with the Nikon D60 as your first digital SLR, one of them may provide the kind of introductory material you need to get up to speed. Four of these dSLR guides are offered by Course Technology PTR, and each approaches topics from a different perspective. They include:

David Busch's Quick Snap Guide to Using Digital SLR Lenses
A bit overwhelmed by the features and controls of digital SLR lenses, and not quite sure when to use each type? This book explains lenses, their use, and lens technology in easy-to-access, two- and four-page spreads, each devoted to a different topic, such as depth-of-field, lens aberrations, or using zoom lenses. If you have a friend or significant other who is less versed in photography, but who wants to borrow and use your Nikon D60 from time to time, this book can save you a ton of explanation.

Quick Snap Guide to Digital SLR Photography
Consider this a prequel to the book you're holding in your hands. It, too, might make a good gift for a spouse or friend who may be using your D60, but who lacks even basic knowledge about digital photography, digital SLR photography, and Nikon photography. It serves as an introduction that summarizes the basic features of digital SLR cameras in general (not just the D60), and what settings to use and when, such as continuous autofocus/single autofocus, aperture/shutter priority, EV settings, and so forth. The guide also includes recipes for shooting the most common kinds of pictures, with step-by-step instructions for capturing effective sports photos, portraits, landscapes, and other types of images. (Here is where you will find those bullet-point checklists I've left out of *this* book.)

Mastering Digital SLR Photography, Second Edition
This book is an introduction to digital SLR photography, with nuts-and-bolts explanations of the technology, more in-depth coverage of settings, and whole chapters on the most common types of photography. While not specific to the Nikon D60, this book can show you how to get more from its capabilities.

Digital SLR Pro Secrets
This is my more advanced guide to dSLR photography with greater depth and detail about the topics you're most interested in. If you've already mastered the basics in *Mastering Digital SLR Photography*, this book will take you to the next level.

Who Are You?

When preparing a guidebook for a specific camera, it's always wise to consider exactly who will be reading the book. Indeed, thinking about the potential audience for *David Busch's Nikon D60 Guide to Digital SLR Photography* is what led me to taking the approach and format I use for this book. I realized that the needs of readers like you had to be addressed both from a functional level (what you will use the D60 for) as well as from a skill level (how much experience you may have with digital photography, dSLRs, or Nikon cameras specifically).

From a functional level, you probably fall into one of these categories:

- Professional photographers who understand photography and digital SLRs, and simply want to learn how to use the Nikon D60 as a backup camera, or as a camera for their personal "off-duty" use.

- Individuals who want to get better pictures, or perhaps transform their growing interest in photography into a full-fledged hobby or artistic outlet with a Nikon D60 and advanced techniques.

- Those who want to produce more professional-looking images for their personal or business website, and feel that the Nikon D60 will give them more control and capabilities.

- Small business owners with more advanced graphics capabilities who want to use the Nikon D60 to document or promote their business.

- Corporate workers who may or may not have photographic skills in their job descriptions, but who work regularly with graphics and need to learn how to use digital images taken with a Nikon D60 for reports, presentations, or other applications.

■ Professional webmasters with strong skills in programming (including Java, JavaScript, HTML, Perl, etc.) but little background in photography, but who realize that the D60 can be used for sophisticated photography.

■ Graphic artists and others who already may be adept in image editing with Photoshop or another program, and who may already be using a film SLR (Nikon or otherwise), but who need to learn more about digital photography and the special capabilities of the D60 dSLR.

Addressing your needs from a skills level can be a little trickier, because the D60 is such a great camera that a full spectrum of photographers will be buying it, from absolute beginners who have never owned a digital camera before up to the occasional professional with years of shooting experience who will be using the Nikon D60 as a backup body. (I have to admit I tend to carry my D60 with me everywhere, even if I intend to take most of my photos with another camera, such as my Nikon D300.)

Before tackling this book, it would be helpful for you to understand the following:

■ **What a digital SLR is:** It's a camera that generally shows an optical (not LCD) view of the picture that's being taken through the (interchangeable) lens that actually takes the photo, thanks to a mirror that reflects an image to a viewfinder, but flips up out of the way to allow the sensor to be exposed. Some dSLRs (like the Nikon D300), also have a *live view* option that flips up the mirror to allow a real-time display on the LCD.

■ **How digital photography differs from film:** The image is stored not on film (which I call the *first* write-once optical media), but on a memory card as pixels that can be transferred to your computer, and then edited, corrected, and printed without the need for chemical processing.

■ **What the basic tools of correct exposure are:** Don't worry if you don't understand these; I'll explain them later in this book. But if you already know something about shutter speed, aperture, and ISO sensitivity, you'll be ahead of the game. If not, you'll soon learn that shutter speed determines the amount of time the sensor is exposed to incoming light; the f/stop or aperture is like a valve that governs the quantity of light that can flow through the lens; the sensor's sensitivity (ISO setting) controls how easily the sensor responds to light. All three factors can be varied individually and proportionately to produce a picture that is properly exposed (neither too light nor too dark).

It's tough to provide something for everybody, but I am going to try to address the needs of each of the following groups and skill levels:

- **Digital photography newbies:** If you've used only point-and-shoot digital cameras, or have worked only with non-SLR film cameras, you're to be congratulated for selecting one of the very best entry-level digital SLRs available as your first dSLR camera. This book can help you understand the controls and features of your D60, and lead you down the path to better photography with your camera. I'll provide all the information you need, but if you want to do some additional reading for extra credit, you can also try one of the other books I mentioned earlier. They complement this book well.

- **Advanced point-and-shooters moving on up:** There are some quite sophisticated pocket-sized digital cameras available, including those with many user-definable options and settings, so it's possible you are already a knowledgeable photographer, even though you're new to the world of the digital SLR. You've recognized the limitations of the point-and-shoot camera: even the best of them have more noise at higher sensitivity (ISO) settings than a camera like the Nikon D60; the speediest still have an unacceptable delay between the time you press the shutter and the photo is actually taken; even a non-interchangeable super-zoom camera with 12X to 20X magnification often won't focus close enough, include an aperture suitable for low-light photography, or take in the really wide view you must have. Interchangeable lenses and other accessories available for the Nikon D60 are another one of the reasons you moved up. Because you're an avid photographer already, you should pick up the finer points of using the D60 from this book with no trouble.

- **Film SLR veterans new to the digital world:** You understand photography, you know about f/stops and shutter speeds, and thrive on interchangeable lenses. If you have used a newer film SLR, it probably has lots of electronic features already, including autofocus and sophisticated exposure metering. Perhaps you've even been using a Nikon film SLR and understand many of the available accessories that work with both film and digital cameras. All you need is information on using digital-specific features, working with the D60 itself, and how to match—and exceed—the capabilities of your film camera with your new Nikon D60.

- **Seasoned dSLR users broadening their experience to include the D60:** Perhaps you started out with the Nikon D70 back in 2004, or a D100 before that. It's very likely that some of you used the 6-megapixel Nikon D40 before the bug to advance to more megapixels bit you. You may have used a digital SLR from Canon or another vendor and are making the switch. You understand basic photography, and want to learn more. And, most of all, you want to transfer the skills you already have to the Nikon D60, as quickly and seamlessly as possible.

■ **Pro photographers and other advanced shooters:** I expect my most discerning readers will be those who already have extensive experience with Nikon intermediate and pro-level cameras. I may not be able to teach you folks much about photography. But, even so, an amazing number of D60 cameras have been purchased by those who feel it is a good complement to their favorite advanced dSLR. Others (like myself) own a camera like the Nikon D300 and find that the D60 fills a specific niche and can function as a terrific backup camera as well; because the D60's 10-megapixel images are often just as good as those produced by more "advanced" models. You pros and semi-pros, despite your depth of knowledge, should find this book useful for learning about the features the D60 has that your previous cameras lack or implement in a different way.

Who Am I?

After spending years as the world's most successful unknown author, I've become slightly less obscure in the past few years, thanks to a horde of camera guidebooks and other photographically oriented tomes. You may have seen my photography articles in *Popular Photography & Imaging* magazine. I've also written about 2,000 articles for magazines like *Petersen's PhotoGraphic* (which is now defunct through no fault of my own), plus *The Rangefinder, Professional Photographer*, and dozens of other photographic publications. But, first, and foremost, I'm a photojournalist and made my living in the field until I began devoting most of my time to writing books. Although I love writing, I'm happiest when I'm out taking pictures, which is why I took 14 days late in 2007 for a solo visit to Spain—not as a tourist, because I've been to Spain no less than a dozen times in the past—but solely to take photographs of the people, landscapes, and monuments that I've grown to love.

Like all my digital photography books, this one was written by a Nikon devotee with an incurable photography bug. My first Nikon SLR was a venerable Nikon F back in the 1960s, and I've owned most of the newer digital models since then. (My current stable consists of a Nikon D3, D2x, D200, D300, D40, and D70—converted to full-time infrared use—in addition to my D60. I had to sell my D50 and D80 to make room for more lenses.)

Over the years, I've worked as a sports photographer for an Ohio newspaper and for an upstate New York college. I've operated my own commercial studio and photo lab, cranking out product shots on demand and then printing a few hundred glossy 8 × 10s on a tight deadline for a press kit. I've served as a photo-posing instructor for a modeling agency. People have actually paid me to shoot their weddings and immortalize them with portraits. I even prepared press kits and articles on photography as a PR consultant for a large Rochester, N.Y., company, which shall remain nameless. My trials and travails with imaging and computer technology have made their way into print in book form an alarming number of times, including a few dozen on scanners and photography.

Like you, I love photography for its own merits, and I view technology as just another tool to help me get the images I see in my mind's eye. But, also like you, I had to master this technology before I could apply it to my work. This book is the result of what I've learned, and I hope it will help you master your Nikon D60 digital SLR, too.

As I write this, I'm currently in the throes of upgrading my website, which you can find at www.nikonguides.com, adding tutorials and information about my other books. There's a lot of information about the Nikon D300 right now, but I'll be adding tips and recommendations about the Nikon D60 (including a list of equipment and accessories that I can't live without) in the next few months. I hope you'll stop by for a visit.

1

Setting Up Your Nikon D60

The Nikon D60 is considerably more camera than any pocket-sized point-and-shoot model, but Nikon has retained the "turn it on and shoot" ease of operation so you can, with about 60 seconds' worth of instruction, go out and begin taking great pictures.

Try it. Insert a memory card and mount the lens (if you bought the D60 at a store, they probably did that for you). Charge the battery and insert it into the camera. Remove the lens cap, turn the camera on (the button's concentric with the shutter release button), and then set the big ol' dial on top to the green AUTO icon. Point the D60 at something interesting and press the shutter release. Presto! A pretty good picture will pop up on the color LCD on the back of the camera. Wasn't that easy?

But if you purchased this book, you're probably not going to be satisfied with pretty good photos. You want to shoot *incredible* images. The D60 can do that, too. All you need is this book and some practice. The first step is to familiarize yourself with your camera. The first three chapters of this book will take care of that. Then, as you gain experience and skills, you'll want to learn more about how to improve your exposures, fine-tune the color, or use the essential tools of photography, such as electronic flash and available light. You'll want to learn how to choose and use lenses, too. All that information can be found in the second part of this book. The Nikon D60 is not only easy to use, it's easy to *learn* to use.

I'm going to divide my introduction to the Nikon D60 into three parts. The first part will cover what you absolutely *need* to know just to get started using the camera (you'll find that in this chapter). The second part offers a more comprehensive look at what you *should* know about the camera and its controls to use its features effectively (that'll be found in Chapter 2). Finally, you'll learn how to make key settings using the menu system, so you'll be able to fine-tune and tweak the D60 to operate exactly the way you want, in Chapter 3. While you probably should master everything in the first two chapters right away, you can take more time to learn about the settings described in Chapter 3, because you won't need to use all those options right away. I've included everything about menus and settings in that chapter so you'll find what you need, when you need it, all in one place.

Some of you may have owned a Nikon digital SLR before. Perhaps you owned a Nikon D50 or D70/D70s for some time and were eager to upgrade to a more modern 10-megapixel model with more features. It's even possible you owned a Nikon D40, enjoyed using it, and wanted more megapixels and some of the added features the D60 offers, such as automatic sensor cleaning and the handy shake-resistant (*vibration reduction*) lens packaged in the D60 kit. A few of you may even be someone like me, who uses a more advanced Nikon dSLR, such as the D300, as a "main" camera, but finds the super-compact D60 an alluring walk-about camera and backup.

If you fall into any of those categories, you may be able to skim through this chapter quickly and move on to the two that follow. The next few pages are designed to get your camera fired up and ready for shooting as quickly as possible. If you're new to digital SLRs, Nikon dSLRs, or even digital photography, you'll want to read through this intro-duction more carefully. After all, the Nikon D60 is not a point-and-shoot camera, although, as I said, you can easily set it up in fully automated Auto mode, or use the semi-automated Program exposure mode and a basic autofocus setting for easy capture of grab shots. But, if you want a little more control over your shooting, you'll need to know more. So I'm going to provide a basic pre-flight checklist that you need to com-plete before you really spread your wings and take off. You won't find a lot of detail in this chapter. Indeed, I'm going to tell you just what you absolutely *must* understand, accompanied by some interesting tidbits that will help you become acclimated to your D60. I'll go into more depth and even repeat some of what I explain here in later chap-ters, so you don't have to memorize everything you see. Just relax, follow a few easy steps, and then go out and begin taking your best shots—ever.

First Things First

The Nikon D60 comes in an impressive gold box filled with stuff, including connect-ing cords, booklets, a CD, and lots of paperwork. The most important components are the camera and lens (unlike some other Nikon models, the D60 is most often sold in a kit with a lens), battery, battery charger, and, if you're the nervous type, the neck strap. You'll also need a Secure Digital memory card, as one is not included. If you purchased your D60 from a camera shop, as I did, the store personnel probably attached the neck strap for you, ran through some basic operational advice that you've already forgotten, tried to sell you a Secure Digital card, and then, after they'd given you all the help you could absorb, sent you on your way with a handshake.

Perhaps you purchased your D60 from one of those mass merchandisers that also sell washing machines and vacuum cleaners. In that case, you might have been sent on your way with only the handshake, or, maybe, not even that if you resisted the hard-sell efforts to sell you an extended warranty. You save a few bucks at the big-box stores, but you don't get the personal service a professional photo retailer provides. It's your choice. There's a third alternative, of course. You might have purchased your camera from a mail order or Internet source, and your D60 arrived in a big brown (or purple/red or yellow/red) truck. Your only interaction when you took possession of your camera was to scrawl your signature on an electronic clipboard.

In all three cases, the first thing to do is to carefully unpack the camera and double-check the contents with the checklist on one end of the box, helpfully designated under the [**Supplied Accessories**] bracketed heading. While this level of setup detail may seem as superfluous as the instructions on a bottle of shampoo, checking the contents *first* is always a good idea. No matter who sells a camera, it's common to open boxes, use a particular camera for a demonstration, and then repack the box without replacing all the pieces and parts afterwards. Someone might actually have helpfully checked out your camera on your behalf—and then mispacked the box. It's better to know *now* that something is missing so you can seek redress immediately, rather than discover two months from now that the video cable you thought you'd never use (but now *must* have) was never in the box. I once purchased a brand-new Nikon dSLR kit that was supposed to include a second focusing screen; it wasn't in the box, but because I discovered the deficiency right away, the dealer ordered a replacement for me post haste.

At a minimum, the box should hold the following:

- **Nikon D60 digital camera.** It almost goes without saying that you should check out the camera immediately, making sure the color LCD on the back isn't scratched or cracked, the Secure Digital and battery doors open properly, and, when a charged battery is inserted and lens mounted, the camera powers up and reports for duty. Out-of-the-box defects like these are rare, but they can happen. It's probably more common that your dealer played with the camera or, perhaps, it was a customer return. That's why it's best to buy your D60 from a retailer you trust to supply a factory-fresh camera.

- **Rechargeable Li-ion battery EN-EL9.** You'll need to charge this 7.4V, 1000mAh (milliampere hour) battery before using it. I'll offer instructions later in this chapter.

- **Quick charger MH-23.** This charger is required to vitalize the EN-EL9 battery.

- **Video cable EG-D100.** Use this cable to connect your D60 to a standard definition (analog) television through the set's yellow RCA video jack when you want to view the camera's output on a larger screen.

- **USB cable UC-E4.** You can use this cable to transfer photos from the camera to your computer (I don't recommend that because direct transfer uses a lot of battery power), to upload and download settings between the camera and your computer (highly recommended), and to operate your camera remotely using Nikon Camera Control Pro software (not included in the box). This cable is a standard one that works with the majority of digital cameras—Nikon and otherwise—so if you already own one, you now have a spare.

- **Neck strap.** Nikon provides you with a neck strap emblazoned with your camera model. It's not very adjustable, but it is useful for showing off to your friends exactly which nifty new camera you bought. I never attach the Nikon strap to my cameras (although once I put a D3 strap on a Nikon D40 as a jest), and instead opt for a more serviceable strap from Op-Tech (www.optechusa.com) or Upstrap (www.upstrap-pro.com). A typical Op-Tech strap is shown in Figure 1.1 attached to my *other* dSLR. I prefer it because it can more easily be adjusted in length, and it has better shoulder padding.

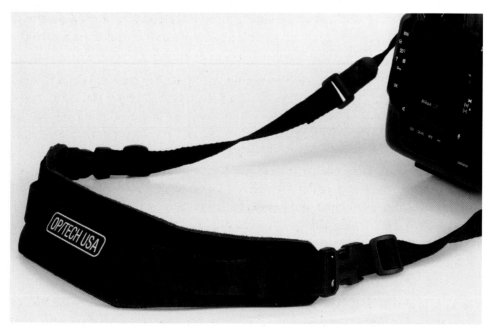

Figure 1.1
Third-party neck straps like this Op-Tech model are often preferable to the Nikon-supplied strap.

- **BF-1A body cap/rear lens cap.** The body cap keeps dust from infiltrating your camera when a lens is not mounted. Always carry a body cap (and rear lens cap, also supplied with the D60) in your camera bag for those times when you need to have the camera bare of optics for more than a minute or two. (That usually happens when repacking a bag efficiently for transport, or when you are carrying an extra body or two for backup.) The body cap/lens cap nest together for compact storage.

- **DK-6 rubber eyecup.** This is the square rubber eyecup that comes installed on the D60. It slides on and off the viewfinder.

- **DK-5 eyepiece cap.** This small piece can be clipped over the viewfinder window to prevent strong light sources from entering the viewing system when your eye is not pressed up against it, potentially affecting exposure measurement. That can be a special problem when the camera is mounted on a tripod, because additional illumination from the rear can make its way to the 420-segment CCD that interprets light reaching the focusing screen. I pack this widget away to keep from losing it. As a practical matter, you'll never find it when you really need it, and covering the viewfinder with your hand (hover *near* the viewfinder window rather than touch it, to avoid shaking a tripod-mounted camera) works almost as well.

- **BS-1 accessory shoe cover.** This is a sliding plastic piece that fits into the accessory shoe on top of the camera, and protects its contents from damage. You can remove it (and probably lose it) when you attach an optional external electronic flash to the shoe. I always, without fail, tuck it into the same place each time (in my case, my right front pants pocket), and have yet to lose one.

- **User manual.** Even if you have this book, you'll probably want to check the user's guide that Nikon provides, if only to confirm the actual nomenclature for some obscure accessory, or to double-check an error code. Google "Nikon D60 manual PDF" to find a downloadable, non-printable version that you can store on your laptop, a CD-ROM, or other media in case you want to access this reference when the paper version isn't handy. If you have an old Secure Digital card that's too small to be usable on a modern dSLR (I still have some 128MB and 256MB cards), you can store the PDF on that. But an even better choice is to put the manual on a low-capacity USB "thumb" drive, which you can buy for less than $10. You'll then be able to access the reference anywhere you are, because you can always find someone with a computer that has a USB port and Adobe Acrobat Reader available. You might not be lucky enough to locate a computer with a Secure Digital reader.

- **Quick guide.** This little booklet tucked away in the camera's paperwork offers a reasonable summary of the Nikon D60's basic commands and settings, and can be stowed in your camera bag more easily than a "field guide" or even this book.

- **Software CD-ROM.** Here you'll find the Nikon Software Suite, which includes various drivers required by some operating systems; Nikon Transfer (to move your files from camera or memory card to your computer); Nikon ViewNX (a useful image management program); as well as various third-party utilities (some of which you may already have installed on your computer), such as DirectX9, QuickTime, and Kodak EasyShare software. I'll cover all the Nikon software offerings later in this book.

- **Warranty and registration card.** Don't lose these! You can register your Nikon D60 by mail or online (in the USA, the URL is www.nikonusa.com/register) and may need the information in this paperwork (plus the purchase receipt/invoice from your retailer) should you require Nikon service support.

Don't bother rooting around in the box for anything beyond what I've listed previously. There are a few things Nikon classifies as optional accessories, even though you (and I) might consider some of them essential. Here's a list of what you *don't* get in the box, but might want to think about as an impending purchase. I'll list them roughly in the order of importance:

- **Secure Digital card.** First-time digital camera buyers are sometimes shocked that their new tool doesn't come with a memory card. Why should it? The manufacturer doesn't have the slightest idea of how much storage you require, or whether you want a slow/inexpensive card or one that's faster/more expensive, so why should they pack one in the box and charge you for it?

- **Extra EN-EL9 battery.** Even though you might get 500 to more than 1,000 shots from a single battery, it's easy to exceed that figure in a few hours of shooting sports at 3 fps. Batteries can unexpectedly fail, too, or simply lose their charge from sitting around unused for a week or two. Buy an extra (I own four, in total), keep it charged, and free your mind from worry.

- **Add-on speedlight.** One of the best uses for your Nikon D60's built-in electronic flash is as a remote trigger for an off-camera speedlight. Your built-in flash can function as the main illumination for your photo, or be softened and used to fill in shadows. But, you'll have to own one or more external flash units to gain that flexibility. If you do much flash photography at all, consider an add-on speedlight as an important accessory.

- **Wireless Remote Control ML-L3.** Use this infrared trigger (see Figure 1.2) to take a picture without the need to touch the camera itself. In a pinch, you can use the D60's self-timer to minimize vibration when triggering the camera. But when you want to take a photo at the exact moment you desire (and not when the self-timer happens to trip), or need to eliminate all possibility of human-induced camera shake, you need this infrared control.

Figure 1.2
The Nikon
Wireless
Remote
Control
ML-L3 lets
you trigger
your camera
remotely.

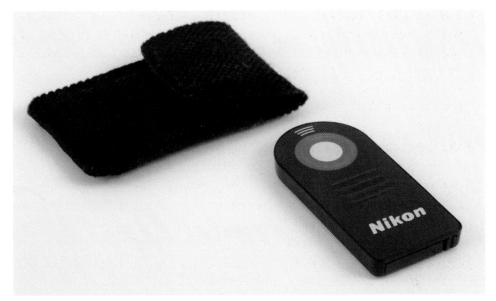

■ **AC Adapter EH-5a/Power Connector EP-4.** These two optional devices are used together to power the Nikon D60 independently of the batteries. There are several typical situations where this capability can come in handy: when you're cleaning the sensor manually and want to totally eliminate the possibility that a lack of juice will cause the fragile shutter and mirror to spring to life during the process; when indoors shooting tabletop photos, portraits, class pictures, and so forth for hours on end; when using your D60 for remote shooting as well as time-lapse photography; for extensive review of images on your television; or for file transfer to your computer. These all use prodigious amounts of power, which can be provided by this AC adapter. (Beware of power outages and blackouts when cleaning your sensor, however!)

■ **DR-6 right-angle viewer.** Used with the Nikon Eyepiece Adapter DK-22, it fastens in place of the standard square rubber eyecup and provides a 90-degree view for framing and composing your image at right angles to the original viewfinder. It's useful for low-level (or high-level) shooting. (Or, maybe, shooting around corners!)

■ **SC-28 TTL flash cord.** Allows using Nikon speedlights off-camera, while retaining all the automated features.

■ **SC-29 TTL flash cord.** Similar to the SC-28, this unit has its own AF-assist lamp, which can provide extra illumination for the D60's autofocus system in dim light (which, not coincidentally, is when you'll probably be using an electronic flash).

- **Nikon Capture NX software.** Nikon's NEF (Raw) conversion and image tweaking software is an extra-cost option that most D60 owners won't need until they progress into extensive image editing. I'll describe this utility's functions in Chapter 8.

- **Camera Control Pro 2 software.** This is the utility you'll use to operate your camera remotely from your computer. Nikon charges extra for this software, too, but you'll find it invaluable if you're hiding near a tethered, tripod-mounted camera while shooting, say, close-ups of hummingbirds. There are lots of applications for remote shooting, and you'll need Camera Control Pro to operate your camera.

Initial Setup

Once you've unpacked and inspected your camera, the initial setup of your Nikon D60 is fast and easy. Basically, you just need to charge the battery, attach a lens, and insert a Secure Digital card. I'll address each of these steps separately, but if you already are confident you can manage these setup tasks without further instructions, feel free to skip this section entirely. I realize that some readers are ambitious, if inexperienced, and should, at the minimum, skim the contents of the next section, because I'm going to list a few options that you might not be aware of.

Mastering the Multi-Selector

I'll be saving descriptions of most of the controls used with the Nikon D60 until Chapter 2, which provides a complete "roadmap" of the camera's buttons and dials and switches. However, you may need to perform a few tasks during this initial setup process, and most of them will require the Menu button and the multi-selector pad. The Menu button is easy to find: it's located to the left of the LCD, the second button from the top. It requires almost no explanation; when you want to access a menu, press it. To exit most menus, press it again.

The multi-selector pad may remind you of the similar control found on many point-and-shoot cameras, and other digital SLRs. It consists of a thumbpad-sized button with indentations at the North, South, East, and West positions, plus a button in the center marked "OK." (See Figure 1.3.)

The multi-selector on the D60 functions slightly differently than its counterpart on some other cameras. For example, some point-and-shoot models assign a function, such as white balance or ISO setting, to one of the directional buttons (usually in conjunction with a function key of some sort). The use of the multi-selector varies, even within the Nikon dSLR line up. For example, many Nikon digital SLRs, such as the Nikon D50/D70/D80 have no center button in the multi-selector at all. (Their OK/Enter button is located elsewhere.) Other Nikon cameras (such as the D300 and D3) allow assigning a function of your choice to the multi-selector center button.

Figure 1.3
The multi-selector pad has four directional buttons for navigating up/down/left/right, and an OK button to confirm your selection.

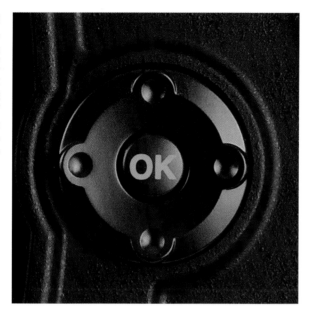

With the D60 (as well as the D40/D40x) the multi-selector is used exclusively for navigation, for example, to navigate among menus on the LCD or to choose one of the three focus points, to advance or reverse display of a series of images during picture review, or to change the kind of photo information displayed on the screen. The OK button is used to confirm your choices.

So, from time to time in this chapter (and throughout this book) I'll be referring to the multi-selector and its left/right/up/down buttons, and center OK button.

Setting the Clock

It's likely that your Nikon D60's internal clock hasn't been set to your local time, so you may need to do that first. If so, the flashing CLOCK indicator on the color LCD will be the giveaway. You'll find complete instructions for setting the four options for the date/time (time zone, actual date and time, the date format, and whether you want the D60 to conform to Daylight Savings Time) in Chapter 3. However, if you think you can handle this step without instruction, press the Menu button to the left of the LCD, and then use the multi-selector to scroll down to the Setup menu (it's marked with a wrench icon), press the multi-selector button to the right, and then press the down button to scroll down to World Time and press the right button again. The options will appear on the screen that appears next. Keep in mind that you'll need to reset your camera's internal clock from time to time, as it is not 100 percent accurate. Of course, your camera will not explode if the internal clock is inaccurate, but your images will have the wrong time stamped on them.

Battery Included

Your Nikon D60 is a sophisticated hunk of machinery and electronics, but it needs a charged battery to function, so rejuvenating the EN-EL9 lithium-ion battery pack furnished with the camera should be your first step. A fully charged power source should be good for a minimum of 500 shots, based on standard tests defined by the Camera & Imaging Products Association (CIPA) document DC-002. In the real world, of course, the life of the battery will depend on how often you review the shots you've taken on the LCD screen, how many pictures you take with the built-in flash, and many other factors. You'll want to keep track of how many pictures *you* are able to take in your own typical circumstances, and use that figure as a guideline, instead.

A BATTERY AND A SPARE

I always recommend purchasing Nikon brand batteries (for about $40) over less-expensive third-party packs, even though the $30 substitute batteries may offer more capacity at a lower price (some top the 1,000 mAh offered by the Nikon battery). My reasoning is that it doesn't make sense to save $10 on a component for a sophisticated camera, especially since batteries have been known to fail in potentially harmful ways. You need only look as far as Nikon's own recall of its earlier EN-EL3 batteries, which forced the company to ship out thousands of free replacement cells. You're unlikely to get the same support from a third-party battery supplier that sells under a half-dozen or more different brand names, and may not even have an easy way to get the word out that a recall has been issued.

If your pictures are important to you, always have at least one spare battery available, and make sure it is an authentic Nikon product.

All rechargeable batteries undergo some degree of self-discharge just sitting idle in the camera or in the original packaging. Lithium-ion power packs of this type typically lose a few percent of their charge every day, even when the camera isn't turned on. Li-ion cells lose their power through a chemical reaction that continues when the camera is switched off. So, it's very likely that the battery purchased with your camera is at least partially pooped out, so you'll want to revive it before going out for some serious shooting.

Charging the Battery

When the battery is inserted into the MH-23 charger properly (it's impossible to insert it incorrectly), a Charge light begins flashing, and remains flashing until the status lamp glows steadily indicating that charging is finished. (See Figure 1.4.) When the battery is charged, slide the latch on the bottom of the camera and ease the battery in, as shown in Figure 1.5.

Figure 1.4
The flashing status light will illuminate while the battery is being charged.

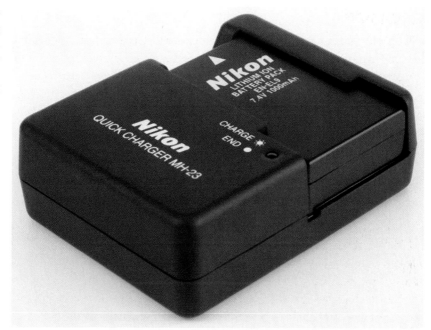

Figure 1.5
Insert the battery in the camera; it only fits one way.

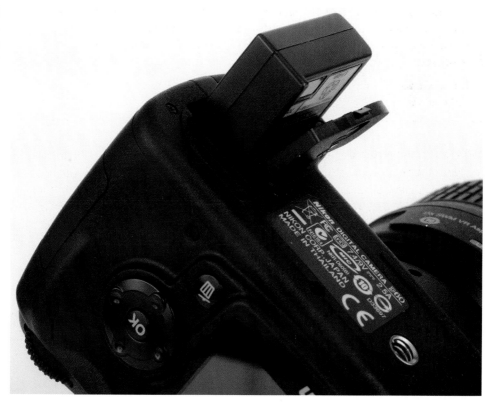

Final Steps

Your Nikon D60 is almost ready to fire up and shoot. You'll need to select and mount a lens, adjust the viewfinder for your vision, and insert a Secure Digital card. Each of these steps is easy, and if you've used any Nikon before, you already know exactly what to do. I'm going to provide a little extra detail for those of you who are new to the Nikon or SLR worlds.

Mounting the Lens

As you'll see, my recommended lens mounting procedure emphasizes protecting your equipment from accidental damage and minimizing the intrusion of dust. If your D60 has no lens attached, select the lens you want to use and loosen (but do not remove) the rear lens cap. I generally place the lens I am planning to mount vertically in a slot in my camera bag, where it's protected from mishaps, but ready to pick up quickly. By loosening the rear lens cap, you'll be able to lift it off the back of the lens at the last instant, so the rear element of the lens is covered until then.

After that, remove the body cap by pressing the release button next to the lens mount, and rotating the cap towards the release button. You should always mount the body cap when there is no lens on the camera, because it helps keep dust out of the interior of the camera. (While the D60's automatic sensor-cleaning mechanism works fine, the less dust it has to contend with, the better.) The body cap also protects the camera's innards from damage caused by intruding objects (including your fingers, if you're not cautious).

Once the body cap has been removed, remove the rear lens cap from the lens, set it aside, and then mount the lens on the camera by matching the alignment indicator on the lens barrel with the white dot on the camera's lens mount. (See Figure 1.6.) Rotate the lens toward the shutter release until it seats securely. Some lenses are trickier to mount than others, especially telephoto lenses with special collars for attaching the lens itself to a tripod.

Set the focus mode switch on the lens to AF or M/A (Autofocus). If the lens hood is bayoneted on the lens in the reversed position (which makes the lens/hood combination more compact for transport), twist it off and remount with the "petals" (if present) facing outward. (See Figure 1.7.) A lens hood protects the front of the lens from accidental bumps, and reduces flare caused by extraneous light arriving at the front of the lens from outside the picture area.

Adjusting Diopter Correction

Those of us with less than perfect eyesight can often benefit from a little optical correction in the viewfinder. Your contact lenses or glasses may provide all the correction you need, but if you are a glasses wearer and want to use the D60 without your glasses,

Figure 1.6
Match the indicator on the lens with the white dot on the camera mount to properly align the lens with the bayonet mount.

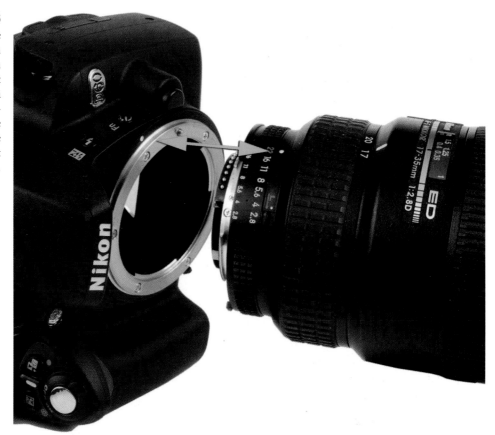

Figure 1.7
A lens hood protects the lens from extraneous light and accidental bumps.

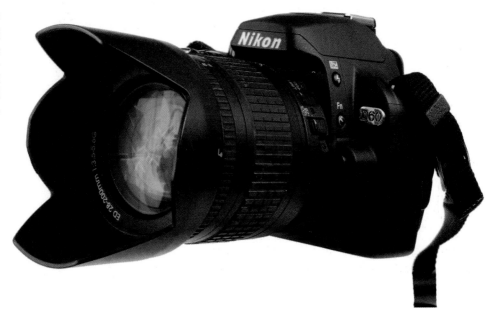

you can take advantage of the camera's built-in diopter adjustment, which can be varied from −1.7 to +0.5 correction. Press the shutter release halfway to illuminate the indicators in the viewfinder, then slide the diopter adjustment switch next to the viewfinder up or down (see Figure 1.8) while looking through the viewfinder until the indicators appear sharp. Should the available correction be insufficient, Nikon offers nine different Diopter-Adjustment Viewfinder Correction lenses for the viewfinder window, ranging from −5 to +3, at a cost of $15–$20 each.

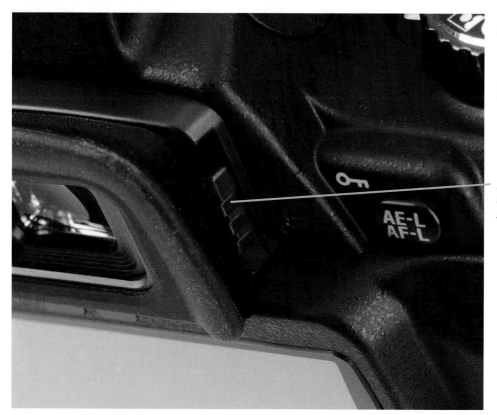

Figure 1.8
Viewfinder diopter correction from −1.7 to +0.5 can be dialed in.

Diopter correction slider

Inserting a Secure Digital Card

You've probably set up your D60 so you can't take photos without a Secure Digital card inserted. (There is a **No memory card** entry, Custom Setting menu **CSM #6** that enables/disables shutter release functions when a memory card is absent—learn about that in Chapter 3). So, your final step will be to insert a Secure Digital card. Slide the cover on the right side of the camera towards the back, and then open it. (You should only remove the memory card when the camera is switched off, or, at the very least, the yellow-green card access light [just to the right of the LCD and "trash can" icon on the back of the camera] that indicates the D60 is writing to the card is not illuminated.)

MORE ABOUT CSM OPTIONS IN CHAPTER 3

You'll find a complete list of Custom Setting menu options and parameters in Chapter 3.

Insert the memory card with the label facing the back of the camera oriented so the edge with the gold edge connectors goes into the slot first. (See Figure 1.9.) Close the door, and, if this is your first use of the card, format it (described next). When you want to remove the memory card later, press the card inwards, and it will pop right out.

Formatting a Memory Card

There are three ways to create a blank Secure Digital card for your D60, and two of them are at least partially wrong. Here are your options, both correct and incorrect:

■ **Transfer (move) files to your computer.** When you transfer (rather than copy) all the image files to your computer from the Secure Digital card (either using a direct cable transfer or with a card reader, as described later in this chapter), the old image files are erased from the card, leaving the card blank. Theoretically. Unfortunately, this method does *not* remove files that you've labeled as Protected (by pressing the Protect button to the right of the viewfinder window [it's marked with a key icon] while viewing the image on the LCD), nor does it identify and lock out parts of your SD card that have become corrupted or unusable since the last time you formatted the card. Therefore, I recommend always formatting the card, rather than simply moving the image files, each time you want to make a blank card. The only exception is when you *want* to leave the protected/unerased images on the card for awhile longer, say, to share with friends, family, and colleagues.

■ **(Don't) Format in your computer.** With the SD card inserted in a card reader or card slot in your computer, you can use Windows or Mac OS to reformat the memory card. Don't! The operating system won't necessarily arrange the structure of the card the way the D60 likes to see it (in computer terms, an incorrect *file system* may be installed). The only way to ensure that the card has been properly formatted for your camera is to perform the format in the camera itself. The only exception to this rule is when you have a seriously corrupted memory card that your camera refuses to format. Sometimes it is possible to revive such a corrupted card by allowing the operating system to reformat it first, then trying again in the camera.

■ **Setup menu format.** To use the recommended methods to format a memory card, press the **Menu** button, use the up/down buttons of the multi-selector (that thumb-pad-sized control to the right of the LCD) to choose the **Setup** menu (which is represented by that wrench icon), navigate to the **Format memory card** entry with the right button of the multi-selector, and select **Yes** from the screen that appears. Press **OK** (in the center of the multi-selector pad) to begin the format process.

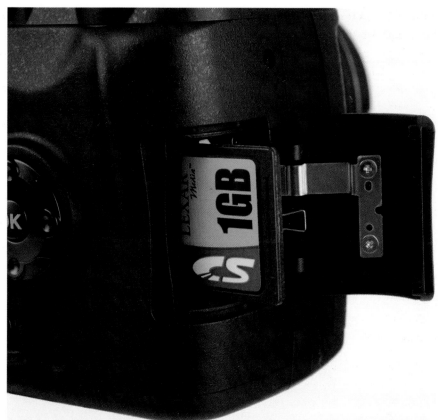

Figure 1.9
The Secure Digital card is inserted with the label facing the back of the camera.

HOW MANY SHOTS?

The D60 provides a fairly accurate estimate of the number of shots remaining on the LCD, as well as at the lower-right edge of the viewfinder display when the display is active. (Tap the shutter release button to activate it.)

It is only an estimate, because the actual number will vary, depending on the capacity of your memory card, the file format(s) you've selected (more on those later), and the content of the image itself. (Some photos may contain large areas that can be more efficiently squeezed down to a smaller size.)

For example, a 1GB card can hold about 133 shots in the format known as JPEG Fine at the D60's maximum resolution (Large) format; 260 shots using the Normal JPEG setting; or 503 shots with Basic JPEG setting. When numbers exceed 1,000, the D60 displays a figure and decimal point, followed by a K superscript, so that 1,900 shots (or thereabouts) is represented by [1.9]^K on the LCD and viewfinder.

Table 1.1 shows the typical number of shots you can expect using a humongous 8GB SD memory card (which I expect will be a popular size card among D60 users as prices continue to plummet during the life of this book). All figures are by actual count with my own 8GB SD card. Take those numbers and cut them in half if you're using a 4GB SD card; multiply by 25 percent if you're using a 2GB card, or by 12.5 percent if you're working with a 1GB SD card. (You can use the Shooting menu's Image Quality option to change the file/formats in column 1, and to change the image sizes in columns 2, 3, and, 4, or change either value using the Quick Settings display, described next under Release Modes.)

Table 1.1 Typical Shots with an 8GB Memory Card

	Large	Medium	Small
JPEG Fine	1,000	1,800	4,000
JPEG Normal	2,000	3,500	7,300
JPEG Basic	4,000	6,900	12,400
RAW	655	N/A	N/A
RAW+JPEG Basic	579	N/A	N/A

Release Modes

This shooting mode determines when (and how often) the D60 makes an exposure. If you're coming to the dSLR world from a point-and-shoot camera, you might have used a model that labels these options as Drive modes, dating back to the film era when cameras could be set for single-shot or "motor drive" (continuous) shooting modes. Your D60 has five release (shooting) modes: Single Shot, Continuous Shooting (Burst), Self-Timer, Two-Second Delayed Remote, and Quick Response Remote. (The latter two require the use of the ML-L3 infrared remote control.)

There are several ways to specify one of the five release modes. You can use the Custom Settings menu (as described in Chapter 3) to choose one of the five modes as the default; thereafter, that mode will be invoked when you press the Fn button located near the D60's chrome nameplate on the front of the camera. Or, you can use the Quick Settings display, which allows you to change many of the D60's basic settings.

I'll show you how to use the Quick Settings display first, because it's a useful tool when you want to change many of the basic options, before explaining each of the release modes.

Using the Quick Settings Display

When you press the Zoom In/Info button on the back of the camera (the bottom button on the left side of the LCD), the Shooting Information display (shown in Figure 1.10) appears. It is a useful status screen that you can use to view many current active settings. Press the Info button a second time, and the display switches to the Quick Setting screen (Figure 1.11), which allows you to modify the most frequently accessed options.

EYE SENSOR HAS ITS EYE ON YOU

There is an "eye sensor" located under the viewfinder that activates when you bring the D60's viewing window to your eye. If the exposure meters are active (just tap the shutter button to activate them), the eye sensor will turn off the Shooting Information display on the LCD (to save battery power). When you remove the viewfinder from your eye, the information display in the viewfinder switches off, and the Shooting Information display comes back. I'll show you how to disable this feature in the Setup menu in Chapter 3.

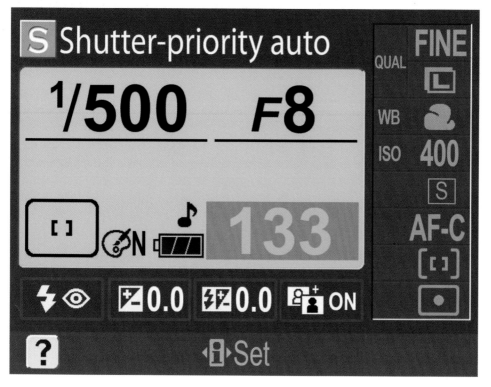

Figure 1.10
The Shooting Information display shows the status of your current settings.

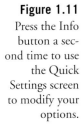

Figure 1.11
Press the Info button a second time to use the Quick Settings screen to modify your options.

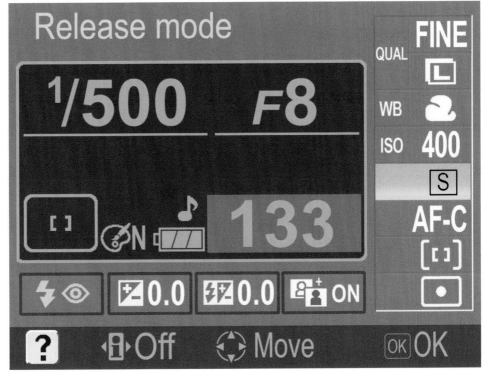

To change release modes, follow these steps:

1. If the LCD screen is blank, press the Zoom In/Info button twice to access the Quick Settings screen.

2. Use the multi-selector pad's left/right/up/down buttons to navigate to the settings at the side of the screen, and up to the Release Mode option. (It's the fifth entry down from the top.)

3. Press the OK button in the center of the multi-selector pad to produce the Release Mode screen, which has four options.

4. To activate the self-timer, select the icon resembling a clock face with the timer delay period next to it. This is **10s** by default, but can be changed to 2, 5, or 20 seconds in the Custom Settings menu entry CSM #16 (as described in Chapter 3).

5. Press the OK button to confirm your choice.

6. Press the Info button to exit the screen.

The release modes available from the Quick Settings menu are:

- **Single Frame.** In this single-shot mode, the default, the D60 takes one picture each time you press the shutter release button down all the way. If you press the shutter and nothing happens (which is very frustrating!), you may be using a focus mode that requires sharp focus to be achieved before a picture can be taken. This is called focus priority, and it is discussed in more detail under "Choosing Focus Modes," later in this chapter.

- **Continuous Shooting.** This shooting mode can be set to produce bursts of up to three frames per second, useful for grabbing action shots of sports, or for capturing fleeting expressions (especially of children).

- **Self-Timer.** You can use the self-timer as a replacement for a remote release, to reduce the effects of camera/user shake when the D60 is mounted on a tripod or, say, set on a firm surface, or when you want to get in the picture yourself. The picture will be taken after about 10 seconds (or 2, 5, or 20 seconds if you've changed the default value as described in Chapter 3). A white lamp on the front of the camera will blink while the timer counts down, then remain on continuously for about two seconds just before the picture is taken. Any time you use the camera on a tripod (with the self-timer or otherwise) make sure there is no bright light shining on the viewfinder window; if so, cover it or locate that eyepiece cap and block the window. Self-Timer mode is not "sticky." After you take one picture with the self-timer, the D60 returns to Single Frame mode.

- **Two-Second Delayed Remote.** Set this release mode, and the D60 will take a picture two seconds after you press the button on the ML-L3 infrared remote control. This mode is "sticky." It remains in force until you turn it off manually, or simply turn off the D60 and turn it back on.

- **Quick Release Remote.** With this choice activated, the D60 takes the photo as soon as you press the button on the ML-L3 infrared remote control. This mode is also "sticky." It remains in force until you turn it off manually, or simply turn off the D60 and turn it back on.

Note

If you plan to dash in front of the camera to join the scene, consider using manual focus so the D60 won't refocus on your fleeing form and produce unintended results. (Nikon really needs to offer an option to autofocus at the *end* of the self-timer cycle.)

Selecting a Shooting Mode

The Nikon D60 has two types of shooting modes, Advanced modes/Exposure modes, and a second set, which Nikon now labels Point-and-Shoot modes (originally called Digital Vari-Program modes). The Advanced modes include Programmed-Auto (or Program mode), Aperture Priority Auto, Shutter Priority Auto, and Manual exposure mode. These are the modes you'll use most often after you've learned all your D60's features, because they allow you to specify how the camera chooses its settings when making an exposure, for greater creative control.

The Point-and-Shoot modes take full control of the camera, make all the decisions for you, and don't allow you to override the D60's settings. They are most useful while you're learning to use the camera, because you can select an appropriate mode (Auto, Auto/No Flash, Portrait, Landscape, Child, Sports, Close-up, or Night Portrait) and fire away. You'll end up with decent photos using appropriate settings, but your opportunities to use a little creativity (say, to overexpose an image to create a silhouette, or to deliberately use a slow shutter speed to add a little blur to an action shot) are minimal. Nikon originally called these modes "Digi-Vari Program" or "DVP" modes, but the rest of the civilized world knows them as Scene modes.

Choosing a "Scene" Mode

The eight Point-and-Shoot/Digital Vari-Program/Scene modes can be selected by rotating the mode dial on the top right of the Nikon D60 to the appropriate icon (shown in Figure 1.12):

- **Auto.** In this mode, the D60 makes all the exposure decisions for you, and will pop up the internal flash if necessary under low-light conditions. The camera automatically focuses on the subject closest to the camera (unless you've set the lens to Manual focus), and the autofocus assist illuminator lamp on the front of the camera will light up to help the camera focus in low-light conditions.

- **Auto (Flash Off).** Identical to Auto mode, except that the flash will not pop up under any circumstances. You'd want to use this in a museum, during religious ceremonies, concerts, or any environment where flash is forbidden or distracting.

- **Portrait.** Use this mode when you're taking a portrait of a subject standing relatively close to the camera and want to de-emphasize the background, maximize sharpness, and produce flattering skin tones. The built-in flash will pop up if needed.

- **Landscape.** Select this mode when you want extra sharpness and rich colors of distant scenes. The built-in flash and AF-assist illuminator are disabled.

- **Child.** Use this mode to accentuate the vivid colors often found in children's clothing, and to render skin tones with a soft, natural-looking texture. The D60 focuses on the closest subject to the camera. The built-in flash will pop up if needed.

- **Sports.** Use this mode to freeze fast-moving subjects. The D60 selects a fast shutter speed to stop action, and focuses continuously on the center focus point while you have the shutter release button pressed halfway. However, you can select one of the other two focus points to the left or right of the center by pressing the multi-selector left/right buttons. The built-in electronic flash and focus assist illuminator lamp are disabled.

- **Close-up.** This mode is helpful when you are shooting close-up pictures of a subject from about one foot away or less, such as flowers, bugs, and small items. The D60 focuses on the closest subject in the center of the frame, but you can use the multi-selector right and left buttons to focus on a different point. Use a tripod in this mode, as exposures may be long enough to cause blurring from camera movement. The built-in flash will pop up if needed.

- **Night Portrait.** Choose this mode when you want to illuminate a subject in the foreground with flash (it will pop up automatically, if needed), but still allow the background to be exposed properly by the available light. The camera focuses on the closest main subject. Be prepared to use a tripod or a vibration-resistant lens like the 18-55 VR kit lens to reduce the effects of camera shake. (You'll find more about VR and camera shake in Chapter 6.)

Choosing an Advanced Mode

If you're very new to digital photography, you might want to set the camera to P (Program mode) and start snapping away. That mode will make all the appropriate settings for you for many shooting situations. If you have more photographic experience, you might want to opt for one of the semi-automatic modes, or even Manual mode. These, too, are described in more detail in Chapter 6. These advanced modes all let you apply a little more creativity to your camera's settings. Figure 1.13 shows the position of the modes described next.

- **M (Manual).** Select when you want full control over the shutter speed and lens opening, either for creative effects or because you are using a studio flash or other flash unit not compatible with the D60's automatic flash metering.

- **A (Aperture Priority).** Choose when you want to use a particular lens opening, especially to control sharpness or how much of your image is in focus. Specify the f/stop you want, and the D60 will select the appropriate shutter speed for you.

Figure 1.12
Rotate the mode dial to select an automated "Scene" mode.

Auto

Auto (Flash Off)

Portrait

Landscape

Child

Sports

Close-up

Night Portrait

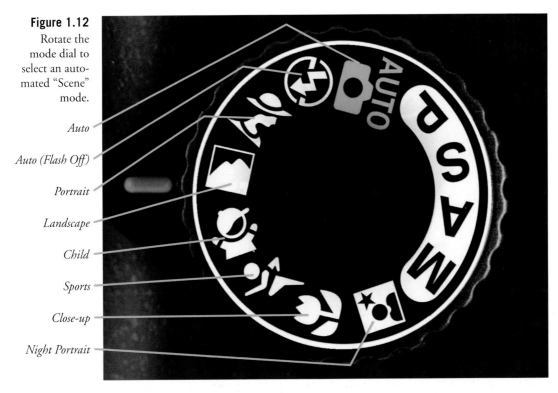

Figure 1.13
Rotate the mode dial to select an advanced mode.

Manual

Aperture Priority

Shutter Priority

Program

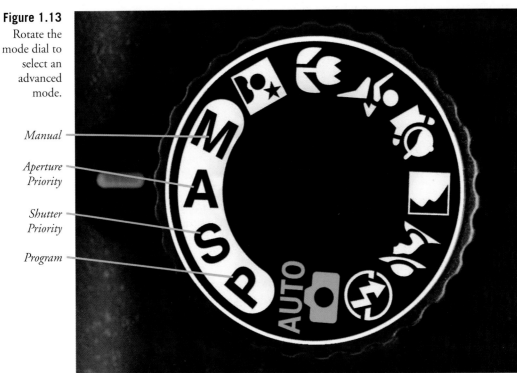

- **S (Shutter Priority).** This mode is useful when you want to use a particular shutter speed to stop action or produce creative blur effects. Choose your preferred shutter speed, and the D60 will select the appropriate f/stop for you.

- **P (Program).** This mode allows the D60 to select the basic exposure settings, but you can still override the camera's choices to fine-tune your image, while maintaining metered exposure.

Choosing a Metering Mode

The metering mode you select determines how the D60 calculates exposure. You might want to select a particular metering mode for your first shots, although the default Matrix metering is probably the best choice as you get to know your camera. (It is used automatically in any of the D60's DVP/scene modes.) I'll explain when and how to use each of the three metering modes later. To change metering modes, use the Quick Setting screen. (You can also specify metering mode using the Custom Setting menu, as I'll describe in Chapter 3.)

1. Press the Info button twice and navigate to the metering selection (it's at the bottom of the right-hand column) using the multi-selector buttons.

2. Press OK to select the option.

3. Use the multi-selector up/down buttons to choose Matrix, Center-Weighted, or Spot metering (described below and shown in Figure 1.14).

4. Press OK to confirm your choice.

5. Press the Info button to exit, or just tap the shutter release button.

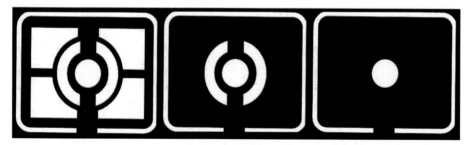

Figure 1.14
Metering modes are (left to right): Matrix, Center-Weighted, Spot.

- **Matrix metering.** The standard metering mode; the D60 attempts to intelligently classify your image and choose the best exposure based on readings from a 420-segment color CCD sensor that interprets light reaching the viewfinder using a database of hundreds of thousands of patterns.

- **Center-Weighted Averaging metering.** The D60 meters the entire scene, but gives the most emphasis to the central area of the frame, measuring about 8mm.

- **Spot metering.** Exposure is calculated from a smaller 3.5 mm central spot, about 2.5 percent of the image area.

You'll find a detailed description of each of these modes in Chapter 6.

Choosing Focus Modes

The Nikon D60 can focus your pictures for you, or allow you to manually focus the image using the focus ring on the lens. (I'll help you locate this ring in Chapter 2.) Switching between Automatic and Manual focus is easy. You can move the AF/MF (Autofocus/Manual focus) or M/A-M (Manual Fine-tune Autofocus/Manual) switch on the lens mounted on your camera.

When using autofocus, you have additional choices. The D60 has three autofocus zones (shown as a row of horizontal brackets in the viewfinder) that can be used to zero in on a particular subject area in your image to focus on. (See Figure 1.15.) In addition, you can select *when* the D60 applies its focusing information to your image prior to exposure.

Figure 1.15
The D60 can select which of three focus zones to use, or allow you to make the choice, depending on the Autofocus Area mode you specify.

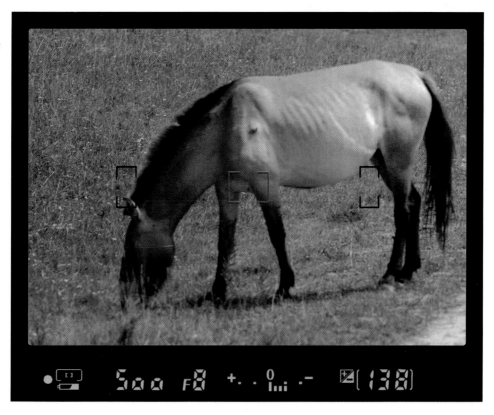

Choosing Autofocus Area Mode

I'll explain autofocus in more depth in Chapter 4, but you can still learn to set the AF-Area mode now, using the Quick Settings screen.

1. Press the Info button twice and navigate to the AF-Area mode selection (it's seventh from the top of the right-hand column) using the multi-selector buttons.

2. Press OK to select the option.

3. Use the multi-selector up/down buttons to choose Closest Subject, Dynamic Area, or Single Point options (described below).

4. Press OK to confirm your choice.

5. Press the Info button to exit, or just tap the shutter release button.

The three modes are as follows:

■ **Closest Subject.** The D60 selects the focus point containing the subject that is nearest to the camera. This mode is used automatically in Auto, Auto (Flash Off), Portrait, Landscape, Child, and Night Portrait scene modes. It is the default mode for Program, Shutter Priority, Aperture Priority, and Manual exposure modes, but you can select one of the other two modes. You cannot choose the focus point in this mode.

■ **Dynamic Area.** You can choose which of the three focus points will be used using the multi-selector, but if the subject moves from the point you have specified, the D60 will focus based on information from one of the other two focus zones. This mode is best for subjects that are moving unpredictably, as in sports activities. In fact, this mode is applied automatically with the Sports scene setting.

■ **Single Point.** You choose which of the three focus points are used. This mode is best for stationary subjects, and is used automatically in Close-up scene mode.

Choosing Focus Mode

When you are using Program, Aperture Priority, Shutter Priority, or Manual exposure mode, you can select the Autofocus mode *when* the D60 measures and locks in focus prior to pressing the shutter release down all the way and taking the picture. The focus mode is chosen using the Quick Settings screen. (You can also choose the focus mode in a slightly slower way using the Custom Setting menu, as I'll describe in Chapter 3.)

1. Press the Info button twice and navigate to the Focus Mode selection (it's sixth from the top of the right-hand column) using the multi-selector buttons.

2. Press OK to select the option.

3. Use the multi-selector up/down buttons to choose AF-A, AF-C, AF-S, or M (described next).

4. Press OK to confirm your choice.

5. Press the Info button to exit, or just tap the shutter release button.

The four focus modes are as follows:

- **Automatic Autofocus (AF-A).** This default setting switches between AF-C and AF-S, as described below.

- **Continuous-Servo Autofocus (AF-C).** This mode, sometimes called *Continuous Autofocus*, sets focus when you partially depress the shutter button (or other auto-focus activation button), but continues to monitor the frame and refocuses if the camera or subject is moved. This is a useful mode for photographing sports and moving subjects.

- **Single-Servo Autofocus (AF-S).** This mode, sometimes called *Single Autofocus*, locks in a focus point when the shutter button is pressed down halfway, and the focus confirmation light glows at bottom left in the viewfinder. The focus will remain locked until you release the button or take the picture. This mode is best when your subject is relatively motionless.

- **Manual focus (M).** When focus is set to manual, you always focus manually using the focus ring on the lens. The focus confirmation indicator in the viewfinder provides an indicator when correct focus is achieved.

Note

Note that the Autofocus/Manual focus switch on the lens and the setting made in camera body must agree; if either is set to Manual focus, then the D60 defaults to Manual focus regardless of how the other is set.

Adjusting White Balance and ISO

There are a few other settings you can make if you're feeling ambitious, but don't feel ashamed if you postpone using these features until you've racked up a little more experience with your D60.

If you like, you can custom-tailor your white balance (color balance) and ISO (sensitivity) settings. I'll explain more about what these settings are, and why you might want to change them, in Chapter 3. To start out, it's best to set white balance (WB) to Auto, and ISO to ISO 200 for daylight photos, and ISO 400 for pictures in dimmer light. (Don't be afraid of ISO 1600, however; the D60 does a *much* better job of producing

low-noise photos at higher ISOs than most other cameras.) You'll find complete recommendations for both these settings in Chapter 4. You can adjust either one now using
the Quick Settings screen, as described multiple times in this chapter. I won't repeat the
instructions again. The WB (for white balance) and ISO settings are third and fourth
from the top of the right-hand column in the Quick Settings screen (respectively).

Reviewing the Images You've Taken

The Nikon D60 has a broad range of playback and image review options, and I'll cover
them in more detail in Chapter 3. For now, you'll want to learn just the basics. Here is
all you really need to know at this time, as shown in Figure 1.16:

■ Press the Playback button (marked with a white right-pointing triangle) at the
  upper-left corner of the back of the camera to display the most recent image on the
  LCD.

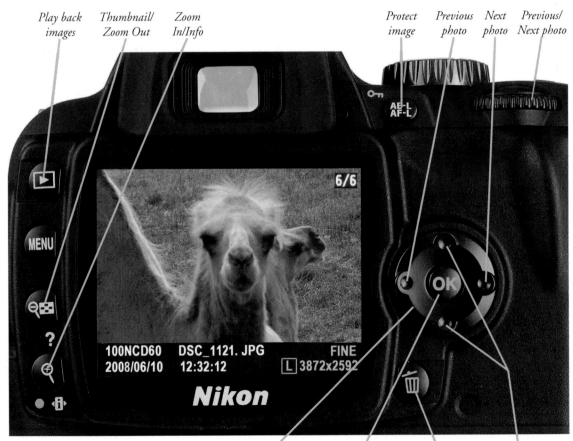

Figure 1.16 Review your images.

- Spin the command dial left or right to review additional images. You can also use the multi-selector left/right buttons. Press right to advance to the next image, or left to go back to a previous image.

- Press the multi-selector button up or down to change among overlays of basic image information or detailed shooting information.

- Press the Zoom button repeatedly to zoom in on the image displayed; the Zoom Out button reduces the image. A thumbnail representation of the whole image appears in the lower-right corner with a yellow rectangle showing the relative level of zoom. At intermediate zoom positions, the yellow rectangle can be moved around within the frame using the multi-selector.

- Press the Protect button to mark an image and shield it from accidental erasure (but not from reformatting of the memory card).

- Press the Trash button twice to remove the photo currently being displayed.

- Press the Playback button again, or just tap the shutter release button to exit playback view.

You'll find information on viewing thumbnail indexes of images, automated playback, and other options in Chapter 3.

Using the Built-in Flash

Working with the D60's built-in flash (as well as external flash units like the Nikon SB-400) deserves a chapter of its own, and I'm providing one (see Chapter 7). But the built-in flash is easy enough to work with that you can begin using it right away, either to provide the main lighting of a scene or as supplementary illumination to fill in the shadows.

The built-in flash will pop up automatically as required in Auto, Portrait, Child, Close-up, and Night Portrait DVP/Scene modes. To use the built-in flash in Manual, Aperture Priority, Shutter Priority, or Program modes, just press the flash pop-up button (shown in Figure 1.17). When the flash is fully charged, a lightning bolt symbol will flash at the right side of the viewfinder display. When using P (Program), A (Aperture Priority) exposure modes, the D60 will select a shutter speed for you automatically from the range 1/250 to 1/60 seconds. In S (Shutter Priority) and M (Manual) modes, you select the shutter speed from 1/250 to 30 seconds.

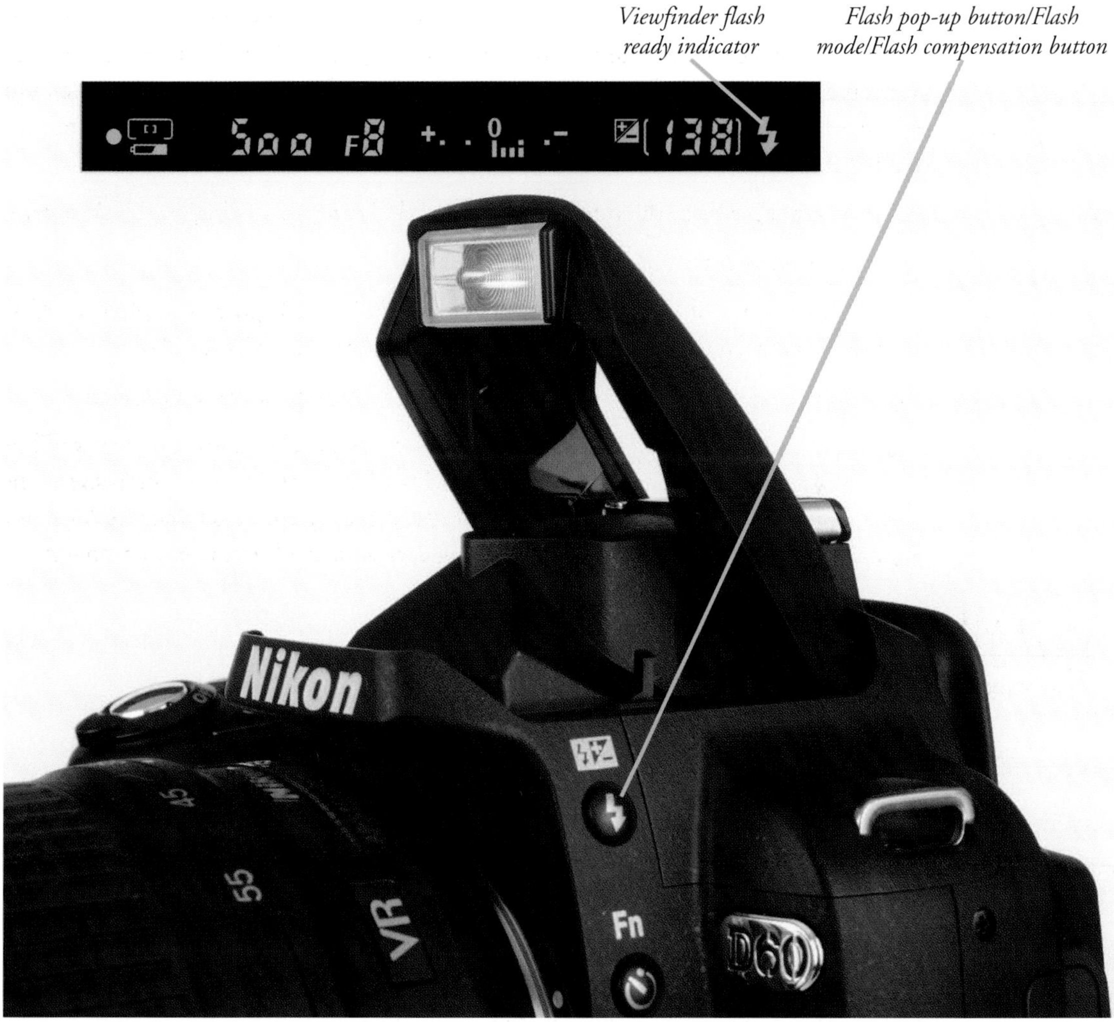

Viewfinder flash ready indicator

Flash pop-up button/Flash mode/Flash compensation button

Figure 1.17 The pop-up electronic flash can be used as the main light source or for supplemental illumination.

Transferring Photos to Your Computer

The final step in your picture-taking session will be to transfer the photos you've taken to your computer for printing, further review, or image editing. Your D60 allows you to print directly to PictBridge-compatible printers and to create print orders right in the camera, plus you can select which images to transfer to your computer. I'll outline those options in Chapter 3.

I always recommend using a card reader attached to your computer to transfer files, because that process is generally a lot faster and doesn't drain the D60's battery. However, you can also use a cable for direct transfer, which may be your only option when you have the cable and a computer, but no card reader (perhaps you're using the computer of a friend or colleague, or at an Internet café).

To transfer images from the camera to a Mac or PC computer using the USB cable:

1. Turn the camera off.

2. Pry back the rubber cover that protects the D60's USB port, and plug the USB cable furnished with the camera into the USB port. (See Figure 1.18.)

3. Connect the other end of the USB cable to a USB port on your computer.

4. Turn the camera on. The operating system itself, or installed software such as Nikon Transfer or Adobe Photoshop Elements Transfer usually detects the camera and offers to copy or move the pictures. Or, the camera appears on your desktop as a mass storage device, enabling you to drag and drop the files to your computer.

Figure 1.18
Images can be transferred to your computer using a USB cable.

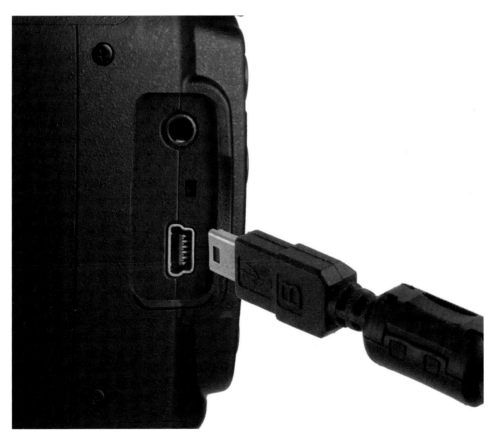

To transfer images from a Secure Digital card to the computer using a card reader, as shown in Figure 1.19, do the following:

1. Turn the camera off.

2. Slide open the memory card door and remove the SD card.

3. Insert the Secure Digital card into your memory card reader. Your installed software detects the files on the card and offers to transfer them. The card can also appear as a mass storage device on your desktop, which you can open and then drag and drop the files to your computer.

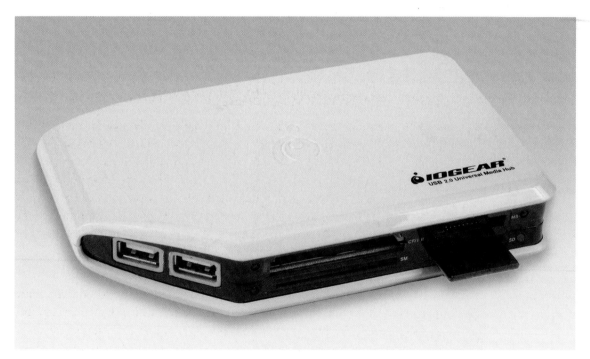

Figure 1.19 A card reader is the fastest way to transfer photos.

2

Nikon D60 Roadmap

With the D60, Nikon has done a rather amazing job of creating a super-compact digital SLR that retains the convenience and easy access to essential controls. Its layout, first seen in the Nikon D40/D40x, simplifies options through a clever arrangement of two dials, a thumb pad, and about a dozen logically laid out buttons. Most of the Nikon D60's key functions and settings that are changed frequently can be accessed directly using the array of dials, buttons, and knobs that populate the camera's surface, or through the Quick Settings screen on the LCD. With so many quick-access controls available, you'll find that the bulk of your shooting won't be slowed down by a visit to the vast thicket of text options called Menu-land.

If you want to operate your D60 efficiently, you'll need to learn the location, function, and application of all these controls. What you really need is a street-level roadmap that shows where everything is, and how it's used. But what Nikon gives you in the user's manual is akin to a world globe with an overall view and many cross-references to the pages that will tell you what you really need to know. Check out the **Getting to Know the Camera** pages in Nikon's manual, which compress views of the front, back, top, and bottom of the D60 into two tiny black-and-white line drawings. There are more than 40 callouts pointing to various buttons and dials crammed into the pair of illustrations. If you can find the control you want within this cramped layout, you'll still need to flip back and forth among multiple pages (individual buttons can have several different cross-references!) to locate the information.

Most other third-party books follow this format, featuring black-and-white photos or line drawings of front, back, and top views, and many labels. I originated the up-close-and-personal full-color, street-level roadmap (rather than a satellite view) that I use in this book and my previous camera guidebooks. I provide you with many different views, like the one shown in Figure 2.1, and lots of explanation accompanying each zone of the camera, so that by the time you finish this chapter, you'll have a basic understanding of every control and what it does. I'm not going to delve into menu functions here—you'll find a discussion of your setup, shooting, and playback menu options in Chapter 3. Everything here is devoted to the button pusher and dial twirler in you.

You'll also find this "roadmap" chapter a good guide to the rest of the book, as well. I'll try to provide as much detail here about the use of the main controls as I can, but some topics (such as autofocus and exposure) are too complex to address in depth right away. So, I'll point you to the relevant chapters that discuss things like setup options, exposure, use of electronic flash, and working with lenses with the occasional cross-reference.

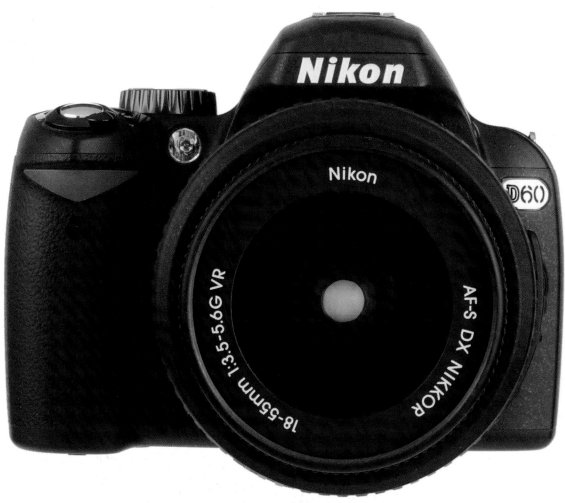

Figure 2.1

Nikon D60: Front View

This is the side of the D60 seen by your victims as you snap away. For the photographer, though, the front is the surface your fingers curl around as you hold the camera, and there are really only a few buttons to press, all within easy reach of the fingers of your left and right hands. There are additional controls on the lens itself. You'll need to look at several different views to see everything.

Figure 2.2 shows a front view of the Nikon D60 from a 45-degree angle. The main components you need to know about are as follows:

■ **Shutter button.** Angled on top of the handgrip is the shutter release button, which has multiple functions. Press this button down halfway to lock exposure and focus. Press it down all the way to actually take a photo or sequence of photos if you're using the Continuous Shooting mode. Tapping the shutter button when the D60's exposure meters have turned themselves off reactivates them, and a tap can be used to remove the display of a menu or image from the rear color LCD.

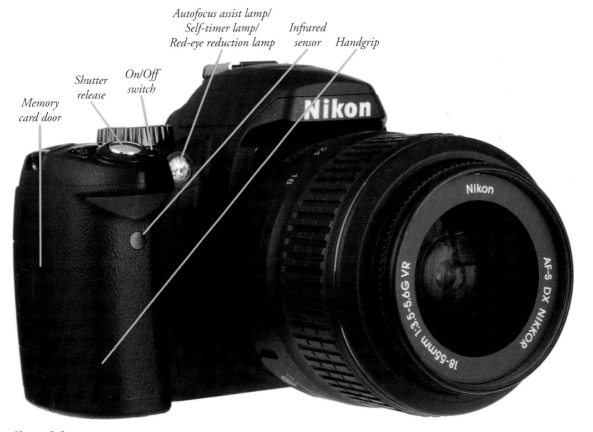

Figure 2.2

- **Red-eye reduction/self-timer/autofocus assist lamp.** This LED provides a blip of light shortly before a flash exposure to cause the subjects' pupils to close down, reducing the effect of red-eye reflections off their retinas. When using the self-timer, this lamp also flashes to mark the countdown until the photo is taken, and serves to provide some extra illumination in dark environments to assist the autofocus system.

- **Handgrip.** This provides a comfortable handhold, and also contains the D60's battery.

- **Memory card door.** Slide this door toward the back of the camera to provide access to the SD memory card slot.

- **Infrared sensor.** You can trigger the D60 remotely using the optional ML-L3 infrared remote control, which is detected by this sensor.

You'll find more controls on the other side of the D60, shown in Figures 2.3 and 2.4. The main points of interest shown include:

- **Self-Timer/Fn (Function button).** This conveniently located button can be programmed to perform any one of several functions (including changing the image quality, setting ISO, or specifying white balance), but its default behavior is to activate the self-timer (which is then triggered when you press the shutter release button). I recommend retaining the default self-timer behavior.

- **Lens release button.** Press this button to unlock the lens, and then rotate it away from the shutter release button to dismount your optics.

- **Flash pop-up/Flash mode button.** This button releases the built-in flash so it can flip up and start the charging process. If you decide you do not want to use the flash, you can turn it off by pressing the flash head back down. Hold down this button while spinning the command dial to chose a flash mode. I'll explain how to use the various flash modes (red-eye reduction, front/rear curtain sync, and slow sync) in Chapter 8, along with some tips for adjusting flash exposure.

- **Pop-up flash.** The flash elevates from the top of the camera, theoretically reducing the chances of red-eye reflections, because the higher light source is less likely to reflect back from your subjects' eyes into the camera lens. In practice, the red-eye effect is still possible (and likely), and can be further minimized with the D60's red-eye reduction lamp (which flashes before the exposure, causing the subjects' pupils to contract), and the after-shot red-eye elimination offered in the Retouch menu. (Your image editor may also have anti-red-eye tools.) Of course, the best strategy is to use an external speedlight that mounts on the accessory shoe on top of the camera (and thus is even higher) or a flash that is off-camera entirely.

Figure 2.3

Flash mode/
Flash compensation button

Function/
Self-timer button

Lens release
button

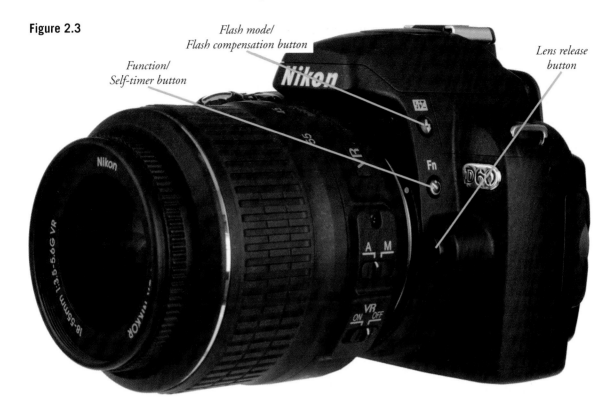

Figure 2.4

Pop-up electronic
flash unit

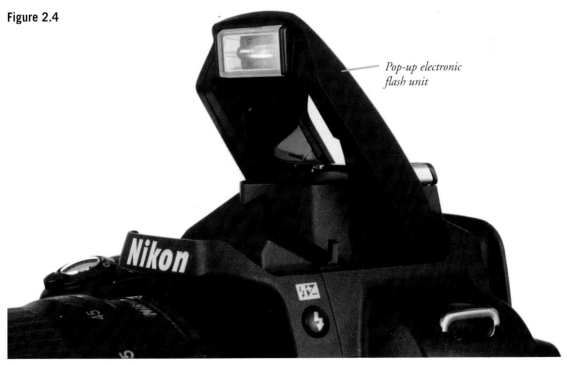

The main feature on the side of the Nikon D60 is a rubber cover (see Figure 2.5) that protects the two connector ports and reset button underneath from dust and moisture. The features, shown in Figure 2.6, with the rubber cover removed, are as follows:

- **Video port.** You can link this connector with a television to view your photos on a large screen.

- **Reset button.** Press this to reset all settings in the camera to their default values.

- **USB port.** Plug in the USB cable furnished with your Nikon D60 and connect the other end to a USB port in your computer to transfer photos, or to interface with the Nikon Camera Control Pro software described in Chapter 8.

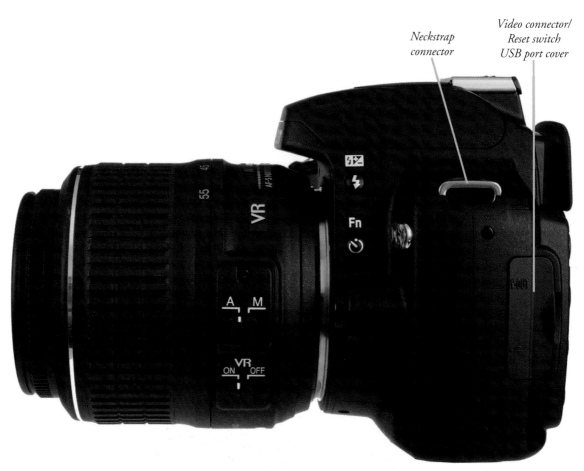

Neckstrap
connector

Video connector/
Reset switch
USB port cover

Figure 2.5

Figure 2.6

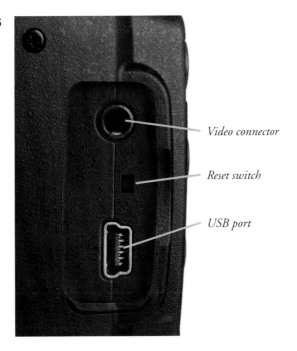

Video connector

Reset switch

USB port

The Nikon D60's Business End

The back panel of the Nikon D60 (see Figure 2.7) bristles with almost a dozen different controls, buttons, and knobs. That might seem like a lot of controls to learn, but you'll find that it's a lot easier to press a dedicated button and spin a dial than to jump to a menu every time you want to access one of these features.

Figure 2.7

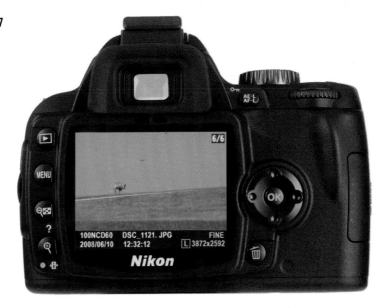

You can see the controls clustered along the top edge of the back panel in Figure 2.8. The key buttons and components and their functions are as follows:

■ **Viewfinder eyepiece.** You can frame your composition by peering into the viewfinder. It's surrounded by a soft rubber eyecup that seals out extraneous light when pressing your eye tightly up to the viewfinder, and it also protects your eyeglass lenses (if worn) from scratching. It can be removed and replaced by the DK-5 eyepiece cap when you use the camera on a tripod, to ensure that light coming from the back of the camera doesn't venture inside and possibly affect the exposure reading. Shielding the viewfinder with your hand may be more convenient (unless you're using the self-timer to get in the photo yourself).

■ **Diopter adjustment slider.** Move this slider up or down to adjust the diopter correction for your eyesight, as described in Chapter 1.

■ **Protect Image/AE-L/AF-L lock.** This triple-duty button can be used to protect an image from accidental erasure. When reviewing a picture on the LCD, press once to protect the image, a second time to unprotect it. A key symbol appears when the image is displayed to show that it is protected. (This feature safeguards an image from erasure when deleting or transferring pictures only; when you format a card, protected images are removed along with all the others.) When shooting pictures, the button locks the exposure or focus that the camera sets when you partially depress the shutter button. The exposure lock indication (AE-L icon) appears in the viewfinder. If you want to recalculate exposure or autofocus with the shutter button still partially depressed, press the button again. The exposure/autofocus will be unlocked when you release the shutter button or take the picture. To retain the exposure/autofocus lock for subsequent photos, keep the button pressed while shooting.

■ **Command dial.** The command dial is used to set or adjust many functions, such as shutter speed, either alone or when another button is depressed simultaneously.

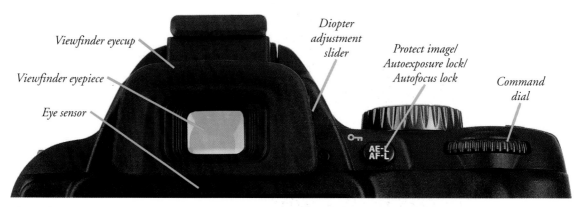

Figure 2.8

You'll be using the five buttons to the left of the LCD monitor (shown in Figure 2.9) quite frequently, so learn their functions now.

- **LCD.** View your images and navigate through the menus on this screen.

- **Playback button.** Press this button to review images you've taken, using the controls and options I'll explain in the next section. To remove the displayed image, press the Playback button again, or simply tap the shutter release button.

- **Menu button.** Summons/exits the menu displayed on the rear LCD of the D60. When you're working with submenus, this button also serves to exit a submenu and return to the main menu.

- **Thumbnail/Zoom Out/Help button.** In Playback mode, use this button to change from full-screen view to six or nine thumbnails, or to zoom out. I'll explain zooming and other playback options in the next section. When viewing most menu items on the LCD, pressing this button produces a concise Help screen with tips on how to make the relevant setting.

Figure 2.9

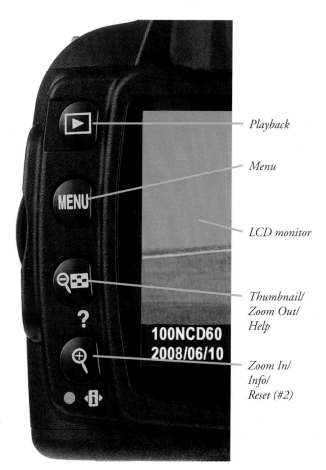

Playback

Menu

LCD monitor

Thumbnail/
Zoom Out/
Help

Zoom In/
Info/
Reset (#2)

■ **Zoom In button.** In Playback mode, press to zoom in on an image. When shooting pictures, press this button to restore the Shooting Information display; press a second time to produce the Quick Settings screen used to make many camera settings, such as metering mode, white balance, or ISO. Hold down this button at the same time as the Active D-Lighting/Reset #1 button on top of the camera (southwest of the shutter release button) to reset the D60 to its default settings.

■ **Info/Help/Protect button.** Press this button to activate the Shooting Information display. Press again to remove the information display (or simply tap the shutter release button). The display will also clear after the period you've set for LCD display (the default value is 20 seconds). The information display can be set to alternate between modes that are best viewed under bright daylight, as well as in dimmer illumination.

More controls reside on the right side of the back panel, as shown in Figure 2.10. The key controls and their functions are as follows:

Figure 2.10

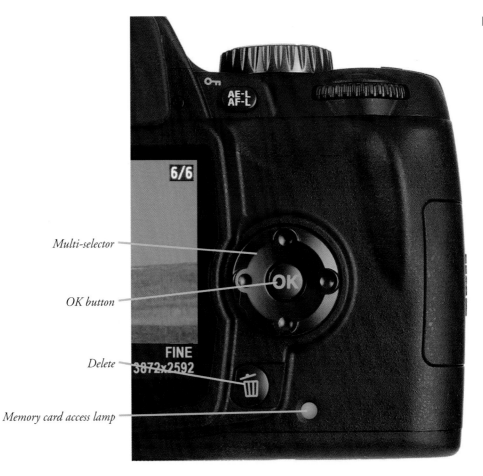

Multi-selector

OK button

Delete

Memory card access lamp

- **Multi-selector.** This joypad-like button can be shifted up/down and side to side to provide several functions, including AF point selection, scrolling around a magnified image, or trimming a photo. Within menus, pressing the up/down buttons moves the on-screen cursor up or down; pressing towards the right selects the highlighted item and displays its options; pressing left cancels and returns to the previous menu.

- **OK button.** Use this button to confirm a selection. When working with menus, press the Menu button instead to back out without making a selection.

- **Access lamp.** When lit or blinking, this lamp indicates that the memory card is being accessed.

- **Trash.** Press to erase the image shown on the LCD. A display will pop up on the LCD asking you to press the Trash button once more to delete the photo, or press the Playback button to cancel.

Playing Back Images

Reviewing images is a joy on the Nikon D60's big 2.5-inch LCD. Here are the basics involved in reviewing images on the LCD screen (or on a television screen you have connected with a cable). You'll find more details about some of these functions later in this chapter, or, for more complex capabilities, in the chapters that I point you to. This section just lists the must-know information.

- **Start review.** To begin review, press the Playback button at the upper-left corner of the back of the D60. The most-recently viewed image will appear on the LCD.

- **Playback folder.** Image review generally shows you the images in the currently selected folder on your memory card. A given card can contain several folders (a new one is created anytime you exceed 999 images in the current folder). You can use the Playback folder menu option in the Playback menu (as I'll explain in Chapter 3) to select a specific folder, or direct the D60 to display images from all the folders on the memory card.

- **View thumbnail images.** To change the view from a single image to four or nine thumbnails, follow the instructions in the "Viewing Thumbnails" section that follows.

- **Zoom in and out.** To zoom in or out, press the Zoom button, following the instructions in the "Zooming the Nikon D60 Playback Display" in the next section. (It also shows you how to move the zoomed area around using the multi-selector pad.)

- **Move back and forth.** To advance to the next image, press the right edge of the multi-selector pad; to go back to a previous shot, press the left edge. When you reach the beginning/end of the photos in your folder, the display "wraps around" to the end/beginning of the available shots.

- **See different types of data.** To change the type of information about the displayed image that is shown, press the up and down portions of the multi-selector pad. To learn what data is available, read the "Working with Photo Information" section later in this chapter.

- **Retouch image.** Press the OK button while a single image is displayed on the screen to jump to the Retouch menu to modify that photograph. (I'll explain the workings of the Retouch menu in Chapter 3.)

- **Remove images.** To delete an image that's currently on the screen, press the Trash button once, and then press it again to confirm the deletion. To select and delete a group of images, use the Delete option in the Playback menu to specify particular photos to remove, as described in more detail in Chapter 3.

- **Cancel playback.** To cancel image review, press the Playback button again, or simply tap the shutter release button.

Zooming the Nikon D60 Playback Display

Here's how to zoom in and out on your images during picture review:

1. When an image is displayed (use the Playback button to start), press the Zoom In button to fill the screen with a slightly magnified version of the image.

2. A navigation window appears in the lower-right corner of the LCD showing the entire image. Keep pressing to continue zooming in.

3. A yellow box in the navigation window shows the zoomed area within the full image. The entire navigation window vanishes from the screen after a few seconds, leaving you with a full-screen view of the zoomed portion of the image.

4. Use the command dial to move to the same zoomed area of the next/previous image.

5. Use the Zoom Out/Thumbnail button to zoom back out of the image.

6. Use the multi-selector buttons to move the zoomed area around within the image. The navigation window will reappear for reference when zooming or scrolling around within the display.

7. To exit zoom in/zoom out display, keep pressing the Zoom Out button until the full screen/full image/information display appears again.

Figure 2.11
The D60 incorporates a small thumbnail image with a yellow box showing the current zoom area.

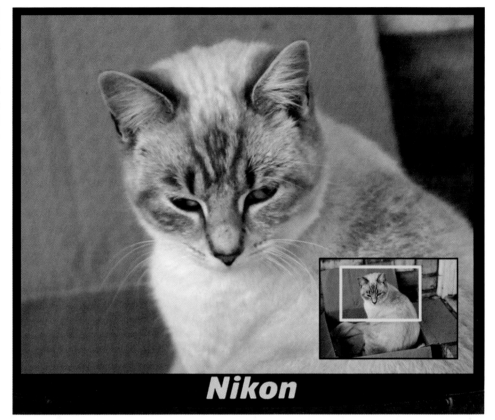

Viewing Thumbnails

The Nikon D60 provides other options for reviewing images in addition to zooming in and out. You can switch between single image view and either four or nine reduced-size thumbnail images on a single LCD screen.

Pages of thumbnail images offer a quick way to scroll through a large number of pictures quickly to find the one you want to examine in more detail. The D60 lets you switch quickly from single- to four- to nine-image views, with a scroll bar displayed at the right side of the screen to show you the relative position of the displayed thumbnails within the full collection of images in the active folder on your memory card. Figure 2.12 offers a comparison between the two levels of thumbnail views. The Zoom In and Zoom Out/Thumbnail buttons are used.

■ **Add thumbnails.** To increase the number of thumbnails on the screen, press the Zoom Out button once or twice. The D60 will switch from single image to four thumbnails to nine thumbnails. Additional presses do nothing (the display doesn't cycle back to single image again).

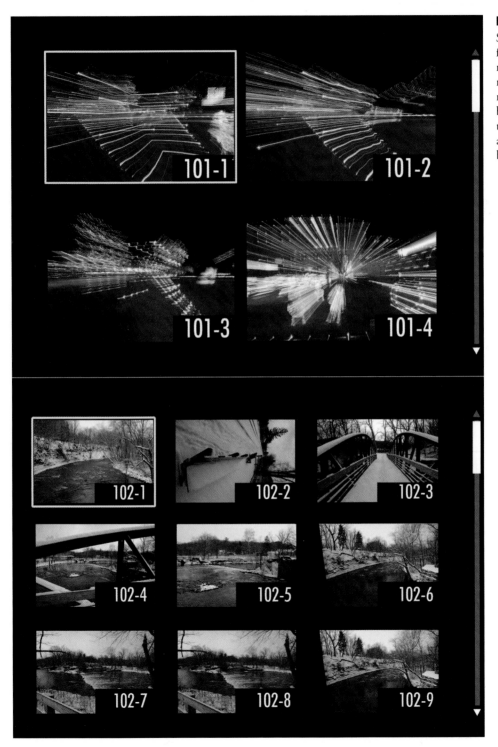

Figure 2.12
Switch between four thumbnails (top) and nine thumbnails (bottom) by pressing the Zoom Out and Zoom In buttons.

- **Reduce number of thumbnails.** To decrease the number of thumbnails on the screen, press the Zoom In button to change from nine thumbnails to four thumbnails, or from four to single-image display. Continuing to press the Zoom In button once you've returned to single-image display starts the zoom process described in the previous section.

- **Move zoomed area.** Use the multi-selector to move the yellow highlight box around among the thumbnails.

- **Protect and delete images.** When viewing thumbnails or a single-page image, press the Protect button to preserve the image against accidental deletion (a key icon is overlaid over the full-page image) or the Trash button (twice) to erase it.

- **Exit image review.** Tap the shutter release button or press the Playback button to exit image review. You don't have to worry about missing a shot because you were reviewing images; a half-press of the shutter release automatically brings back the D60's exposure meters, the autofocus system, and cancels image review.

Working with Photo Information

When reviewing an image on the screen, your D60 can supplement the image itself with a variety of shooting data, ranging from basic information presented at the bottom of the LCD display, to three text overlays that detail virtually every shooting option you've selected. This section will show you the type of information available. Most of the data is self-explanatory, so the labels in the accompanying figures should tell you most of what you need to know. To change to any of these views while an image is on the screen in Playback mode, press the multi-selector up/down buttons (unless you've swapped the up/down functions with the left/right functions in the Custom Settings menu).

- **File information screen.** The basic full image review display is officially called the File Information screen, and looks like Figure 2.13.

- **Shooting Data 1.** This is the first in a series of three screens that collectively provide everything else you might want to know about a picture you've taken. I'm not providing any labels in Figure 2.14, because the information in the first eight lines in the screen should be obvious as you read about metering, exposure modes, lens focal lengths, and flash modes in this book.

- **Shooting Data 2.** This screen shows white balance data and adjustments, ISO, sharpness and saturation settings, and other parameters. (See Figure 2.15.)

- **Shooting Data 3.** The final screen shows your Active D-Lighting setting and any retouching changes you've made. (See Chapter 3 for more information on both.)

- **Highlights.** When the Highlights display is active (see Figure 2.17), any overexposed areas will be indicated by a flashing black border. As I am unable to make the printed page flash, you'll have to check out this effect for yourself.

- **Brightness Histogram.** This shows the image overlaid with a brightness histogram, which you can see in Figure 2.18. The histogram is a kind of chart that represents an image's exposure, and how the darkest areas, brightest areas, and middle tones have been captured. Histograms are easy to work with, and I'll show you how in Chapter 4.

Retouch   Protection   Frame number/
indicator   status   Frames shot

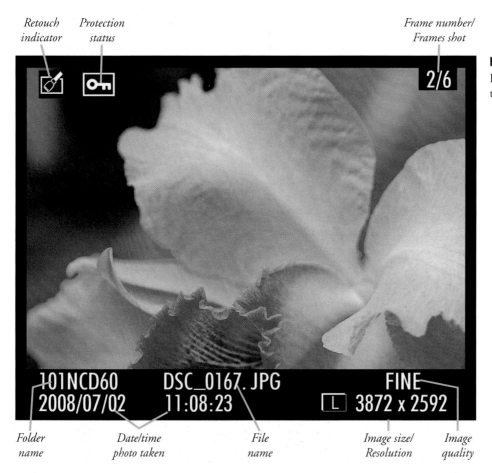

Figure 2.13
File information screen.

Folder   Date/time   File   Image size/   Image
name   photo taken   name   Resolution   quality

Figure 2.14
Shooting data
screen 1.

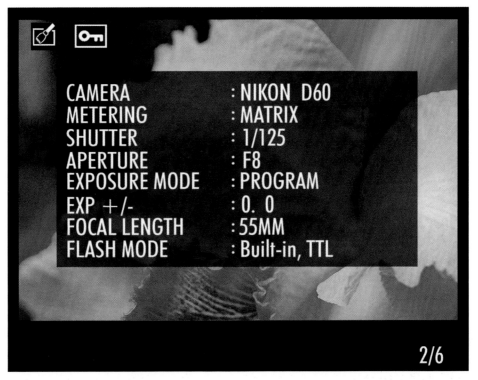

Figure 2.15
Shooting Data
screen 2.

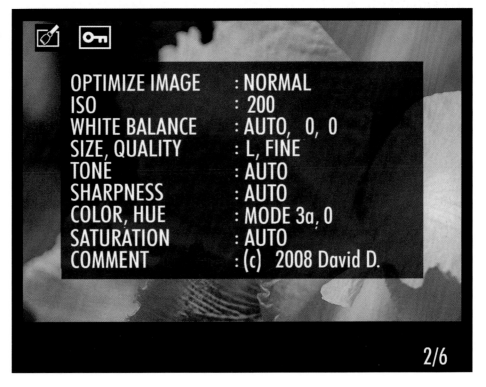

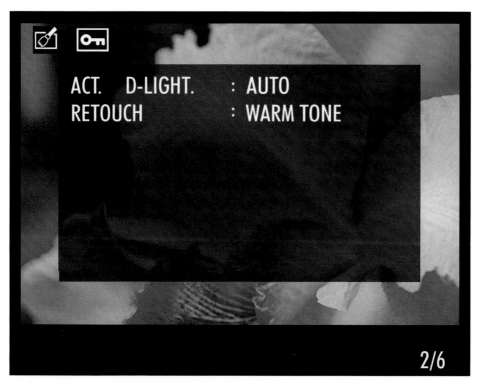

Figure 2.16
Shooting Data
screen 3.

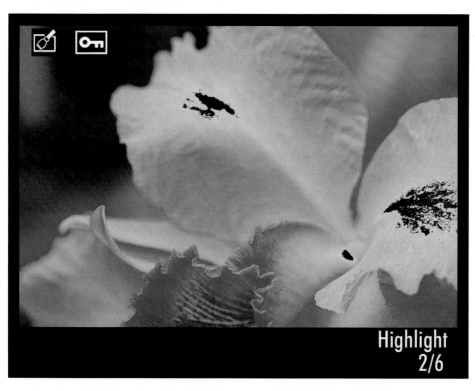

Figure 2.17
Highlights
screen.

Figure 2.18
Luminance
(brightness)
histogram
screen.

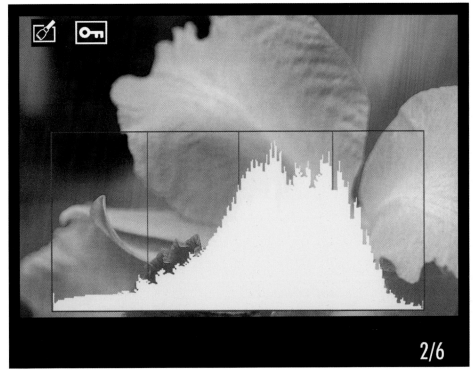

Going Topside

The top surface of the Nikon D60 (see Figure 2.19) has its own set of frequently accessed controls.

- **Accessory shoe.** Slide an electronic flash into this mount when you need a more powerful speedlight. A dedicated flash unit, like the Nikon SB-400, SB-600, or SB-800, can use the multiple contact points shown to communicate exposure, zoom setting, white balance information, and other data between the flash and the camera. There's more on using electronic flash in Chapter 8.

- **Power switch.** Rotate this switch clockwise to turn on the Nikon D60 (and virtually all other Nikon dSLRs).

- **Shutter release button.** Partially depress this button to lock in exposure and focus. Press all the way to take the picture. Tapping the shutter release when the camera has turned off the autoexposure and autofocus mechanisms reactivates both. When a review image is displayed on the back-panel color LCD, tapping this button removes the image from the display and reactivates the autoexposure and autofocus mechanisms.

Figure 2.19

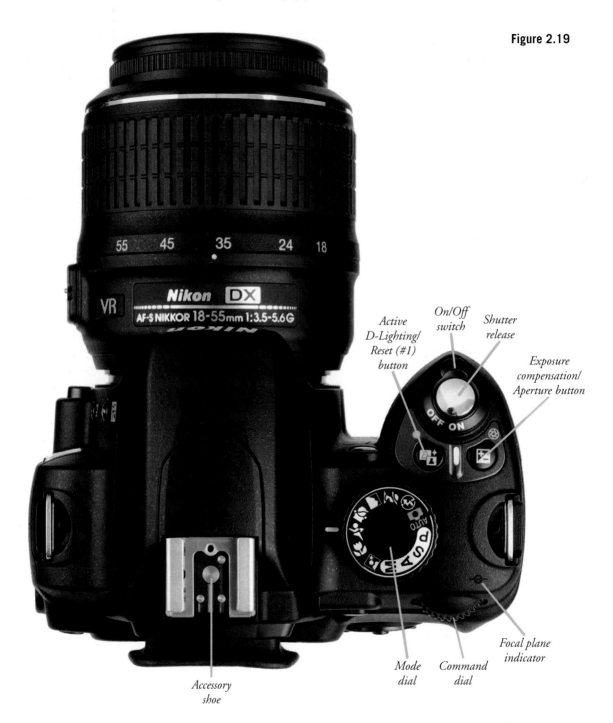

Active
D-Lighting/
Reset (#1)
button

On/Off
switch

Shutter
release

Exposure
compensation/
Aperture button

Mode
dial

Command
dial

Focal plane
indicator

Accessory
shoe

- **Exposure compensation/Aperture button.** Press this button while spinning the command dial to change the aperture in Manual exposure mode (there is no need to press the button to change the aperture in Aperture Priority mode). Hold down this button and spin the command dial to add or subtract exposure when using Program, Aperture Priority, or Shutter Priority modes. This facility allows you to "override" the settings the camera has made and create a picture that is lighter or darker. This is called *exposure compensation.* You can "apply" exposure compensation in Manual mode, too, but in that case the exposure isn't really changed. The D60 simply tells you how much extra or reduced exposure you are requesting, using a display in the viewfinder and LCD, which I'll describe later in this chapter. Finally, the button can be used in conjunction with the flash button on the front of the camera to set flash exposure compensation. Hold down both buttons and spin the command dial to adjust the amount of flash exposure. (I'll explain this process in Chapter 7.)

- **Active D-Lighting/Reset (#1) button.** Hold down this button while spinning the command dial to turn Active D-Lighting on or off. The status appears on the LCD. This button is also used in conjunction with the Zoom In button on the back of the camera to provide a quick two-button reset of the camera to (most of) its factory default settings. Hold down the two buttons, each marked with a green dot, for about two seconds to affect the reset. Only the parameters that can be changed using the Quick Settings display (that is, image quality/size, white balance ISO, release mode, focus mode, AF-area mode, metering mode, flash mode, exposure/flash exposure compensation, Active D-Lighting, and flexible program settings) are returned to their default values.

- **Focal plane indicator.** This indicator shows the *plane* of the sensor, for use in applications where exact measurement of the distance from the focal plane to the subject are necessary. (These are mostly scientific/close-up applications.)

- **Mode dial.** Rotate the mode dial to choose between Program, Aperture Priority, Shutter Priority, and Manual exposure modes, as well as the DVP/scene modes Auto, Auto (No Flash), Portrait, Landscape, Child, Sports, Close-up, and Night Portrait. Your choice will be displayed on the LCD and in the viewfinder, both described in the next sections. You can read more about the Scene modes in Chapter 1.

Lens Components

The lens shown at left in Figure 2.20 is a typical lens that might be mounted on the Nikon D60. It is, in fact, the 18-55mm VR "kit" lens often sold with the camera body. Unfortunately, this particular lens doesn't include all the common features found on the various Nikon lenses available for your camera, so I am including a second lens (shown at right in the figure) that *does* have more features and components. It's not a typical lens that a D60 user might work with, however. This 17-35mm zoom is a pricey "pro" lens that costs about twice as much as the entire D60 camera. Nevertheless, it makes a good example. Components found on this pair of lenses include:

- **Filter thread.** Most lenses have a thread on the front for attaching filters and other add-ons. Some, like the 18-55 VR kit lens, also use this thread for attaching a lens hood (you screw on the filter first, and then attach the hood to the screw thread on the front of the filter). Some lenses, such as the AF-S Nikkor 14-24mm f/2.8G ED lens, have no front filter thread, either because their front elements are too curved to allow mounting a filter and/or because the front element is so large that huge filters would be prohibitively expensive. Some of these front-filter-hostile lenses allow using smaller filters that drop into a slot at the back of the lens.

- **Lens hood bayonet.** Lenses like the 17-35mm zoom shown in the figure use this bayonet to mount the lens hood. Such lenses generally will have a dot on the edge showing how to align the lens hood with the bayonet mount.

- **Focus ring.** This is the ring you turn when you manually focus the lens, or fine-tune autofocus adjustment. It's a narrow ring at the very front of the lens (on the 18-55mm kit lens), or a wider ring located somewhere else.

- **Focus scale.** This is a readout found on many lenses that rotates in unison with the lens' focus mechanism to show the distance at which the lens has been focused. It's a useful indicator for double-checking autofocus, roughly evaluating depth-of-field, and for setting manual focus guesstimates. Chapter 6 deals with the mysteries of lenses and their controls in more detail.

- **Zoom setting.** These markings on the lens show the current focal length selected.

- **Zoom ring.** Turn this ring to change the zoom setting.

- **Autofocus/Manual switch.** Allows you to change from automatic focus to manual focus.

- **Aperture ring.** Some lenses have a ring that allows you to set a specific f/stop manually, rather than use the camera's internal electronic aperture control. An aperture ring is useful when a lens is mounted on a non-automatic extension ring, bellows, or other accessory that doesn't couple electronically with the camera. Aperture rings also allow using a lens on an older camera that lacks electronic control. In recent

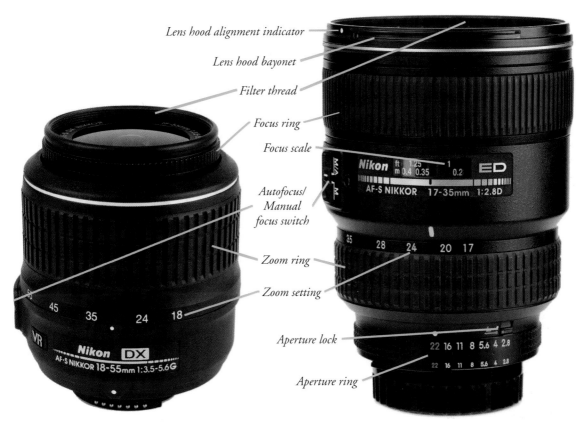

Lens hood alignment indicator

Lens hood bayonet

Filter thread

Focus ring

Focus scale

Autofocus/
Manual
focus switch

Zoom ring

Zoom setting

Aperture lock

Aperture ring

Figure 2.20

years, Nikon has been replacing lenses that have aperture rings with versions that only allow setting the aperture with camera controls.

■ **Aperture lock.** If you want your D60 (or other Nikon dSLR) to control the aperture electronically, you must set the lens to its smallest aperture (usually f/22 or f/32) and lock it with this control.

■ **Focus limit switch.** Some lenses have this switch (shown in Figure 2.21), which limits the focus range of the lens, thus potentially reducing focus seeking when shooting distant subjects. The limiter stops the lens from trying to focus at closer distances (in this case, closer than 2.5 meters).

■ **Vibration reduction switch.** Lenses with Nikon's Vibration Reduction (VR) feature include a switch for turning the stabilization feature on and off, and, in some cases, for changing from normal vibration reduction to a more aggressive "active" VR mode useful for, say, shooting from moving vehicles. More on VR and other lens topics in Chapter 6.

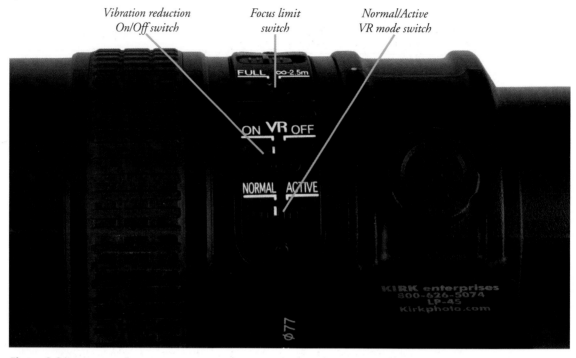

Figure 2.21

The back end of a lens intended for use on a Nikon camera has other components that you seldom see (except when you swap lenses), shown in Figure 2.22, but still should know about:

- **Lens bayonet mount.** This is the mounting mechanism that attaches to a matching mount on the camera. Although the lens bayonet is usually metal, some lenses use a rugged plastic for this key component.

- **Automatic diaphragm lever.** This lever is moved by a matching lever in the camera to adjust the f/stop from wide open (which makes for the brightest view) to the *taking aperture*, which is the f/stop that will be used to take the picture. The actual taking aperture is determined by the camera's metering system (or by you when the D60 is in Manual mode), and is communicated to the lens through the electronic contacts described next. (An exception is when the aperture ring on the lens itself is unlocked and used to specify the f/stop.) However, the spring-loaded physical levers are what actually push the aperture to the selected f/stop.

- **Electronic contacts.** These metal contacts pass information to matching contacts in the camera body allowing a firm electrical connection so that exposure, distance, and other information can be exchanged between the camera and lens.

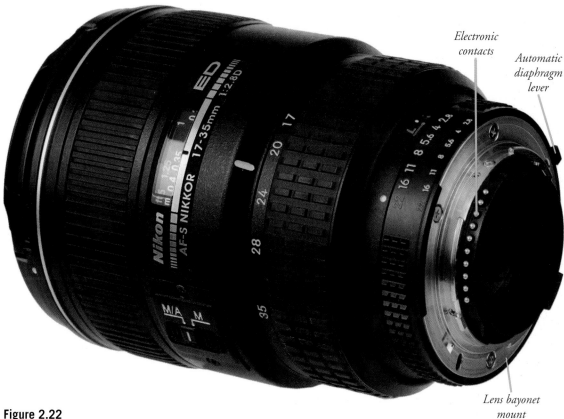

Electronic contacts

Automatic diaphragm lever

Lens bayonet mount

Figure 2.22

Underneath Your Nikon D60

There's not a lot going on with the bottom panel of your Nikon D60. You'll find the battery compartment access door and a tripod socket, which secures the camera to a tripod. The socket accepts other accessories, such as flash brackets and quick release plates that allow rapid attaching and detaching of the D60 from a matching platform affixed to your tripod.

Figure 2.23 shows the underside view of the camera.

Figure 2.23

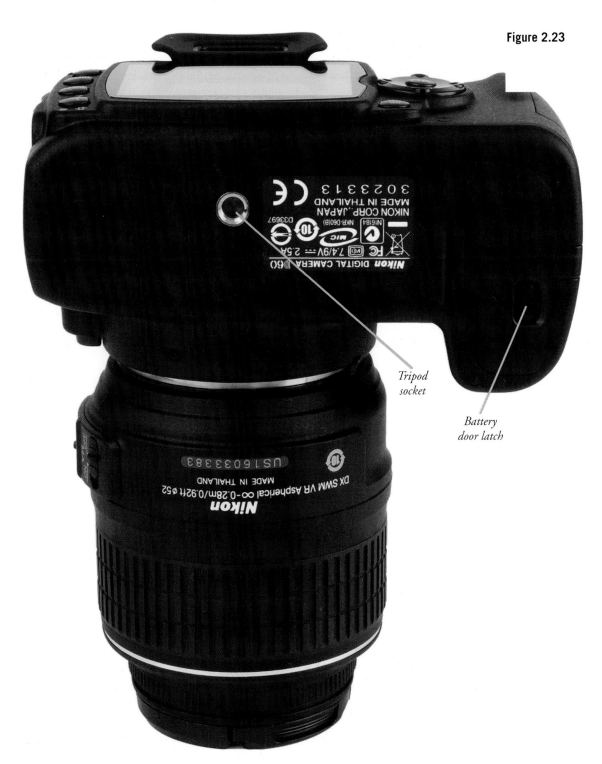

Tripod socket

Battery door latch

Looking Inside the Viewfinder

Much of the important shooting status information is shown inside the viewfinder of the Nikon D60. Not all of this information will be shown at any one time. Figure 2.24 shows what you can expect to see.

These readouts include:

■ **Focus points.** Can display the three areas used by the D60 to focus. The camera can select the appropriate focus zone for you, or you can manually select one or all of the zones.

■ **Active focus point.** The currently selected focus point can be highlighted with red illumination, depending on focus mode.

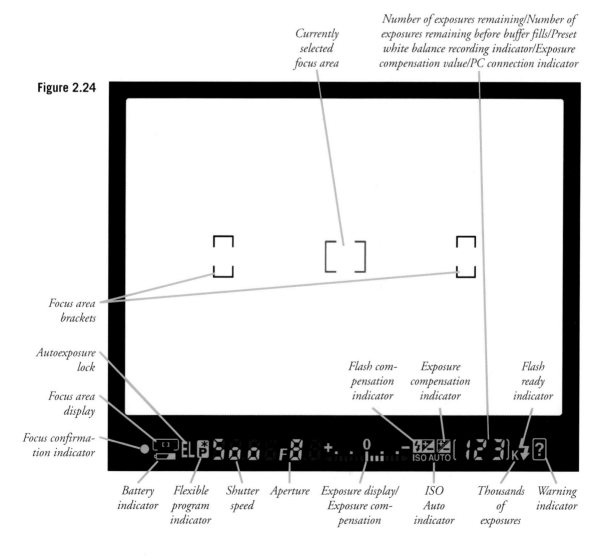

Figure 2.24

- **Battery indicator.** Appears when the D60's battery becomes depleted.

- **Focus indicator.** This green dot stops blinking when the subject covered by the active autofocus zone is in sharp focus, whether focus was achieved by the AF system, or by you using manual focusing.

- **Autoexposure lock.** Shows that exposure has been locked.

- **Shutter speed.** Displays the current shutter speed selected by the camera, or by you in Manual exposure mode.

- **Aperture.** Shows the current aperture chosen by the D60's autoexposure system, or specified by you when using Manual exposure mode.

- **Automatic ISO indicator.** Is shown as a reminder that the D60 has been set to adjust ISO sensitivity automatically.

- **Electronic analog exposure display.** This scale shows the current exposure level, with the bottom indicator centered when the exposure is correct as metered. The indicator may also move to the left or right to indicate over- or underexposure (respectively). The scale is also used to show the amount of exposure compensation dialed in.

- **Flash compensation indicator.** Appears when flash EV changes have been made.

- **Exposure compensation indicator.** This is shown when exposure compensation (EV) changes have been made. It's easy to forget you've dialed in a little more or less exposure, and then shoot a whole series of pictures of a different scene that doesn't require such compensation. Beware!

- **Flash ready indicator.** This icon appears when the flash is fully charged.

- **Exposures remaining/maximum burst available.** Normally displays the number of exposures remaining on your memory card, but while shooting it changes to show a number that indicates the number of frames that can be taken in Continuous Shooting mode using the current settings. This indicator also shows other information, such as exposure/flash compensation values, and whether the D60 is connected to a PC through a USB cable.

LCD Readouts

The Shooting Information displayed on the LCD displays status information about most of the shooting settings (see Figure 2.25). Some of the items on the status LCD also appear in the viewfinder, such as the shutter speed and aperture and the exposure level. This display remains active for about eight seconds, then shuts off if no operations are performed with the camera, or if the eye sensor detects that you're looking through the viewfinder. The display also turns off when you press the shutter release halfway. You can re-activate the display by pressing the Zoom In/Info, Zoom Out, D-Lighting, or Self-timer/Fn buttons (except when the behavior of the latter button has been set to White balance compensation). The display also appears when the exposure compensation/aperture button is pressed in P, S, or A exposure modes, or when the Flash button is pressed in any exposure mode other than Auto (Flash Off). In other words, the Shooting Information display appears whenever you're likely to need it, and can be summoned at other times by pressing the Zoom In/Info button. (Remember, you can press the button a second time to access the Quick Settings screen.)

The Nikon D60 offers three different formats for display of this information on the LCD. (See Chapter 3 for an explanation of how to change among this trio of formats.) There is a Graphics mode, which uses a pleasant but non-intuitive display mixing text, graphical elements, and icons. You can also choose a Wallpaper mode, which overlays the informational display on a background derived from one of your own photographs. I prefer the Classic format, which offers the most information in the most legible format. Included is a thicket of information:

■ **Exposure mode.** This indicator tells you whether the D60 is set for one of the DVP/Scene modes, or for Program, Aperture Priority, Shutter Priority, or Manual exposure modes. An asterisk appears next to the P when you have used Flexible Program mode, which allows you to depart from the camera's programmed exposure setting to set a different combination of shutter speed/aperture that produces the same exposure. You'll find more about this feature in Chapter 4.

■ **Image size.** Shows whether the D60 is shooting Large (3872 x 2592 pixels), Medium (2896 x 1944 pixels), or Small (1926 x 1296 pixels) sizes.

■ **Image quality.** Shows current image quality, including JPEG, RAW, and RAW+Basic.

■ **White balance setting.** One of the white balance settings will appear here, depending on the selection you've made.

- **Shooting mode.** Indicates whether the D60 is set for Single Frame, Continuous Shooting, or one of the Self-Timer/Remote modes.

- **Focus mode.** Shows AF-C, AF-S, AF-A, and Manual focus modes.

- **Autofocus-area indicator.** Displays the autofocus area status, from among Closest Subject, Dynamic Area, and Single Point zone selection modes.

- **Metering mode.** Indicates whether Matrix, Center-Weighted, or Spot metering has been selected.

- **ISO Auto indicator.** Displayed when you've set the D60 to adjust ISO for you automatically.

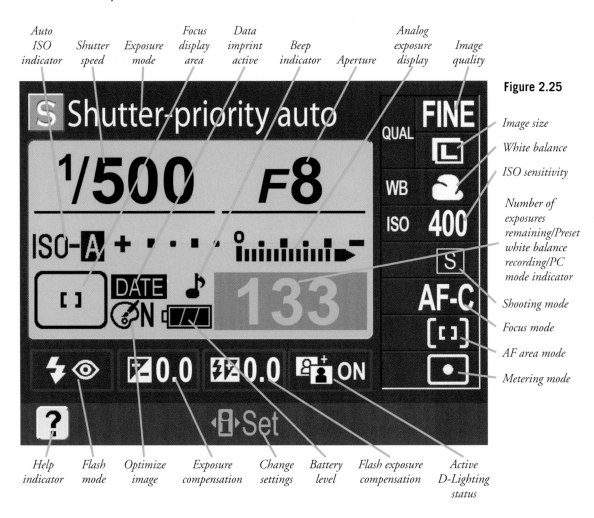

Figure 2.25

■ **Electronic analog display/additional functions.** This is a continuous scale that shows that correct exposure is achieved when the indicator is in the center, and how many stops off exposure is when the indicator veers to the right (underexposure) or left (overexposure). This scale is also used to display other information, such as exposure compensation and bracketing progress.

■ **Exposure compensation.** Appears when you've dialed in exposure compensation. Monitor this indicator, as it's easy to forget that you've told the Nikon D60 to use more or less exposure than what its (reasonably intelligent) metering system would otherwise select.

■ **Flash compensation.** Reminds you that you've tweaked the D60's electronic flash exposure system with more or less exposure requested.

■ **Number of exposures/additional functions.** This indicator shows the number of exposures remaining on your memory card, as well as other functions, such as the number of shots remaining until your memory buffer fills.

■ **Battery status.** Three segments show the approximate battery power remaining.

■ **Flash mode.** The current mode for the D60's built-in electronic flash unit is shown here.

■ **Active D-Lighting status.** Shows whether this feature is active or turned off.

■ **Beep indicator.** Indicates that a helpful beep will sound during the countdown in Self-Timer or Delayed Remote Control mode, or just once in Quick Response Remote mode. The beep also chirps when the D60 successfully focuses when using Sports scene mode, as well as in AF-S or AF-A Autofocus modes. No beep sounds in AF-C mode, or when the subject is moving while in AF-A mode (because the D60 effectively switches to AF-C mode at that point).

■ **Aperture/additional functions.** The selected f/stop appears here, along with a lot of other alternate information, as shown in the label in the figure.

■ **Shutter speed/additional functions.** Here you'll find the shutter speed, ISO setting, color temperature, and other useful data.

■ **Help indicator.** Press the Help button to receive more information about a setting.

■ **Change settings.** Press the Info button while this screen is displayed to access the Quick Settings screen.

3

Setting Up Your Nikon D60

For an entry-level camera, the Nikon D60 has a remarkable number of options and settings you can use to customize the way your camera operates. Not only can you change shooting settings used at the time the picture is taken, but you can adjust the way your camera behaves. Indeed, if your D60 doesn't operate in exactly the way you'd like, chances are you can make a small change in the Playback, Shooting, Custom Setting, and Setup menus that will tailor the D60 to your needs. If you don't like the menus themselves, you can customize which items appear using the D60's My Menu option.

This chapter will help you sort out the settings for all the D60's menus. These include the Playback and Shooting menus, which determine how the D60 displays images on review, and how it uses many of its shooting features to take a photo. Later in the chapter, I'll show you how to use the Custom Setting menu to set power-saving timers, choose a metering mode, and set other functions. In the section on the Setup menu, you'll discover how to format a memory card, set the date/time and LCD brightness, and do other maintenance tasks. You'll learn how to use the Retouch menu to remove red-eye and fix up photos right in your camera.

As I've mentioned before, this book isn't intended to replace the manual you received with your D60, nor have I any interest in rehashing its contents. You'll still find the original manual useful as a standby reference that lists every possible option in exhaustive (if mind-numbing) detail—without really telling you how to use those options to take better pictures. There is, however, some unavoidable duplication between the

Nikon manual and this chapter, because I'm going to explain all the key menu choices and the options you may have in using them. You should find, though, that I will give you the information you need in a much more helpful format, with plenty of detail on why you should make some settings that are particularly cryptic.

I'm not going to waste a lot of space on some of the more obvious menu choices in these chapters. For example, you can probably figure out, even without my help, that the Beep option in Custom Setting menu **CSM #1** deals with the solid-state beeper in your camera that sounds off during various activities (such as the self-timer countdown). You can certainly decipher the import of the two options available for the Beep entry (On and Off). In this chapter, I'll devote no more than a sentence or two to the blatantly obvious settings and concentrate on the more confusing aspects of D60 setup, such as autofocus. I'll start with an overview of using the D60's menus themselves.

Anatomy of the Nikon D60's Menus

The D60 has one of the best-designed menu systems of any digital SLR in its price class, with a remarkable amount of consistency with other cameras in the Nikon product line. In fact, if you used any other Nikon dSLR before you purchased your Nikon D60, you're probably already familiar with the basic menu lineup. Press the Menu button, located third from the bottom at the left side of the LCD. The menus consist of a series of five separate screens with rows of entries, as shown in Figure 3.1. (Note that when the D60 is set on Auto, some menu choices are not available.)

There are three columns of information in each menu screen.

- The left-hand column includes an icon representing each of the top-level menu screens. From the top in Figure 3.1, they are Playback (right-pointing triangle icon), Shooting (camera icon), Custom Setting (pencil icon), Setup (wrench), and Retouch (a paintbrush), with Help access represented by a question mark at the bottom of the column.

- The center column includes the name representing the function of each choice in the currently selected menu. For example, **Delete** represents the menu entry for removing individual photos or multiple images, while **Print set (DPOF)** indicates the menu entry used for choosing photos for printing.

- The right-hand column has an icon or text that shows either the current setting for that menu item or text or an icon that represents the function of that menu entry. In Figure 3.1, a trash can icon shows that you can use the **Delete** entry for removing images, while the text **ON** appears next to the **Rotate tall** entry, indicating that the D60 has been set to rotate vertical images to display them in their proper orientation on the LCD.

Figure 3.1
The most-
recently
accessed menu
appears when
you press the
Menu button.

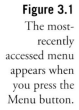

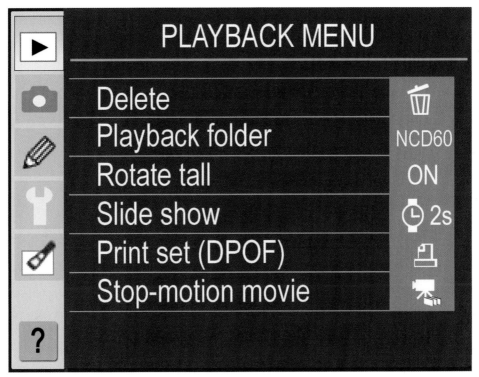

Navigating among the various menus is easy and follows a consistent set of rules.

■ **Press Menu to start.** Press the Menu button to display the main menu screens.

■ **Navigate with the multi-selector pad.** The multi-selector pad, located to the right of the LCD, has indents at the up/down/left/right positions. Press these "buttons" to navigate among the menu selections. Press the left button to move highlighting to the left column; then press the up/down buttons to scroll up or down among the five top-level menus.

■ **Highlighting indicates active choice.** As each top-level menu is highlighted, its icon will first change from black and white to yellow/amber, white, and black. As you use the multi-selector's right button to move into the column containing that menu's choices, you can then use the up/down buttons to scroll among the individual entries, as shown in Figure 3.2. If more than one screen full of choices is available, a scroll bar appears at the far right of the screen, with a position slider showing the relative position of the currently highlighted entry. (You'll see the scroll bar in an upcoming menu screen.)

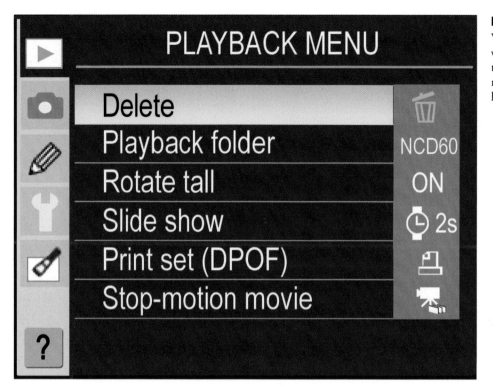

Figure 3.2
When working
within a menu,
the selected
menu entry is
highlighted.

Tip

You can remove or restore various items in each of the top-level menus using the
CSM/Setup Menu entry in the Setup menu. For example, if you never make
stop-motion movies, you can hide that entry. I'll show you how to do that later
in this chapter.

■ **Select a menu item.** To work with a highlighted menu entry, press the OK button
in the center of the multi-selector on the back of the D60 or just press the right
button on the multi-selector. Any additional screens of choices will appear, as shown
in Figure 3.3. You can move among them using the same multi-selector movements.

■ **Choose your menu option.** You can confirm a selection by pressing the OK button or, frequently, by pressing the right button on the multi-selector once again.
Some functions require scrolling to a Done menu choice, or include an instruction
to Set a choice using some other button.

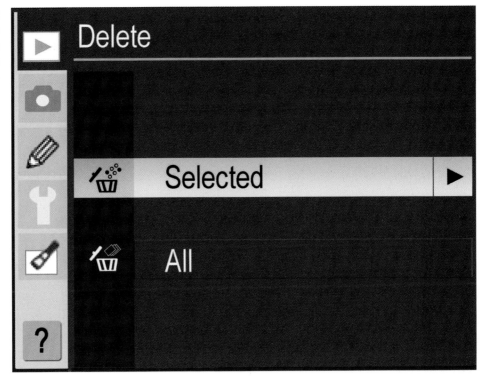

- **Leaving the menu system.** Pressing the multi-selector left button usually backs you out of the current screen, and pressing the Menu button again usually does the same thing. You can exit the menu system at any time by tapping the shutter release button. If you haven't confirmed your choice for a particular option, no changes will be made.

- **Quick return.** The Nikon D60 "remembers" the top-level menu and specific menu entry you were using (but not any submenus) the last time the menu system was accessed (even if you have subsequently turned the camera off), so pressing the Menu button brings you back to where you left off. So, if you were working with, say, the Delete option in the Playback menu, the next time you press the Menu button, the Playback menu and Delete entry will be highlighted (as in Figure 3.2), but not the specific submenu (Figure 3.3) that you might have selected.

The top-level menus are color coded, and a bar in that color is displayed underneath the menu title when one of those menus is highlighted. The colors are Playback menu (blue); Shooting menu (green); Custom Setting menu (red); Setup menu (orange); Retouch menu (purple); and My Menu (gray).

Playback Menu Options

The blue-coded Playback menu has six entries used to select options related to the display, review, and printing of the photos you've taken. Unless you've hidden a menu entry (as described under the Setup menu options), the choices you'll find include:

- Delete
- Playback folder
- Rotate Tall
- Slide Show

- Slide Show
- Print set (DPOF)
- Stop-Motion Movie

Delete

Choose this menu entry and you'll be given two choices (as shown earlier in Figure 3.3): Selected and All. If you choose Selected, you'll see an image selection screen like the one shown in Figure 3.4. Then, follow these instructions:

1. **Review thumbnails.** Use the multi-selector left/right buttons to scroll among the available images. (You cannot use the up/down buttons to skip up or down a row of images; only the left/right buttons can be used to advance/reverse among the thumbnails.)

2. **Examine image.** When you highlight an image you think you might want to delete, press the Zoom button to temporarily enlarge that image so you can evaluate it further. When you release the button, the selection screen returns.

3. **Mark/unmark images.** To mark an image for deletion, press the multi-selector up button (*not* the Trash button). A trash can icon will appear overlaid on that image's thumbnail. To unmark an image, press the multi-selector up or down button.

4. **Remove images.** When you've finished marking images to delete, press **OK**. A final screen will appear asking you to confirm the removal of the image(s). Choose **Yes** to delete the image(s) or **No** to cancel deletion, and then press **OK**. If you selected Yes, then you'll return to the Playback menu; if you choose No, you'll be taken back to the selection screen to mark/unmark images.

5. To back out of the selection screen, press the Menu button.

Tip

Using the Delete menu option to remove images will have no effect on images that have been marked as protected with the Protect key.

Figure 3.4
Images selected
for deletion are
marked with a
trash can icon.

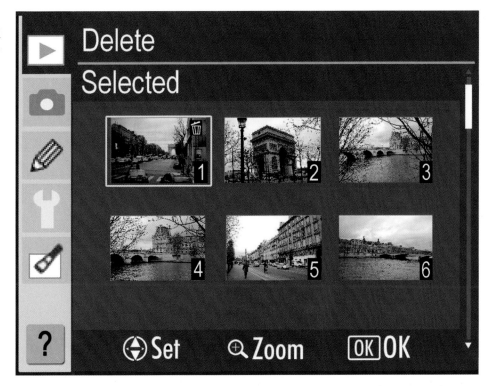

Keep in mind that deleting images through the Delete process is slower than just wiping out the whole card with the Format command, so using Format is generally much faster than choosing Delete: All, and also is a safer way of returning your memory card to a fresh, blank state.

Playback Folder

Images created by your Nikon D60 are deposited into folders on your memory card. These folders have names like 100NCD60 or 101NCD60, but you can change those default names to something else using the Folders option in the Setup menu, described later in this chapter.

With a freshly formatted memory card (formatting is covered under the Setup menu), the D60 starts with a default name: 100NCD60. When that folder fills with the maximum of 999 images, the camera automatically creates a new folder numbered one higher, such as 101NCD60. If you use the same memory card in another camera, that camera will also create its own folder (say, 102NCD40 for a Nikon D40). Thus you can end up with several folders on the same memory card, at least one for each camera the card is used in, until you eventually reformat the card and folder creation starts anew. Later in this chapter, in the section on the Setup menu, I'll show you how to create folders with names you select yourself.

This menu item allows you to choose which folders are accessed when displaying images using the D60's Playback facility. Your choices are as follows:

- **Current.** The D60 will display only images in the current folder, as specified in the Setup menu (described later in this chapter). For example, if you have been shooting heavily at an event and have already accumulated more than 999 shots and the D60 has created a new folder for the overflow, you'd use this setting to view only the most recent photos, which reside in that new current folder. You can change the current folder to any other specific folder on your memory card using the Folders option in the Setup menu, described later in this chapter.

- **All.** All folders containing images that the D60 can read will be accessed, regardless of which camera created them. You might want to use this setting if you swap memory cards among several cameras and want to be able to review all the photos. You will be able to view images even if they were created by a non-Nikon camera if those images conform to a specification called the Design Rule for Camera File systems (DCF).

Rotate Tall

When you rotate the D60 to photograph vertical subjects in portrait (tall), rather than landscape (wide) orientation, you probably don't want to view them tilted onto their sides later on, either on the camera LCD or within your image viewing/editing application on your computer. The D60 is way ahead of you. It has a directional sensor built in that can detect whether the camera was rotated when the photo was taken and hide this information in the image file itself.

The orientation data is applied in two different ways. It can be used by the D60 to automatically rotate images when they are displayed on the camera's LCD monitor, or you can ignore the data and let the images display in non-rotated fashion (so you have to rotate the camera to view them in their proper orientation). Your image editing application, such as Adobe Photoshop Elements, can also use the embedded file data to automatically rotate images on your computer screen.

But either feature works only if you've told the D60 to place orientation information in the image file so it can be retrieved when the image is displayed. You must set **Auto image rotation** to **On** in the Setup menu (I'll show you how to do that later in this chapter). Once you've done that, the D60 will embed information about orientation in the image file, and both your D60 and your image editor can rotate the images for you as the files are displayed.

This menu choice deals only with whether the image should be rotated when displayed on the *camera LCD monitor*. (If you de-activate this option, your image editing software can still read the embedded rotation data and properly display your images.) When Rotate Tall is turned off, the Nikon D60 does not rotate pictures taken in vertical orientation, displaying them as shown in Figure 3.5. The image is large on your LCD screen, but you must rotate the camera to view it upright.

When Rotate Tall is turned on, the D60 rotates pictures taken in vertical orientation on the LCD screen so you don't have to turn the camera to view them comfortably. However, this orientation also means that the longest dimension of the image is shown using the shortest dimension of the LCD, so the picture is reduced in size, as you can see in Figure 3.6.

Figure 3.5
With Rotate Tall turned off, vertical images appear large on the LCD, but you must turn the camera to view them upright.

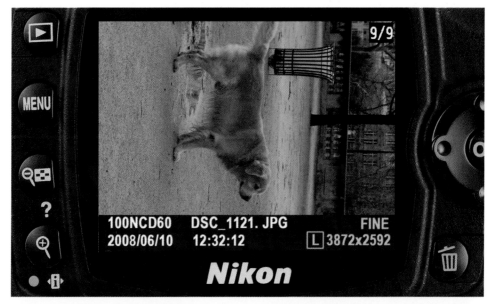

Figure 3.6
With Rotate Tall turned on, vertical images are shown in a smaller size, but oriented for viewing without turning the camera.

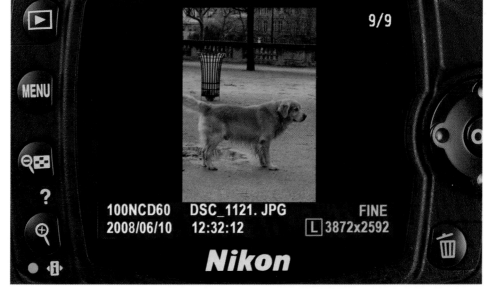

So, turn this feature **On** (as well as Auto image rotation in the Setup menu), if you'd rather not turn your camera to view vertical shots in their natural orientation, and don't mind the smaller image. Turn the feature **Off** if, as I do, you'd rather see a larger image and are willing to rotate the camera to do so.

Slide Show

The D60's Slide Show feature is a convenient way to review images in the current play-back folder one after another, without the need to manually switch between them. To activate, just choose **Start** from this entry in the Playback menu. If you like, you can choose **Frame interval** before commencing the show in order to select an interval of 2, 3, 5, or 10 seconds between "slides."

During playback, you can press the **OK** button to pause the "slide show" (in case you want to examine an image more closely). When the show is paused, a menu pops up, as shown in Figure 3.7, with choices to restart the show (by pressing the OK button again); change the interval between frames; or to exit the show entirely.

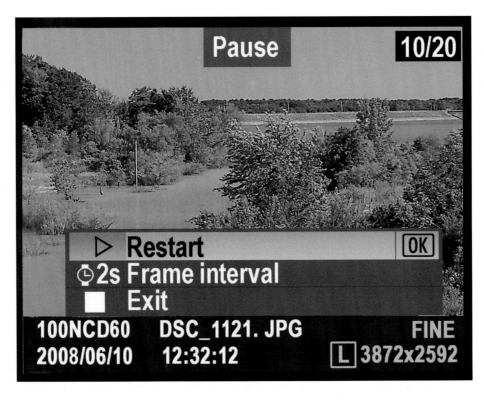

Figure 3.7
Press the OK button to pause the slide show, change the interval between slides, or to exit the presentation.

As the images are displayed, press the up/down multi-selector buttons to change the amount of information presented on the screen with each image. For example, you might want to review a set of images and the settings used to shoot them. At any time during the show, press the up/down buttons until the informational screen you want is overlaid on the images.

As the slide show progresses, you can press the left/right multi-selector buttons to move back to a previous frame or jump ahead to the next one. The slide show will then proceed as before. Press the Menu button to exit the slide show and return to the menu, or the Playback button to exit the menu system totally. As always, while reviewing images you can tap the Menu button to exit the show and return to the menus, or tap the shutter release button if you want to remove everything from the screen and return to shooting mode.

At the end of the slide show, as when you've paused it, you'll be offered the choice of restarting the sequence, changing the frame interval, or exiting the slide show feature completely.

Print Set (DPOF)

You can print directly from your camera to a printer compatible with a specification called *PictBridge* (most recent printers are, and have a connector for that mode). You can also move your memory card and give it to your retailer for printing in their lab or in-store printing machine, or insert the card into a stand-alone picture kiosk and make prints yourself. In all these cases, you can easily specify exactly which photos you want printed, and how many copies you'd like of each picture. This menu item does all the work for you.

The Nikon D60 supports the DPOF (Digital Print Order Format) that is now almost universally used by digital cameras to specify which images on your memory card should be printed, and the number of prints desired of each image. This information is recorded on the memory card and can be interpreted by a compatible printer when the camera is linked to the printer using the USB cable, or when the memory card is inserted into a card reader slot on the printer itself. Photo labs and stand-alone kiosks are also equipped to read this data and make prints when you supply your memory card to them.

When you choose this menu item, you're presented with a set of screens that looks very much like the Delete photos screens described earlier (I used the same set of example pictures for the illustration), only you're selecting pictures for printing rather than deleting them. The first screen you see when you choose **Print Set (DPOF)** asks if you'd like to **Select/set** pictures for printing, or **Deselect all?** images that have already been marked.

Choose **Select/set** to choose photos and specify how many prints of each you'd like. Choose **Deselect all?** to cancel any existing print order and start over. If you want to select photos for printing, follow these steps when the screen shown in Figure 3.8 appears:

1. **View images on your card.** Use the multi-selector left/right keys (and not the up/down keys) to scroll among the available images.

2. **Evaluate specific photos.** When you highlight an image you might want to print, press the Zoom button to temporarily enlarge that image so you can evaluate it further. When you release the button, the selection screen returns.

3. **Mark images for printing and specify number of copies.** To mark a highlighted image for printing, press the multi-selector up/down buttons to choose the number of prints you want, up to 99 per image. The up button increases the number of prints; the down button decreases the amount. A printer icon and the number specified will appear overlaid on that image's thumbnail.

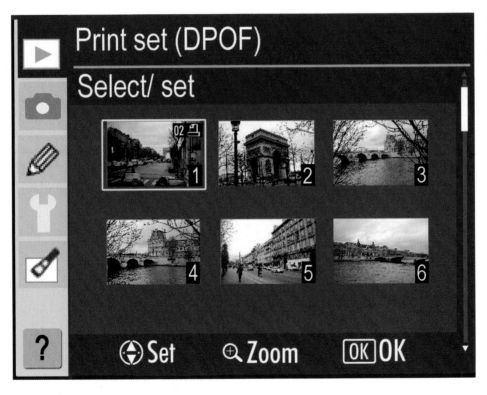

Figure 3.8
Select images for printing.

4. **Unmark images if you change your mind.** To unmark an image for printing, highlight and press the down button until the number of prints reaches zero. The printer icon will vanish.

5. **Finish selecting and marking images.** When you've finished marking images to print, press **OK**.

6. **Specify date or shooting information on the print.** A final screen will appear in which you can request a data imprint (shutter speed and aperture) or imprint date (the date the photos were taken). Use the up/down buttons to select one or both of these options, if desired, and press the left/right buttons to mark or unmark the check boxes. When a box is marked, the imprint information for that option will be included on *all* prints in the print order.

7. **Exit the Print Set screens.** Scroll up to **Done** when finished, and press **OK** or the right cursor button.

Stop-Motion Movie

Stop-motion movies are mini-films created in the Retouch menu, and consist of a series of frames that are displayed quickly, one after another, in flip-book or rough movie fashion. I'll explain how to create stop-motion movies later in this chapter. The Stop-Motion Movie menu choice in the Playback menu is grayed out (inaccessible) unless you have one or more of these movies stored in your current playback folder. There aren't many in the way of options for this menu entry; you can select a movie and play it.

If Stop-Motion Movie is not grayed out, select it and you'll see the Nikon D60's image selection screen, but the thumbnails shown represent the first frame of each movie. Use the multi-selector left/right buttons to navigate to the thumbnail of the movie you want to view. Then, press the Zoom button to see a slightly enlarged thumbnail of the first frame, or press **OK** to start the movie. During playback, a progress bar appears at the bottom of the screen along with a bar containing the standard VCR/DVD-player type Reverse/Pause-Play/Stop/Forward icons. Press the multi-selector left/right buttons to choose one of those actions and the OK button to activate it. I'll show you how to make your own stop-motion movie later in this chapter.

Shooting Menu Options

This concise menu has just seven settings, and five of them—Image Quality, Image Size, White Balance, ISO Sensitivity, and Active D-Lighting—duplicate functions that are more readily available from the Quick Settings screen described in Chapter 1. The two new settings are Optimize Image and Noise Reduction (see Figure 3.9). Taken together, these seven are likely to be the most common settings changes you make, with changes made to one or more of them during a particular session fairly common. You might make such adjustments as you begin a shooting session, or when you move from one type of subject to another. Nikon makes accessing these changes very easy.

I recommend using the Quick Settings screen for making changes to the five entries duplicated there. You can readily see the current settings for any of these—and the other settings visible on the Shooting Information screen—and then press the Info button, use the multi-selector directional buttons to navigate to the entry you want to use, press OK, and make your change in a few seconds. Using the equivalent Shooting menu entries usually takes a little longer.

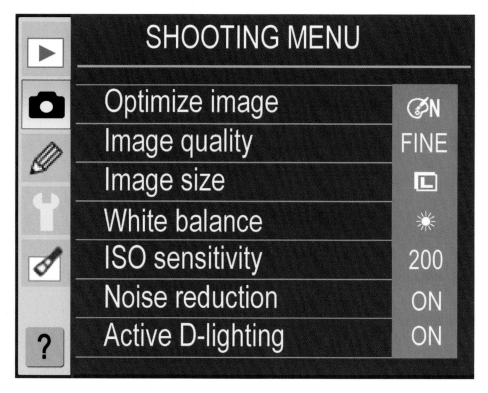

Figure 3.9
Common shooting settings can be changed in this menu.

This section explains the options of the Shooting menu and how to use them. The options you'll find in these green-coded menus (unless you've changed the Shooting menu using the Setup menu option described later in this chapter) include:

- Optimize Image
- Image Quality
- Image Size
- White Balance

- ISO Sensitivity
- Active D-Lighting
- Noise Reduction

Optimize Image

The pictures you take with your D60 can be individually fine-tuned in an image editor, of course, but you can also choose certain kinds of adjustments that are made to every picture, as you shoot. The Optimize Image options found in this menu option have five settings you can use to give your pictures richer color, increased or reduced contrast, or a softer look. There's an additional setting for black-and-white effects, and a custom setting that you can use to adjust parameters (described next) such as color, sharpening, color richness, and contrast yourself. To apply any of these settings to an appropriate shooting situation, just visit this menu entry and select the setting you want to use.

When you select this menu choice, you'll see a total of seven options. Each of these provides varying amounts of five different attributes: sharpness, contrast, color mode, saturation, and hue. The individual parameters affect your images in various ways, with four of them easily illustrated in Figure 3.10:

- **Sharpness.** This affects the contrast of the edges or outlines of your image, making a photo look more or less sharp. At upper left in Figure 3.10, a section of an image has had extra sharpening applied, which you can see by comparing that section with the others in the figure.

- **Contrast.** This factor affects an attribute called *tone compensation*, which controls whether detail is visible or lost in the brightest areas and darkest areas of your image. An image with high contrast shows less detail in the highlights and shadows, but produces a more dramatic appearance. A lower contrast image has more detail in those areas, but, if contrast is too low, the image may appear to be flat and dull. At upper right in Figure 3.10, I've divided the image section into two parts, with higher contrast applied at top, and normal contrast at bottom.

- **Color mode.** This attribute controls which of three different color palettes—sets of available colors—are applied. I'll explain color mode in more detail later in this section, but I haven't illustrated it in the figure, because the differences are subtle.

■ **Saturation.** The richness of the colors is determined by the saturation setting. For example, a deep red rose is fully saturated, while one that appears more pinkish is still, technically, red, but the color is less saturated and more muted. At lower left in Figure 3.10, the saturation has been enhanced.

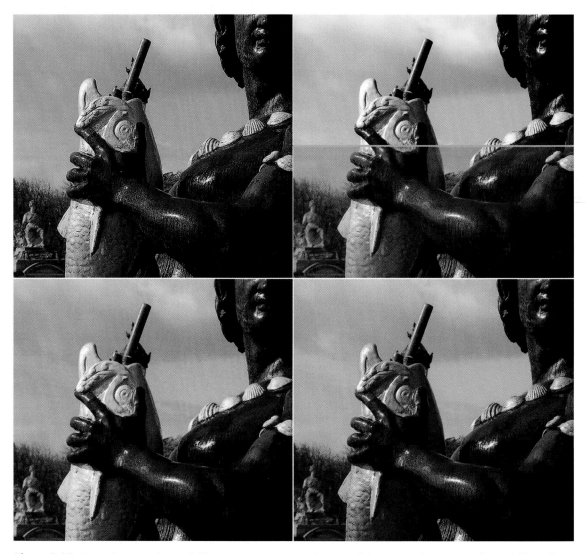

Figure 3.10 Extra sharpness (upper left); contrast adjustment (upper right); enhanced saturation (lower left); and hue modification (lower right).

■ **Hue.** Think of hue as rotating all the colors in an image around a color wheel, as was done for the hue adjustment seen at bottom right in Figure 3.10. Positive hue adjustments bias reds toward the orange end of the spectrum, greens more towards the blue, and blues become purplish, as you can visualize in Figure 3.11. Going the other way around the wheel, reds become more purple, blues more green, and greens become more yellow. I'll describe hue more in the section on using Custom settings.

Figure 3.11
Hue adjust-
ments "rotate"
colors in one
direction or
another along
the perimeter
of this color
wheel.

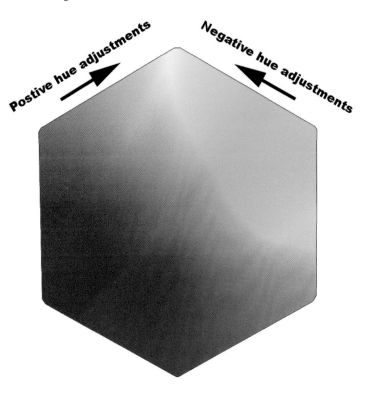

These attributes are tweaked in a variety of ways to produce the individual settings. If you want to adjust them yourself, use the Custom option. Your choices are as follows:

■ **N: Normal.** With the Nikon D60, this default setting produces images that have slightly reduced contrast and saturation, ripe for a bit of fine-tuning in your image editor. If you want to use most of your images "as-is" you might be happier with the Vivid setting as your standard choice.

■ **SO: Softer.** This setting produces pictures that are even lower in contrast and with a little less sharpness, making them perfect for flattering portraits, particularly if you are using the built-in flash (which tends to provide lighting that is a little harsh and higher in contrast).

- **VI: Vivid.** Many find that this setting is a good choice for all-around shooting, because it provides a brighter, more colorful image with a slight increase in sharpness. If you make prints directly from your camera images, you'll probably like this setting.

- **VI+: More vivid.** Everything you get with Vivid, and then some. There may be too much sharpness and saturation boost, but this setting would certainly be useful on a dull, overcast day.

- **PO: Portrait.** While this setting supposedly gives you lower contrast and softness for portraits, the effects may be too little to do much good. I prefer the Softer setting for portraits.

- **BW: Black-and-white.** This setting gives you a black-and-white picture as you shoot. I recommend using it only if you need a quick monochrome image for some reason. You can usually produce a better black-and-white picture in your image editor, particularly if you work from the RAW file. In addition, the Retouch menu has an option for creating a black-and-white copy of any image on your memory card.

- **Custom.** This setting allows you to specify sharpness, contrast, color mode, saturation, and hue yourself. I'll describe how to use it next.

Custom Image Optimization

To create a customized Optimize Image setting, press the Menu button and navigate to the Optimize Image entry in the Shooting menu. Then, press the multi-selector up/down buttons to highlight the Custom entry. Press the right button, and the screen shown in Figure 3.12 appears. It shows six entries: five for parameters you can change, and Done.

To change the attributes of the Custom setting, scroll down to the parameter you want to modify and press the multi-selector right button to invoke a screen with each of the possible values available. Use the multi-selector up/down buttons to scroll among the values, and then press OK to confirm your choice. You'll be returned to the Optimize Image: Custom screen to select more attributes to modify. When you're finished, scroll up to the Done selection and press OK to return to the Shooting menu. At that point, you can press the Menu button or tap the shutter release button to exit the menu system.

The available values you can select are as follows:

- **Image sharpening.** You can choose from Normal (0) to plus/minus 2. Use –1 (low) or –2 (medium low) to produce a softer image, and +1 (medium high) or +2 (high) to add sharpness. Select Auto, and the D60 will choose sharpening for you, based on its interpretation of the image content.

Figure 3.12
Five attributes
can be modi-
fied from the
Optimize
Image: Custom
screen.

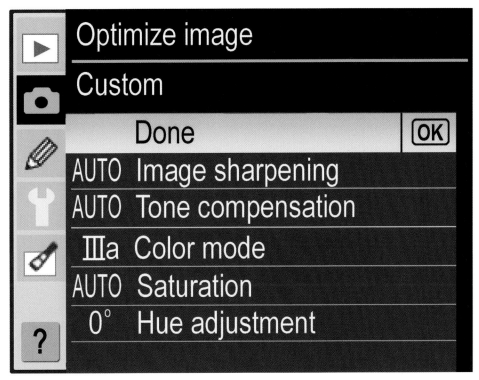

■ **Tone compensation.** The settings of Auto or Normal (0) are usually best, but if you feel that a scene can use a contrast boost to give it more snap, you can choose +1 (medium high), or +2 (more contrast). To reduce contrast, choose –1 (medium low) or –2 (less contrast). Be careful when using tone compensation here if you are also adjusting tonal values by using the D-lighting feature introduced earlier in this chapter and explained in more detail in the section on the Retouch menu.

■ **Color mode.** This option allows you to choose one of three different ranges of colors, called *color spaces*, that the D60 will use. You can choose Ia (sRGB), which is recommended for subjects like images of people that will be printed more or less as they were taken; II (Adobe RGB), which is recommended for images that will be edited and can benefit from the additional colors available; and IIIa (sRGB), the default setting, which is similar to Ia, but with colors better suited for nature and landscape photos. Don't panic! I'll explain the differences between these three color modes next.

■ **Saturation.** Choose from Auto (the D60 selects a suitable color saturation for you); Normal (the default setting, which produces somewhat muted colors); Moderate (for colors that are even more muted); or Enhanced (for more vivid color). You can use saturation in combination with the Tone compensation contrast settings to produce different degrees of color brightness, if you're willing to experiment to see what you like.

■ **Hue adjustment.** Your choices here are from minus 9 degrees (counterclockwise on the color wheel shown in Figure 3.11) to plus 9 degrees (to shift colors in a clockwise direction), in increments of three degrees. (Thus, –9, –6, –3, 0, +3, +6, and +9 degrees are available.) Use this adjustment to add a color bias to your photos.

Color Space

The Nikon D60's Color Mode option gives you three variations of two different color spaces (also called *color gamuts*), named Adobe RGB (because it was developed by Adobe Systems in 1998), and sRGB (supposedly because it is the *standard* RGB color space). These two color gamuts define a specific set of colors that can be applied to the images your D60 captures.

You're probably surprised that the Nikon D60 doesn't automatically capture *all* the colors we see. Unfortunately, that's impossible because of the limitations of the sensor and the filters used to capture the fundamental red, green, and blue colors, as well as that of the phosphors used to display those colors on your camera and computer monitors. Nor is it possible to *print* every color our eyes detect, because the inks or pigments used don't absorb and reflect colors perfectly.

Instead, the colors that can be reproduced by a given device are represented as a color space that exists within the full range of colors we can see. That full range is represented by the odd-shaped splotch of color shown in Figure 3.13, as defined by scientists at an international organization back in 1931. The colors possible with Adobe RGB are represented by the larger, black triangle in the figure, while the sRGB gamut is represented by the smaller white triangle.

Regardless of which triangle—or color space—is used by the D60, you end up with 16.8 million different colors that can be used in your photograph. (No one image will contain all 16.8 million!) But, as you can see from the figure, the colors available will be *different*.

Adobe RGB (Color Mode II) is what is often called an *expanded* color space, because it can reproduce a selection of colors that is spread over a wider range of the visual spectrum. Adobe RGB is useful for commercial and professional printing. You don't need this range of colors if your images will be displayed primarily on your computer screen or output by your personal printer.

The other color space, sRGB (Color Modes Ia and IIIa), is recommended for images that will be output locally on the user's own printer, as this color space matches that of the typical inkjet printer fairly closely. You'd choose between Modes Ia and IIIa based on the type of subject matter you were shooting (as outlined earlier). While both Adobe RGB and sRGB can reproduce the exact same 16.8 million absolute colors, Adobe RGB spreads those colors over a larger portion of the visible spectrum, as you can see in the figure. Think of a box of crayons (the jumbo 16.8 million crayon variety). Some of the

Figure 3.13
The outer fig-
ure shows all
the colors we
can see; the
two inner out-
lines show the
boundaries of
Adobe RGB
(black triangle)
and sRGB
(white
triangle).

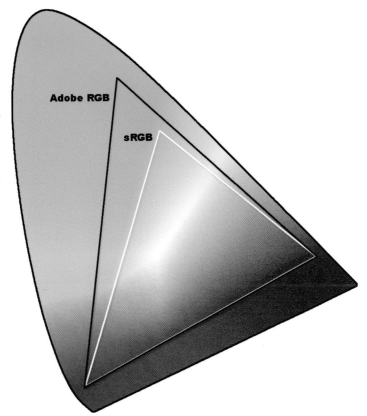

basic crayons from the original sRGB set have been removed and replaced with new
hues not contained in the original box. Your "new" box contains colors that can't be
reproduced by your computer monitor, but which work just fine with a commercial
printing press.

Image Quality

As I noted in Chapter 2, you can choose the image quality settings used by the D60 to
store its files. The quickest way to do that is with the Quick Settings screen. You can
also use this menu option, if you prefer. There is no real advantage to using this menu
instead of the Quick Settings screen. You have two choices to make:

■ **Level of JPEG compression.** To reduce the size of your image files and allow more
photos to be stored on a given memory card, the D60 uses JPEG compression to
squeeze the images down to a smaller size. This compacting reduces the image quality a little, so you're offered your choice of Fine (a 1:4 reduction), Normal (1:8
reduction), and Basic (1:16) compression. You can see an exaggerated version of the
effects of JPEG compression in Figure 3.14. I'll explain more about JPEG compression later in this section.

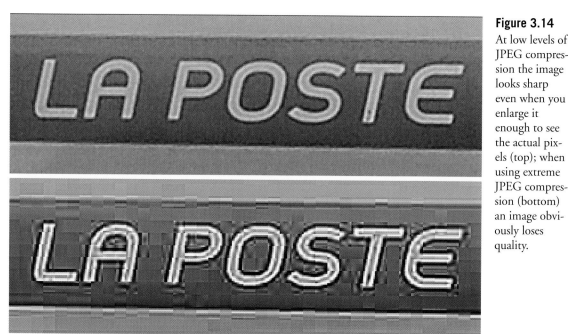

Figure 3.14
At low levels of JPEG compression the image looks sharp even when you enlarge it enough to see the actual pixels (top); when using extreme JPEG compression (bottom) an image obviously loses quality.

- **JPEG, RAW, or both.** You can elect to store only JPEG versions of the images you shoot, or you can save your photos as RAW images, which Nikon calls NEF, for Nikon Electronic Format files. RAW images consume more than twice as much space on your memory card. Or, you can store both RAW and a JPEG Basic file at once as you shoot. Many photographers elect to save *both* JPEG and a RAW, so they'll have a JPEG Basic version that might be usable as-is, as well as the original "digital negative" RAW file in case they want to do some processing of the image later. You'll end up with two different versions of the same file: one with a .jpg extension, and one with the .nef extension that signifies a Nikon RAW file.

To choose the combination you want, access the Shooting menu, scroll to **Image quality**, and select it by pressing **OK** or the multi-selector right button. Scroll to highlight the setting you want, and either press **OK** or push the multi-selector right button to confirm your selection.

In practice, you'll probably use the **JPEG fine** or **NEF (RAW)+JPEG basic** selections most often. Why so many choices, then? There are some advantages to using the JPEG Normal and JPEG Basic settings. Settings that are less than max allow stretching the capacity of your memory card so you can shoehorn quite a few more pictures onto a single memory card. That can come in useful when on vacation and you're running out of storage, or when you're shooting non-critical work that doesn't require 10 megapixels of resolution (such as photos taken for real estate listings, web page display, photo

ID cards, or similar applications). Some photographers like to record RAW+JPEG Basic so they'll have a moderate quality JPEG file for review only and no intention of using for editing purposes, while retaining access to the original RAW file for serious editing.

For most work, using lower resolution and extra compression is false economy. You never know when you might actually need that extra bit of picture detail. Your best bet is to have enough memory cards to handle all the shooting you want to do until you have the chance to transfer your photos to your computer or a personal storage device.

However, reduced image quality can sometimes be beneficial if you're shooting sequences of photos rapidly, as the D60 is able to hold more of them in its internal memory buffer before transferring to the memory card. Still, for most sports and other applications, you'd probably rather have better, sharper pictures than longer periods of continuous shooting. Do you really need 10 shots of a pass reception in a football game, or six slightly different versions of your local basketball star driving in for a lay-up?

JPEG vs. RAW

You'll sometimes be told that Nikon's NEF or RAW files are the "unprocessed" image information your camera produces, before it's been modified. That's nonsense. RAW files are no more unprocessed than camera film is after it's been through the chemicals to produce a negative or transparency. Your digital image undergoes a significant amount of processing before it is saved as a RAW file.

A RAW file is more similar to a film camera's processed negative. It contains all the information captured by the sensor, but with no sharpening and no application of any special filters or other settings you might have specified when you took the picture. Those settings are *stored* with the RAW file so they can be applied when the image is converted to a form compatible with your favorite image editor. However, using RAW conversion software such as Adobe Camera Raw or Nikon Capture NX, you can override those settings and apply settings of your own. You can select essentially the same changes there that you might have specified in your camera's picture-taking options.

RAW exists because sometimes we want to have access to all the information captured by the camera, before the camera's internal logic has processed it and converted the image to a standard file format. RAW doesn't save as much space as JPEG. What it does do is preserve all the information captured by your camera after it's been converted from analog to digital form.

So, why don't we always use RAW? Some photographers avoid using Nikon's RAW NEF files on the misguided conviction that they don't want to spend time in an image editor. But, if your basic settings are okay, such work is *optional*, and needs to be applied only when a particular image needs to be fine-tuned.

Although some photographers do save *only* in RAW format, it's common to use RAW+JPEG Basic, or, if you're confident about your settings, just shoot JPEG and eschew RAW altogether. In some situations, working with a RAW file can slow you down a little. RAW images take longer to store on the memory card, and must be converted from RAW to a format your image editor can handle, whether you elect to go with the default settings in force when the picture was taken, or make minor adjustments to the settings you specified in the camera.

As a result, those who depend on speedy access to images or who shoot large numbers of photos at once may prefer JPEG over RAW. These photographers include wedding and sports shooters, who may take hundreds to more than a thousand pictures within a few hours.

JPEG was invented as a more compact file format that can store most of the information in a digital image, but in a much smaller size. JPEG predates most digital SLRs and was initially used to squeeze down files for transmission over slow dial-up connections. JPEG provides smaller files by compressing the information in a way that loses some image data. JPEG remains a viable alternative because it offers several different quality levels. At the highest-quality Fine level, you might not be able to tell the difference between the original RAW file and the JPEG version. If you don't mind losing some quality, you can use more aggressive Normal compression with JPEG to cut the size again.

Image Size

The next menu command in the Shooting menu lets you select the resolution, or number of pixels captured as you shoot with your Nikon D60. Your choices range from Large (L—3872 × 2592, 10.2 megapixels), Medium (M—2896 × 1944, 5.6 megapixels), and Small (S—1936 × 1296 pixels, 2.5 megapixels). There are no additional options available from the Image Size menu screen. Keep in mind that if you choose NEF (RAW) or NEW (RAW)+JPEG Basic, only the Large image size can be selected. The other size options are grayed out and unavailable.

White Balance

The Shooting menu's White Balance settings are considerably more flexible than those available from the Quick Settings screen, so may want to use this menu entry instead. The Quick Settings screen lets you choose one of six pre-defined settings, plus Auto and PRE (which is a user-definable white balance you can base on the lighting in a scene of your choice). The White Balance menu, on the other hand, gives you the additional option of fine-tuning the white balance precisely.

Different light sources have difference "colors," at least as perceived by your D60's sensor. Indoor illumination tends to be somewhat reddish, while daylight has, in comparison, a more bluish tinge. If the color balance the camera is using doesn't match the light source, you can end up with a color rendition that is off-kilter, as you can see in Figure 3.15.

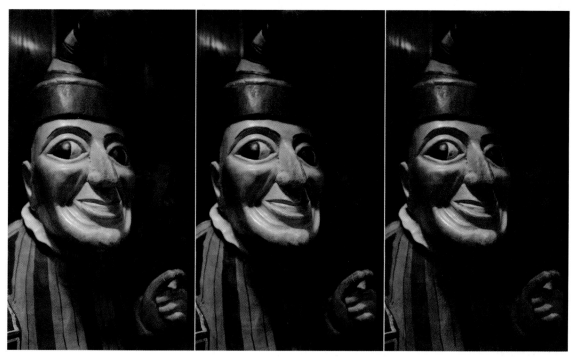

Figure 3.15 Adjusting color temperature can provide different results of the same subject at settings of 3,400K (left), 5,000K (middle), and 2,800K (right).

This menu entry allows you to choose one of the white balance values from among Auto, incandescent, seven varieties of fluorescent illumination (the Quick Settings screen has only a generic fluorescent option), direct sunlight, flash, cloudy, shade, a specific color temperature of your choice, or a preset value taken from an existing photograph or a measurement you make.

In this section I'm going to describe only the menu commands at your disposal for setting white balance. To learn more about the theory behind why and when you should make white balance adjustments, check out the more complete description in Chapter 6.

When you select the White Balance entry on the Shooting menu, you'll see an array of choices like those shown in Figure 3.16. (One additional choice, **PRE Preset Manual** is not visible until you scroll down to it.) Choose the predefined value you want by pressing the multi-selector right button, or press **OK**.

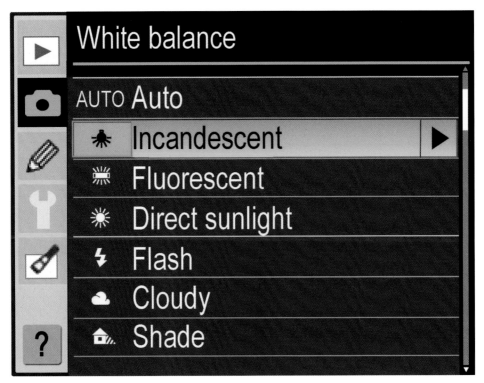

Figure 3.16
The White Balance menu has predefined values, plus the option of setting a preset you measure yourself.

If you choose Fluorescent, you'll be taken to another screen that presents seven different types of lamps, from sodium-vapor through warm-white fluorescent down to high temperature mercury-vapor. If you know the exact type of non-incandescent lighting being used, you can select it, or settle on a likely compromise. Press the multi-selector right button again or press **OK** to select the fluorescent lamp variation you want to use.

When you've finished choosing a fluorescent light source *and for all other pre-defined values* (Auto, incandescent, direct sunlight, flash, cloudy, or shade), you'll next be taken to the fine-tuning screen shown in Figure 3.17 (and which uses the incandescent setting as an example). The screen shows a grid with two axes, a blue/amber axis extending left/right, and a green/magenta axis extending up and down the grid. By default, the grid's cursor is positioned in the middle, and a readout to the right of the grid shows the cursor's coordinates on the A-B axis (yes, I know the display has the end points reversed) and G-M axis at 0,0.

You can use the multi-selector's up/down and right/left buttons to move the cursor to any coordinate in the grid, thereby biasing the white balance in the direction(s) you choose. The amber-blue axis makes the image warmer or colder (but not actually yellow or blue). Similarly, the green/magenta axis preserves all the colors in the original image, but gives them a tinge biased toward green or magenta. Each increment equals about five mired units, but you should know that mired values aren't linear; five mireds

Figure 3.17
Specific white balance settings can be fine-tuned by changing their bias in the amber/blue, magenta/green directions—or along both axes simultaneously.

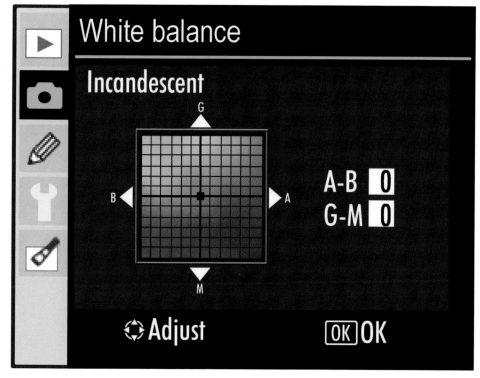

at 2,500K produces a much stronger effect than five mireds at 6,000K. If you really want to fine-tune your color balance, you're better off experimenting and evaluating the results of a particular change.

When you've fine-tuned white balance, an asterisk appears next to the white balance icon in both the Shooting menu and Shooting Information screen shown on the LCD, as a tip-off that this tweaking has taken place.

Using Preset Manual White Balance

If automatic white balance or one of the predefined settings available aren't suitable, you can set a custom white balance using the Preset Manual menu option. You can apply the white balance from a scene, either by shooting a new picture on the spot and using the resulting white balance (**Measure**), or using an image you have already shot (**Use photo**). To perform direct measurement from your current scene using a reference object (preferably a neutral gray or white object), follow these steps:

1. Place the neutral reference under the lighting you want to measure.

2. Choose **Preset manual** from the White Balance screen in the Shooting menu (you may need to scroll down to see it).

3. Select **Measure** from the screen that appears by scrolling to it and pressing the multi-selector right button or pressing **OK**.

4. A warning message appears, **Overwrite existing preset data?** Choose **Yes.**

5. An instructional message appears for a few seconds telling you to take a photo of a white or gray object that fills the viewfinder under the lighting that will be used for shooting. Do that!

6. After you've taken the photo, if the D60 was able to capture the white balance data, a message **Data acquired** appears on the Shooting Information screen, and the PRE white balance setting is shown. (See Figure 3.18.) If the D60 was not able to capture white balance data, a pop-up message appears, and you should try again.

Tip

Nikon describes two other ways of activating the "measure white balance mode," but I don't recommend them. You can jump to the WB option in the Quick Settings screen, select **Preset manual**, and then hold down the **OK** button for a few seconds—usually. The Shooting menu is more reliable. You can also redefine the Self-timer/Fn button in Custom Setting #CSM 11 to activate white balance measurement, but I think the button is far more useful with its default self-timer behavior.

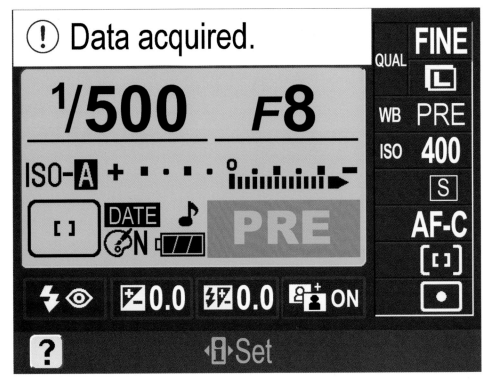

Figure 3.18
When you capture a scene's white balance, it will be stored in the D60's white balance preset.

The preset value you've captured will remain in the D60's memory until you replace that white balance with a new captured value. You can also use the white balance information from a picture you've already taken, using the **Use photo** option, as described next:

1. Choose **Preset Manual** from the White Balance menu.

2. Select Use photo.

3. The most recently shot picture will appear, with a menu offering to use **This image** or **Select image**.

4. Press **OK** to use the displayed image, or choose Select image to specify another picture on your memory card.

5. If you want to select a different image, you can choose which folder on your memory card, then navigate through the selected images, using the standard D60 image selection screen shown several times previously in this chapter. (See Figure 3.4 for a refresher.)

6. When the photo you'd like to use is highlighted, press **OK** to select it.

7. You'll be returned to the Shooting menu, where you can press the Menu button to exit, or just tap the shutter release.

A WHITE BALANCE LIBRARY

Consider dedicating a low-capacity memory card to stow a selection of images taken under a variety of lighting conditions. If you want to "recycle" one of the color temperatures you've stored, insert the card and select it with the **Use photo** option.

ISO Sensitivity Settings

ISO governs how sensitive your Nikon D60 is to light. Low ISO settings, such as ISO 100 or ISO 200 mean that the camera must have more light available to take a picture, or that you must use wider lens openings or slower shutter speeds. Faster ISO settings, on the other hand, let you take pictures in lower light levels, with faster shutter speeds (say, to freeze action) or with smaller lens openings (to produce a larger range in which objects are in sharp focus). I'll explain all these factors in more detail in Chapter 4.

This menu entry allows you to set an ISO sensitivity value, from ISO 100 (at the low end) through ISO 1600, plus Hi 1, which is the equivalent of ISO 3200 (at the high end). You can also choose Auto, which allows the Nikon D60 to change the ISO setting as you shoot if the setting you have made isn't high enough to produce the best combination of shutter speed and lens opening for a sharp picture. You can define when and how the D60 applies its automatic ISO capabilities using the Custom Settings menu entry CSM #10, explained later in this chapter.

Noise Reduction

Visual noise is that awful graininess caused by long exposures and high ISO settings, and which shows up as multicolored specks in images. This setting helps reduce noise, which is rarely desirable in a digital photograph. There are easier ways to add texture to your photos.

High ISO noise commonly appears when you raise your camera's sensitivity setting above ISO 800. This type of visual noise appears as a result of the amplification needed to increase the sensitivity of the sensor. While higher ISOs do pull details out of dark areas, they also amplify non-signal information randomly, creating noise.

A similar noisy phenomenon occurs during long time exposures, which allow more photons to reach the sensor, increasing your ability to capture a picture under low-light conditions. However, the longer exposures also increase the likelihood that some pixels will register random phantom photons, often because the longer an imager is "hot" the warmer it gets, and that heat can be mistaken for photons.

While high ISO settings are the usual culprit, some noise is created when you're using shutter speeds longer than eight seconds. Extended exposure times allow more photons to reach the sensor, but increase the likelihood that some photosites will react randomly even though not struck by a particle of light. Moreover, as the sensor remains switched on for the longer exposure, it heats, and this heat can be mistakenly recorded as if it were a barrage of photons.

While noise reduction does minimize the grainy effect, it can do so at the cost of some sharpness. This menu setting can be used to activate or deactivate the D60's noise-canceling operation.

- **Off.** This default setting disables noise reduction. Use it when you want the maximum amount of detail present in your photograph, even though higher noise levels will result. This setting also eliminates the delay caused by the noise reduction process that occurs after the picture is taken (this delay is roughly the same amount of time that was required for the exposure). If you plan to use only lower ISO settings (thereby reducing the noise caused by high ISO values), the noise levels produced by longer exposures may be acceptable. For example, you might be shooting a waterfall at ISO 100 with the camera mounted on a tripod, using a neutral density filter and a long exposure to cause the water to blur. (Try exposures of 2 to 16 seconds, depending on the intensity of the light and how much blur you want.) (See Figure 3.19.) To maximize detail in the non-moving portions of your photos for the exposures that are eight seconds or longer, you can switch off long exposure noise reduction.

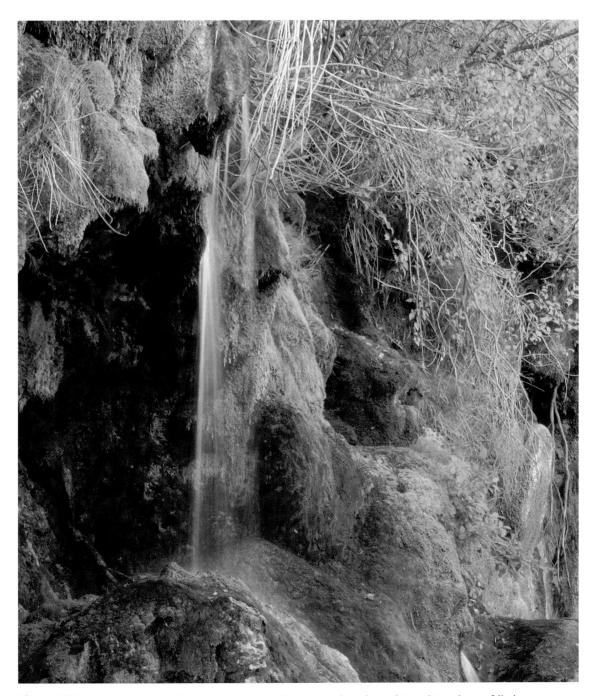

Figure 3.19 A long exposure with the camera mounted on a tripod produces this traditional waterfall photo.

■ **On.** When exposures are eight seconds or longer, the Nikon D60 takes a second, blank exposure to compare that to the first image. (While the second image is taken, the warning **Job nr** appears in the viewfinder.) Noise (pixels that are bright in a frame that *should* be completely black) in the "dark frame" image is subtracted from your original picture, and only the noise-corrected image is saved to your memory card. Because the noise-reduction process effectively doubles the time required to take a picture, you won't want to use this setting when you're rushed. Some noise can be removed later on, using tools like Bibble Pro or the noise reduction features built into Nikon Capture NX.

Active D-Lighting

D-lighting is a feature that improves the rendition of detail in highlights and shadows when you're photographing high contrast scenes (those that have dramatic differences between the brightest areas and the darkest areas that hold detail). It's been available as an internal retouching option that could be used *after* the picture has been taken, and has been found in Nikon's lower-end cameras (by that I mean the Coolpix point-and-shoot line) for some time, and has gradually worked its way up through the company's dSLR products, most recently becoming available in the Nikon D60, D300, and D3. You'll find this post-shot feature in the Retouch menu, which I'll describe later in the chapter.

A new wrinkle, however, is the *active D-Lighting* capability introduced with Nikon's newest cameras, which, unlike the Retouch menu post-processing feature, applies its improvements *while you are actually taking the photo.* That's good news and bad news. It means that, if you're taking photos in a contrasty environment, active D-lighting can automatically improve the apparent dynamic range of your image as you shoot, without additional effort on your part. However, you'll need to disable the feature once you leave the high contrast lighting behind, and the process does take some time to apply as you shoot. You wouldn't want to use active D-lighting for continuous shooting of sports subjects, for example. There are many situations in which the selective application of D-lighting using the Retouch menu is a better choice.

For best results, use your D60's Matrix metering mode (described in more detail in Chapter 4), so the active D-lighting feature can work with a full range of exposure information from multiple points in the image. Active D-lighting works its magic by subtly *underexposing* your image so that details in the highlights (which would normally be overexposed and become featureless white pixels) are not lost. At the same time, it adjusts the values of pixels located in midtone and shadow areas so they don't become too dark because of the underexposure. Highlight tones will be preserved, while shadows will eventually be allowed to go dark more readily. Bright beach or snow scenes, especially those with few shadows (think high noon, when the shadows are smaller) can benefit from using active D-lighting. Figure 3.20 shows a typical example.

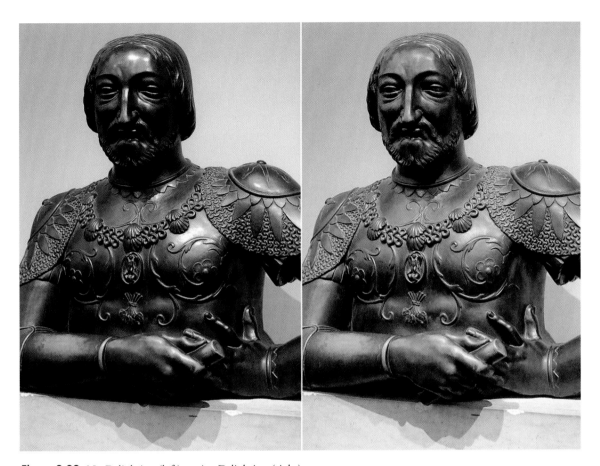

Figure 3.20 No D-lighting (left); active D-lighting (right).

You have just two choices: Off and On. You'll want to experiment to see which types of situations can benefit your shooting the most.

The Custom Setting Menu

Unlike the Shooting menu options, which you are likely to modify frequently as your picture-taking environment changes, the Custom Setting menu (see Figure 3.21) provides a roster of slightly more stable groups of preferences that let you tailor the behavior of your camera in a variety of different ways for longer-term use.

Some options are minor tweaks useful for specific shooting situations. You can turn off the autofocus assist lamp, the back panel LCD's shooting information display, and the D60's built-in beeper when you are shooting an acoustic music concert, when you'd rather not disrupt the environment. Others make the camera more convenient to use. Perhaps you'd like to assign a frequently used feature to the Func button.

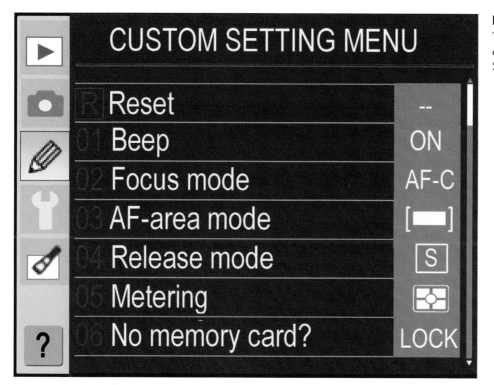

Figure 3.21
The first page
of the Custom
Setting menu.

This section concentrates on explaining all the options of the Custom Setting menu
and, most importantly, when and why you might want to use each setting. As with the
Shooting menu, some of the Custom Setting options duplicate those found in the
Quick Settings screen. When making those settings, use whichever method you find
most convenient.

Tip

If you have specified **Simple** menu display rather than **Full** menu display in the
Setup menu (explained later in this chapter), only the first six items of the Custom
Setting menu will appear. Change to **Full** to make all the CSM entries available.

Reset

If you select **Yes,** all the Custom Settings options will be reset to their default values. It has no effect on the settings in other menus, or any of the other camera settings. If that's what you want, try the two-button reset described in Chapter 1, holding down the D-Lighting button (just southwest of the shutter release) and Zoom button (the bottom button to the left of the LCD), both marked with green dots, for about two seconds.

You'd want to use this Reset option when you've made a bunch of changes to your Custom Settings (say, while playing around with them as you read this chapter), and now want to put them back to the factory defaults. Your choices are **Yes** and **No.**

01: Beep

The Nikon D60's internal beeper provides a (usually) superfluous chirp to signify various functions, such as the countdown of your camera's self-timer or autofocus confirmation in AF-S mode or AF-A mode with a static subject. You can (and probably should) switch it off if you want to avoid the beep because it's annoying, impolite, or distracting (at a concert or museum), or undesired for any other reason. It's one of the few ways to make the D60 a bit quieter. (I've actually had new dSLR owners ask me how to turn off the "shutter sound" the camera makes; such an option was available in the point-and-shoot camera they'd used previously.) Your choices are **On** and **Off.** When the beeper is active, a musical note icon is shown in the Shooting Information display.

02: Focus Mode

When using a non-Scene mode (Program, Shutter Priority, Aperture Priority, or Manual exposure), you can choose from among AF-A, AF-S, AF-C, or Manual focus modes. Each of these modes can be selected using the Quick Settings screen, as described in Chapter 1, or chosen here. The first three modes are available only when the autofocus switch on the D60's lens is set to A (autofocus) or M/A (autofocus with manual override). To review the four modes:

- **Automatic Autofocus (AF-A)**. When you press the shutter release halfway, the camera shifts into AF-S mode (as described below). If the subject begins to move, the D60 changes to AF-C mode for as long as the subject continues its motion. This default mode is a good choice for general shooting when you don't know whether your subject will be stationary.

- **Continuous-Servo Autofocus (AF-C)**. When the D60 is set to this mode, the camera sets focus when you partially depress the shutter button, but continues to monitor the frame and refocuses if the camera or subject is moved. This is a useful mode for photographing sports and moving subjects.

- **Single-Servo Autofocus (AF-S).** In this mode, the Nikon D60 locks in a focus point when the shutter button is pressed down halfway, and the focus confirmation light glows at bottom left in the viewfinder. The focus will remain locked until you release the button or take the picture. This mode is best when your subject is relatively motionless, because it is fast.

- **Manual focus (M).** When the focus mode is set to manual, or when the switch on your lens is set to M, or you have mounted a lens that does not offer autofocus on your D60, you always focus manually using the focus ring on the lens. The focus confirmation indicator in the viewfinder provides an indicator when correct focus is achieved. Lenses that don't provide autofocus features include lenses that do not have an autofocus motor built in. Nikon lenses with the AF-S designation in their name do have this autofocus motor; lenses labeled as AF do not. Don't confuse AF-S (so-called because they are autofocus lenses with a Nikon Silent-Wave motor) with the AF-S (autofocus single-servo) mode. Older, manual focus lenses that totally lack AF features also must be focused manually (obviously).

03: AF Area Mode

This entry is a duplication of the autofocus area mode options in the Quick Settings menu, as described in Chapter 1. You can also choose any of these modes from the Custom Setting menu. You'll find more about autofocus and focus modes in Chapter 6. To recap, the three choices are:

- **Closest Subject.** The D60 selects the focus point containing the subject that is nearest to the camera. This mode is used automatically in Auto, Auto (Flash Off), Portrait, Landscape, Child, and Night Portrait scene modes. It is the default mode for Program, Shutter Priority, Aperture Priority, and Manual exposure modes, but you can select one of the other two modes. It's an excellent choice when you are confident that the closest object in the frame will also be your center of interest, regardless of its position within the picture. You have to trust the D60's "smarts" when using this mode, because you cannot select the focus area manually.

- **Dynamic area.** In this autofocus area mode, you can choose which of the three focus points will be used using the multi-selector left/right buttons. However, if the subject moves from the point you have specified, the D60 will focus based on information from one of the other two focus zones. This mode is best for subjects that are moving unpredictably, as in sports activities. In fact, this mode is applied automatically with the Sports scene setting.

- **Single point.** You choose which of the three focus points are used. This mode is best for stationary subjects, because you can select the focus zone when you frame the photo, and the D60 won't depart from that in calculating autofocus. This mode is used automatically in Close-up scene mode.

04: Release Mode

The release mode determines when (and how often) the D60 makes an exposure. You can choose one of these modes from the Quick Settings screen, as described in Chapter 1, or specify a mode here. The D60's five release (shooting) modes are:

■ **Single Shot.** This is the default setting. One picture is taken every time you press the shutter release button down all the way. The Nikon D60 operates so quickly, though, that you can easily take a series of shots in fast-moving situations simply by operating the shutter button rapidly.

■ **Continuous Shooting (burst).** When this setting is chosen, the D60 takes a series of shots at approximately three frames per second for as long as you hold down the shutter release button, or until the camera's built-in memory (called a *buffer*) fills. When that happens, you must wait while pictures are transferred from the buffer to your memory card. As soon as some pictures are transferred, continuous shooting can resume. An indicator in the lower-right corner of the viewfinder shows how many more pictures the buffer can accept before the D60's continuous shooting rate begins to slow. However, the D60 can take a maximum of 100 pictures in continuous mode.

> **Tip**
>
> Continuous shooting mode is disabled when you are using flash; electronic flash can't recycle quickly enough to keep up with a three-frames-per-second burst of shots.

■ **Self-Timer.** In this mode, the Nikon D60 waits for a specified period of time after the shutter release is pressed before the picture is taken. You can set this delay to 2, 5, 10 (the default), or 20 seconds using CSM #16 (described later in this section). While the camera is counting down, the AF assist/self-timer lamp on the front of the camera blinks, until the last few seconds, when it remains on until the picture is finally taken. Remember that Nikon recommends attaching the eyepiece cap to the viewfinder eyepiece when shooting photos in this mode, or either of the two remote modes listed next. Light coming in the viewfinder can produce an incorrect exposure.

■ **Delayed Remote.** Use this setting with the Nikon ML-L3 infrared remote control to trigger the camera to take a picture about two seconds after the D60 has locked in focus.

■ **Quick Response Remote.** With this setting, the D60 takes a picture as soon as the button on the ML-L3 infrared remote control is pressed and the camera has achieved sharp focus.

05: Metering

This is a duplicate of the settings you can make from the Quick Settings screen. I'll explain each of the Nikon D60's three metering modes in more detail in Chapter 4. As I explained in Chapter 1, the three modes are:

- **Matrix metering.** The standard metering mode; the D60 attempts to intelligently classify your image and choose the best exposure based on readings from a 420-segment color CCD sensor that interprets light reaching the viewfinder using a database of hundreds of thousands of patterns.

- **Center-Weighted averaging metering.** The D60 meters the entire scene, but gives the most emphasis to the central area of the frame, measuring about 8mm in diameter.

- **Spot metering.** Exposure is calculated from a smaller 3.5 mm central spot, about 2.5 percent of the image area.

06: No Memory Card?

This entry gives you the ability to snap off "pictures" without a memory card installed—or, alternatively, to lock the camera shutter release if no card is present. It is sometimes informally called Play mode, because you can experiment with your camera's features or even hand your D60 to a friend to let them fool around, without any danger of pictures actually being taken.

Back in our film days, we'd sometimes finish a roll, rewind the film back into its cassette surreptitiously, and then hand the camera to a child to take a few pictures—without actually wasting any film. It's hard to waste digital film, but "shoot without card" mode is still appreciated by some, especially camera vendors who want to be able to demo a camera at a store or trade show, but don't want to have to equip each and every demonstrator model with a memory card. Choose **Enable release** to activate "play" mode or **Release locked** to disable it.

The pictures you actually "take" are displayed on the LCD with the legend "Demo" superimposed on the screen, and they are, of course, not saved. Note that if you are using the optional Camera Control Pro 2 software to record photos from a USB-tethered D60 directly to a computer, no memory card is required to unlock the shutter even if **Release locked** has been selected.

07: Image Review

This setting is the first entry in the "second" screen of the Custom Setting menu roster (see Figure 3.22), visible only if you've set menu display to Full in the Setup menu (as I'll describe in the next section). Use this setting to determine whether the Nikon D60 displays a review image of your most recent photo after it has been taken. Your choices are as follows:

■ **On.** With this setting (the default), the D60 will automatically display each image on the LCD as it is taken. The length of time the picture is shown can be set with CSM #15 (described later), to either "short," "normal," or "long" time-frames, or custom times of 8, 12, 20, 60 seconds, or 10 minutes.

■ **Off.** This setting disables automatic display, and is useful under several circumstances. Skipping automatic picture review can save a significant amount of power and extend your battery life. You can always review individual shots by pressing the Playback button. I like to de-activate image review at concerts, plays, and religious ceremonies, particularly those in dark surroundings, to avoid distracting those behind me with the glare of the LCD screen. Turning off picture review can also free you from the attentions of distracting "gawkers" who can't resist leaning over to catch a glimpse of your LCD between shots.

Figure 3.22
The second "page" of the Custom Setting menu screens.

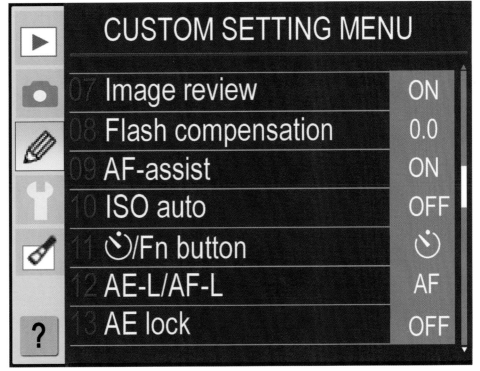

08: Flash Compensation

Flash compensation, which overrides the Nikon D60's metering to provide more or less exposure when using flash, can be set from the Quick Settings screen, or specified here. You can subtract 3.0 "stops" from the metered flash exposure, to counter an overly bright image; or add +1 stops to fix an underexposed image. (A "stop" is the equivalent of one whole shutter speed or lens opening increment, such as the difference between 1/125 second and 1/250 second, or f/8 and f/11.) You can learn more about exposure and exposure compensation in Chapter 4, and quite a bit more about using electronic flash in Chapter 7.

09: AF-Assist

Use this setting to control whether the AF-assist lamp built into the Nikon D60, or the more powerful AF-assist lamp built into Nikon electronic flash units (like the Nikon SB-800) and the Nikon SC-29 coiled remote flash cord (for firing the flash when not mounted on the camera) function in low light situations.

- **On.** This default value will cause the AF-assist illuminator lamp to fire when lighting is poor, but only if Single-Servo Autofocus (AF-S) or Automatic Autofocus (AF-A) are active, or you have selected the center focus point manually and either single-point or dynamic-area autofocus (rather than auto-area autofocus) has been chosen. It does not operate in Manual focus modes, in AF-C mode, or when AF-A has switched to its AF-C behavior, nor when Landscape or Sports DVP/Scene modes are used.

Tip
With some lenses, the lens hood can block the AF-assist lamp's illumination; you may have to remove the hood in low-light situations.

- **Off.** Use this to disable the AF-assist illuminator. You'd find that useful when the lamp might be distracting or discourteous (say, at a religious ceremony or acoustic music concert), or your subject is located closer than one foot, eight inches or farther than about 10 feet. One downside of turning AF-assist off is that the D60 may be unable to focus accurately in situations where it really, really needs the extra light from the supplementary lamp. You may have to focus manually in such situations.

10: ISO Auto

The sensitivity of the Nikon D60's sensor can be increased or decreased, which is what happens when you use the Quick Settings screen to change from, say, ISO 200 to ISO 400 (increasing the sensitivity), or from ISO 800 to ISO 400 (decreasing the sensitivity). I'll explain ISO settings in more detail in Chapter 4.

If you like, the D60 can set the ISO value for you, as conditions require, when you're using Program, Shutter Priority, Aperture Priority, or Manual exposure modes (it does not work with any of the DVP/Scene modes). This feature can be used both with available light shots, and those using electronic flash.

When active, if the ISO rating that you've chosen doesn't provide enough sensitivity to take an optimal picture (that is one that is well-exposed, but also has a shutter speed that's fast enough to stop action, and an aperture that produces an acceptable range of sharpness), the camera can increase the ISO automatically.

This capability can be a convenience (and, at times, a life-saver), but it is also fraught with pitfalls. For example, it is possible that the D60 could, if not given some guidance, choose an ISO setting far higher than what you intended, producing pictures that might be unacceptably grainy for a given purpose. In such cases, you might have preferred to keep your original ISO setting and optimize exposure through some other means, such as supplementary flash or using a tripod with a longer shutter speed.

Fortunately, the D60 does not easily lead you astray. Automatic ISO shifts are possible only if you've activated that feature in this menu, and, when implemented by the camera, you're given fair warning by an ISO-Auto indicator on the Shooting Information screen and in the viewfinder. Better yet, you can lay down some rules that the D60 will use before it meddles with the ISO setting you originally specified.

The ISO Auto screen has four choices. Two of them, **On** and **Off**, are self-explanatory; you can enable or disable the ISO Auto feature by choosing the appropriate option. The other two, **Max. sensitivity** and **Min. shutter speed**, lead you to separate screens you can use to lay down the ground rules. Here's a quick explanation of how your options operate:

■ **Off.** Set ISO sensitivity auto control to off, and the ISO setting will not budge from whatever value you have specified. Use this setting when you don't want any ISO surprises, or when ISO increases are not needed to counter slow shutter speeds. For example, if the D60 is mounted on a tripod, you can safely use slower shutter speeds at a relatively low ISO setting, so there is no need for a speed bump.

■ **On.** At other times, you may want to activate the feature. For example, if you're hand-holding the camera and the D60 set for Program (P) or Aperture Priority (A) mode wants to use a shutter speed slower than, say, 1/30 second, it's probably a good idea to increase the ISO to avoid the effects of camera shake. If you're using a telephoto lens (which magnifies camera shake), a shutter speed of 1/125 second or higher might be the point where an ISO bump would be a good idea. In that case, you can turn the ISO sensitivity auto control on, or remember to boost the ISO setting yourself.

- **Maximum sensitivity.** If the idea of unwanted noise bothers you, you can avoid using an ISO setting that's higher than you're comfortable with. This parameter sets the highest ISO setting the D60 will use in ISO-Auto mode. You can choose from ISO 200, 400, 800, and 1600 as the max ISO setting the camera will use. Use a low number if you'd rather not take any photos at a high ISO without manually setting that value yourself. Dial in a higher ISO number if getting the photo at any sensitivity setting is more important than worrying about noise.

- **Minimum shutter speed.** You can decide the shutter speed that's your personal "danger threshold" in terms of camera shake blurring. That is, if you feel you can't hand-hold the camera at a shutter speed slower than 1/30 second, you can tell the D60 that when the metered exposure will end up with a speed slower than that, ISO-Auto should kick in and do its stuff. When the shutter speed is *faster* (shorter) than the speed you specify, ISO-Auto will not take effect and the ISO setting you've set yourself remains in force. The default value is 1/30 second, because in most situations, any shutter speed longer/slower than 1/30 is to be avoided, unless you're using a tripod, monopod, or looking for a special effect. If you're working with a telephoto lens and find even a relatively brief shutter speed "dangerous," you can set a minimum shutter speed threshold of 1/250 second.

11: Assign FUNC. Button

You can define the action that the Func. button performs when pressed alone, or when pressed while the command dial is rotated. There are five different actions you can define for the button:

- **Self-Timer.** This is the default setting and the one I recommend keeping, unless you never use the self-timer. When the button is pressed, the Nikon D60 shifts into Self-Timer mode, and the next time you press the shutter release button all the way, the self-timer will activate.

- **Release mode.** When this option is selected, pressing the Fn button pops up a modified version of the Quick Settings screen on the LCD, with the Release mode function active. (You can set the mode directly from this Quick Settings screen; it's not necessary to venture into the submenu.) Just rotate the command dial until the release mode you want appears on the LCD. This is an acceptable alternative to the default value if you use the self-timer sometimes, but want to use one of the other release modes from time to time.

- **Qual.** With this setting, when the Fn button is pressed, the Quick Settings screen pops up, and you can rotate the command dial to view and select image quality (RAW, JPEG Fine, JPEG Norm, JPEG Basic, or RAW+Basic) and image size (for JPEG images). When specifying JPEG quality and size, the Quick Settings display cycles among the three quality settings, then moves to the next lower size, allowing you to set both with one (extended) rotation of the command dial. For example, the Fine, Normal, and Basic Large settings are shown first, followed by Fine, Normal, Basic Medium, and Fine, Normal Basic Small. I never use this function key definition; it's easier just to use the Quick Settings menu, and I rarely change image size, anyway.

- **ISO.** Use this option if you want to adjust ISO setting using the Fn key. The Quick Settings screen appears, and you can rotate the command dial to choose an ISO sensitivity.

- **White Balance.** When the Fn button is pressed, you can rotate the command dial to select one of the white balance settings when using Program, Shutter Priority, Aperture Priority, or Manual exposure modes.

12: AE-L/AF-L

When the Nikon D60 is set to its default values, a half-press of the shutter release locks in the current autofocus setting in AF-S mode, or in AF-A mode if your subject is not moving. (The camera will refocus if the subject moves and the D60 is set for AF-C or AF-A mode.) That half-press also activates the exposure meter, but, ordinarily, the exposure changes as the lighting conditions in the frame change.

However, sometimes you want to lock in focus and/or exposure, and then reframe your photo. For that, and for other focus/exposure locking options, Nikon gives you the AE-L/AF-L button (located on the back of the camera to the right of the viewfinder window), and a variety of behavior combinations for it. This CSM setting allows you to define whether the Nikon D60 locks exposure, focus, or both when the button is pressed, so the AE-L/AF-L button can be used for these functions in addition to, or instead of a half-press of the shutter release. It can also be set so that autofocus starts *only* when the button is pressed; in that case, a half-press of the shutter release initiates autoexposure, but the AE-L/AF-L button *must* be pressed to start the autofocusing process. These options can be a little confusing, so I'll offer some clarification:

- **AE/AF lock.** Lock both focus and exposure while the **AE-L/AF-L** button is pressed and held down, even if the shutter release button has not been pressed. This is the default value, and is useful when you want to activate and lock in exposure and focus independently of the shutter release button. Perhaps your main subject is off-center; place that subject in the middle of the frame, lock in exposure and focus, and then reframe the picture while holding the AE-L/AF-L button.

- **AE lock only.** Lock only the exposure while the **AE-L/AF-L** button is pressed. The exposure is fixed when you press and hold the button, but autofocus continues to operate (say, when you press the shutter release halfway) using the AF-A, AF-S, or AF-C mode you've chosen.

- **AF lock only.** Focus is locked in while the **AE-L/AF-L** button is held down, but exposure will continue to vary as you compose the photo and press the shutter release button.

- **AE lock (Hold).** Exposure is locked when the **AE-L/AF-L** button is pressed, and remains locked until the button is pressed again, or the exposure meter-off delay expires. Use this option when you want to lock exposure at some point, but don't want to keep your thumb on the AE-L/AF-L button.

- **AF (AF-ON).** The AE-L/AF-L button is used to initiate autofocus. A half-press of the shutter release button does not activate or change focus. This setting is useful when you want to frame your photo, press the shutter release halfway to lock in exposure, but don't want the D60 to autofocus until you tell it to. I use this for sports photography when I am waiting for some action to move into the frame before starting autofocus. For example, I might press the AE-L/AF-L button just before a racehorse crosses the finish line.

13: AE Lock

This is the first entry in the third page of the Custom Setting menu (see Figure 3.23). When you turn this option **On**, the exposure locks when the shutter release button is pressed halfway. When **Off** (the default), a shutter release half-press does not lock exposure; the camera will continue to adjust exposure until you press the shutter release all the way to take the picture, or take your finger off the button. Set this option to **Off** when you are shooting under lighting conditions that may change suddenly; use **On** when you want the exposure to remain constant even if the lighting changes. You might do this while recording a series of scenes illuminated by the setting sun, and wanted the scene to gradually get darker as the sun sinks behind the horizon. With the default **Off** setting, the D60 would constantly compensate for the waning light, rendering each shot similar in appearance.

14: Built-In Flash

This setting is used to adjust the features of the Nikon D60's built-in pop-up electronic flash, or the optional Nikon SB-400 add-on flash unit, which fits in the accessory shoe on top of the camera. Its settings are in force when you are using Program, Shutter Priority, Aperture Priority, or Manual exposure modes (but not when using any of the DVP/Scene modes). You can read more about using the D60's flash capabilities in Chapter 7.

Figure 3.23
The third page
of the Custom
Setting menu
looks like this.

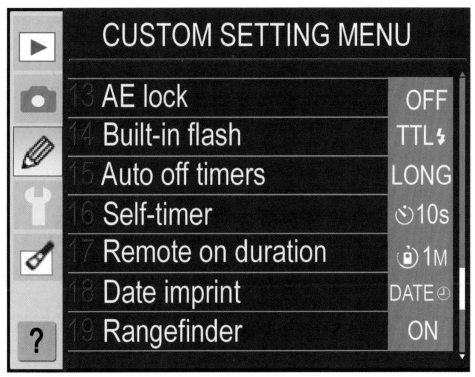

Figure 3.23
The third page of the Custom Setting menu looks like this.

You have two options with this setting:

- **TTL.** When selected, the built-in flash or SB-400 operate in iTTL (intelligent through-the-lens) exposure mode to automatically choose an exposure based on measuring the light from a "preflash" (fired an instant before the picture is taken) as it reflects back to the camera. Use this setting under most circumstances. As you'll learn in Chapter 7, the D60 can even balance the flash output with the daylight or other illumination to allow the flash to fill in dark shadows or provide supplementary light.

- **Manual.** In this mode, the flash always fires using a preselected output level, which ranges from full power to 1/32 power. Use this mode when you want a certain exposure for every shot, say, to deliberately under- or overexpose an image for a special effect.

15: Auto Off Timers

Use this setting to determine how long the D60's LCD and viewfinder displays, and exposure meters continue to operate after the last operation, such as autofocusing, focus point selection, and so forth, was performed. You can choose a short timer to save power, or a longer value to keep the camera "alive" for a longer period of time. When the Nikon

EH5a/EH-5 AC adapter is connected to the D60, the exposure meters will remain on indefinitely, and when the D60 is connected to a computer or PictBridge-compatible printer, the LCD and viewfinder displays do not turn off automatically.

Sports shooters and some others prefer longer delays, because they are able to keep their camera always "at the ready" with no delay to interfere with taking an action shot that unexpectedly presents itself. Extra battery consumption is just part of the price paid. For example, when I am shooting football, a meter-off delay of 16 seconds is plenty, because the players lining up for the snap is my signal to get ready to shoot. But for basketball or soccer, I typically set a longer limit, because action is virtually continuous.

SAVING POWER WITH THE NIKON D60

There are several settings techniques you can use to help you stretch the longevity of your D60's battery. To get the most from each charge, consider these steps:

- **CSM #07.** Turn off automatic image review after each shot. You can still review your images by pressing the Playback button. Or, leave image review on, but set the display for the minimum 4 seconds using **CSM #15.**

- **Auto meter-off-delay.** Set to 4 seconds in **CSM #15** if you can tolerate such a brief active time.

- **Monitor off Delay.** In CSM #15, set for the minimum, four seconds, for playback, menus, and image review. That 2.5-inch LCD uses a lot of juice, so reducing the amount of time it is used when you don't turn it off manually can boost the effectiveness of your battery.

- **Reduce LCD brightness.** In the Setup menu's **LCD Brightness** option, select the lowest of the seven brightness settings that work for you under most conditions. If you're willing to shade the LCD with your hand, you can often get away with lower brightness settings outdoors, which will further increase the useful life of your battery.

- **Turn off the Shooting Information display.** I'll show you how to do that under the Setup menu. You can always turn it on manually by pressing the Info button.

- **Reduce internal flash use.** No flash at all or fill flash use less power than a full blast.

- **Don't let the remote keep your D60 hanging.** Use CSM #17 (described later) to reduce the amount of time the D60 will remain awake waiting for an IR remote control signal.

- **Cancel VR.** Turn off vibration reduction if your lens (such as the 18-55mm VR kit lens) has that feature and you feel you don't need it.

- **Use a card reader.** When transferring pictures from your D60 to your computer, use a card reader instead of the USB cable. Linking your camera to your computer and transferring images using the cable takes longer and uses a lot more power.

Of course, if the meters have shut off, and if the power switch remains in the On position, you can bring the camera back to life by tapping the shutter button. You can select generic times such as Short, Norm, and Long as the autoff delay, or specify custom times for playback/menus, image review, and exposure meters. Your delay options are as follows:

- **Short.** LCD Playback/Menus: 8 seconds; LCD Review: 4 seconds; Exposure Meters: 4 seconds.

- **Norm.** LCD Playback/Menus: 12 seconds; LCD Review: 4 seconds; Exposure Meters: 8 seconds.

- **Long.** LCD Playback/Menus: 20 seconds; LCD Review: 20 seconds; Exposure Meters: 60 seconds.

- **Custom: Playback/menus.** Choose 8, 12, 20, 60 seconds, or 10 minutes.

- **Custom: Image review.** Choose 4, 8, 20, 60 seconds, or 10 minutes.

- **Custom: Auto meter-off.** Choose 4, 8, 20, 60 seconds, or 30 minutes.

16: Self-Timer

This setting lets you choose the length of the self-timer shutter release delay. The default value is 10 seconds. You can also choose 2, 5, or 20 seconds. These are unchanged from the D200. If I have the camera mounted on a tripod or other support and am too lazy to reach for my ML-L3 infrared remote, I can set a two-second delay that is sufficient to let the camera stop vibrating after I've pressed the shutter release. I use a longer delay time if I am racing to get into the picture myself and am not sure I can make it in 10 seconds.

17: Remote On Duration

Use this simple option to specify how long the camera will remain active waiting for a signal from the ML-L3 infrared remote. You can specify 1 minute, 5 minutes (the default value), 10, or 15 minutes. Longer values are useful, say, when you've set the camera up on a tripod and are lying in wait for the elusive snipe to approach your snipe-feeder. It would be a good idea to have a fully charged battery when trying this, however.

18: Date Imprint

You can superimpose the date, time, or both on your photographs, or imprint a date counter that shows the number of days (or years and days, or months, years, and days) between when the picture was taken and a date (in the past or future) that you select. The good news is that this feature can be useful for certain types of photographs used for documentation. While the D60's time/date stamp may not be admissible in a court of law, it makes a convincing (or convenient) in-picture indication of when the shot was made. This feature works only with JPEG images; you cannot use Date Imprint with pictures taken using the RAW or RAW+Basic settings.

The bad news, especially if you use the feature accidentally, is that the imprint is a permanent part of the photograph. You'll have to polish up your Photoshop skills if you want to remove it, or, at the very least, crop it out of the picture area. Date and time are set using the format you specify in the World Time setting of the Setup menu, described in the next section. Your options are:

- **Off.** Deactivates the date/time imprint feature.

- **Date.** The date is overlaid on your image in the bottom-right corner of the frame, and appears in the Shooting Information display. If you've turned on Auto Image Rotation, the date is overlaid at the bottom-right corner of vertically oriented frames. You can see the result in the middle snapshot shown in Figure 3.24.

- **Date/Time.** Both date and time are imprinted, in the same positions. The result is shown in the top picture in the "stack" in Figure 3.24.

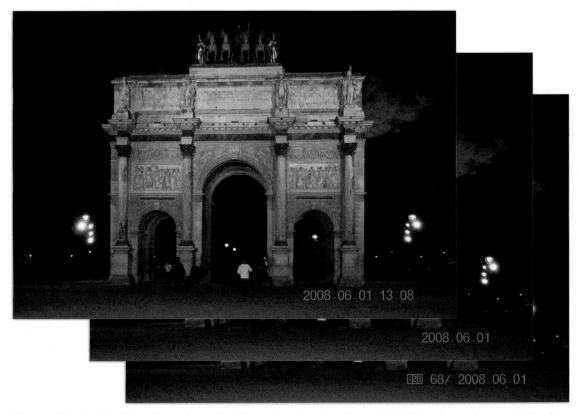

Figure 3.24 This "stack" of photos shows the different date/time imprints available. Top: date and time; middle: date; bottom: date and days elapsed/remaining.

■ **Date Counter.** This option imprints the current date on the image, but also adds the number of days that have elapsed since a particular date in the past that you specify, *or* the days remaining until an upcoming date in the future. The imprinting is shown in the bottom picture in the stack shown in Figure 3.24.

Using the Date Counter

If you're willing to have information indelibly embedded in your images, the Date Counter can be a versatile feature. You can specify several parameters in advance (or at the time you apply the Date Counter) and activate the overprinting *only* when you want it. The parameters, shown in Figure 3.25, are:

■ **Off.** Select this from the main Date Imprint screen. Choosing **Off** disables the imprinting of date, date/time, *and* the Date Counter. When disabled, no date or counter information is shown, regardless of how you have set the other parameters.

■ **Choose Date.** When you enter the Date Counter screen, one option lets you enter up to three different dates for your countdown/countup. When you activate the Date Counter, you can choose from the three dates (or a new date you enter to replace one of the three) and use that for your date counting imprint.

Figure 3.25
You can select dates in the past or future, and specify whether to display number of days, or number of days and months, or days, months, and years.

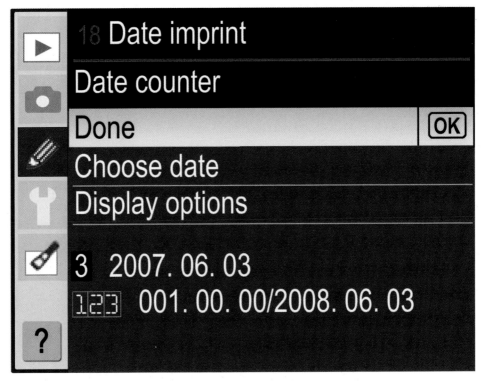

- **Display Options.** Also in the Date Counter screen, you can select Display Options, which allows you to specify **Number of days**, **Years and days**, or **Years, months, and days** for the Date Counter readout imprinted on your images.

- **Done.** When you've finished entering date and display options, choose Done to return to the Custom Setting menu. (You *must* do this. If you press the Menu button or tap the shutter release button at this point, your changes will not be confirmed.)

Here are some applications for the Date Counter:

- **Tracking a newborn.** Enter the child's birthday as one of your three dates. Select Number of Days as your display option for a newborn. Then, as often as you like, activate the Date Counter and take a picture or two. The number of days since the baby's birth will be displayed right on the picture. (Remember to turn the feature off when shooting other pictures of the child, or of other subjects!)

- **Document construction.** Enter the start date of the project, activate the Date Counter, and take pictures of the construction progress. Each photo will show exactly how many days have elapsed since ground was broken (or the cornerstone laid, or that non-bearing wall demolished to begin remodeling).

- **Long-term documentation.** Perhaps you'd like to record the appearance of your favorite nature spot at different times of the year. Choose the first day of Spring as your start date, then shoot pictures at intervals for an entire year, activating the Date Counter as needed. The results will be interesting—and maybe a revelation. With the Years, Months, and Days selected as a display option, you can continue your documentation for years!

- **Countdown.** Something big scheduled for a particular day? Choose that date in the future as your counter, and any photo you take with imprinting activated will show the days remaining until the big day.

19: Rangefinder

This setting enables a useful electronic "rangefinder" in the viewfinder to help you focus manually.

Some lenses don't offer autofocus features with the Nikon D60, because they lack the internal autofocus motor the D60 requires. (They are able to autofocus on other Nikon cameras, except for the D40/D40x, because those cameras include an autofocus motor in the body.) Many Manual focus lenses that never had autofocus features can also be used with the D60 in Manual focus mode. You'll find more information about this limitation in Chapter 6, but all you need to know is that Nikon lenses with the AF-S designation in the lens name *will* autofocus on the D60, while those with the AF, AI, or

AI-S designation will not. Specifications for lenses from other vendors will indicate whether the lens includes an autofocus motor or not.

When a non-autofocus lens is mounted on the Nikon D60, and the camera has been set for any exposure mode except for Manual (M)—that is, any of the DVP/Scene modes, plus Program, Aperture Priority, or Shutter Priority, Manual focus mode is automatically activated. (You'll see **MF** focus in the Shooting Information display, and focus mode selection will be disabled in **CSM #02**.) You can manually focus by turning the focus ring on the lens (set the lens to Manual focus if it is an AF-type lens) and watching the sharpness of the image on the focusing screen. The focus confirmation indicator at the lower-left corner of the viewfinder will illuminate when correct focus is achieved, if your lens has a maximum aperture of f/5.6 or larger (that is, a larger number, such as f/5.6, f/4.5, f/4, and so forth).

Turn the Rangefinder **On** with this Custom Setting option for an additional manual focusing aid. With a manual focus lens and the Rangefinder operating, the analog exposure display at bottom right in the viewfinder will be replaced by a rangefinder focusing scale, shown in Figure 3.26. Indicators on the scale show when the image is in sharp focus, as well as when you have focused somewhat in front of or behind the subject.

Figure 3.26
The Rangefinder pointing to the left with three "bars" shows that the current focus point is slightly in front of correct focus for the subject located in the red-highlighted focus zone.

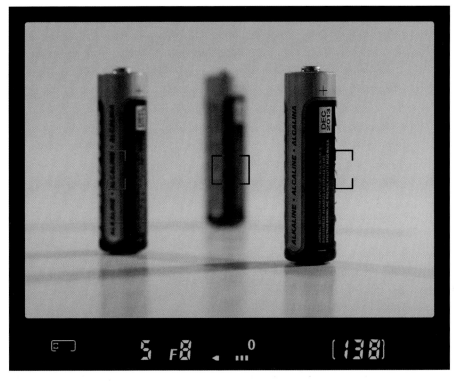

Follow these steps to use the Rangefinder:

1. Press the multi-selector left/right buttons to choose a focus point that coincides with the subject you'd like to be in focus.

2. Rotate the focusing ring, watching the rangefinder scale at the bottom of the viewfinder. If the current sharp focus plane is *in front* of the point of desired focus, the rangefinder scale will point towards the left side of the viewfinder, as you can see in Figure 3.26. The greater the difference, the more bars shown in the rangefinder.

3. When the current focus plane is *behind* the desired point of focus, the rangefinder indicator will point to the right, as you can see in Figure 3.27.

4. When the subject you've selected with the focus zone bracket is in sharp focus, only two bars will appear, centered under the 0 as shown in Figure 3.28, and the focus confirmation indicator will stop blinking.

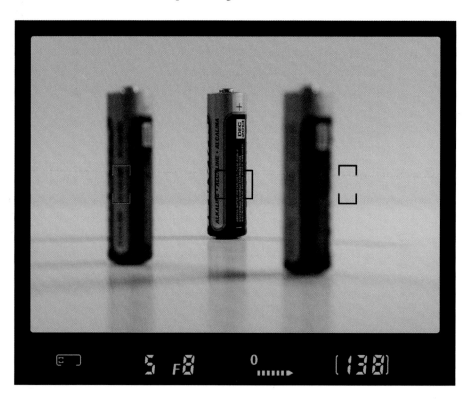

Figure 3.27
The Range-finder will point to the right to show that the current focus plane is behind the correct focus. More "bars" are shown because the current focus is a larger distance from the desired point.

Figure 3.28
When the subject under the highlighted focus bracket is sharply focused, the Rangefinder shows two "bars" centered under the zero, and the focus confirmation indicator stops blinking.

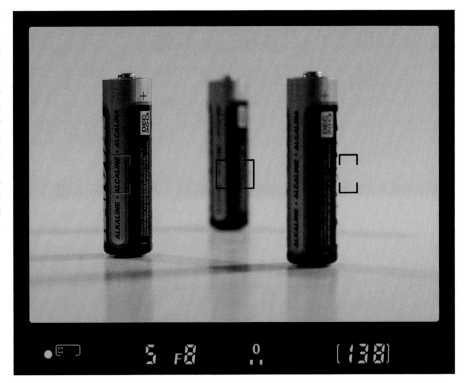

Setup Menu Options

The orange-coded Setup menu (see Figure 3.29 for its first page) has a long list of 17 entries (or just 10 if you've enabled "simple" menus using the CSM/Setup Menu option described below). In this menu you can make additional adjustments on how your camera *behaves* before or during your shooting session, as differentiated from the Shooting menu, which adjusts how the pictures are actually taken. Your choices include:

- CSM/Setup menu
- Format memory card
- Info display format
- Auto shooting info
- Shooting info auto off
- World Time
- LCD brightness
- Video mode
- Language

- Image comment
- Folders
- File No. Sequence
- Clean image sensor
- Mirror lock-up
- Firmware version
- Dust off ref photo
- Auto image rotation

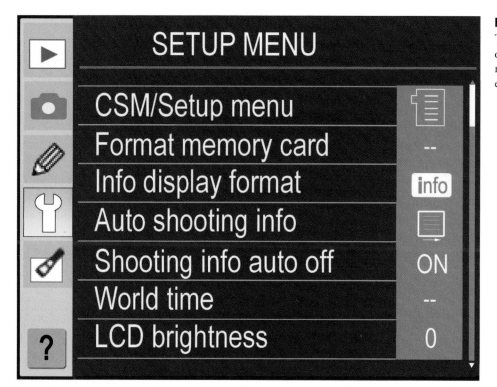

Figure 3.29
The first page
of the Setup
menu has seven
entries.

CSM/Setup Menu

This option allows you to choose from between "simple" menus for the Custom Setting menu and Setup menu, "full" menus, or My Menu options. **Simple** menus show only the first six of 19 total Custom Setting entries, and the first 10 of 17 total Setup menu options. All other menus show all their available options.

The **Full** menu choice displays all of the entries in those menus. When you select My Menu, you can selectively enable or disable most entries that appear in the Playback, Shooting, Custom Setting, Setup, and Retouch menus. One exception is that you cannot remove *this* entry, the CSM/Setup Menu option, from the Setup menu. You'd need it to restore other menu items when you want to make changes!

I can think of only a couple reasons for switching from Full menus to Simple menus. Perhaps you rarely use the extra Custom Setting or Setup menu options and don't want to see them. The Simple choice hides them from you, but keep in mind that undesired menu options reside on the second page, anyway, so if you don't scroll down you won't see them when using Full menus either. And, you'll have to restore the Full menus any time you *do* happen to need one of the hidden menu entries. Another possible reason for switching to Simple menus is because you loan your D60 to an unsophisticated user and want to help them avoid accidentally fiddling with an "inappropriate" menu option.

More useful is the My Menu choice, which lets you disable any entries you want (whether for security or convenience) and provides this access to *any* of the Nikon D60's menus. Suppose you *never* plan to make a Stop-Motion Movie. You can remove its entries from the Playback and Retouch menus, and never have to think about them again. Or, you've set your camera's default language to English, and don't plan on ever changing to a foreign tongue. Banish that entry with My Menu!

Using My Menu

The Nikon D60's My Menu feature allows you to customize which items are displayed in the Playback, Shooting, Custom Setting, Setup, and Retouch menus. You can hide or reveal nearly any entry, so the menus show only the options that you want to appear. Note: Don't confuse the D60's My Menu system with that of some other Nikon digital SLRs, such as the Nikon D300, which have a separate menu called My Menu, which contains only the items you specify.

To set up My Menu options, follow these steps:

1. In the Setup Menu, choose **CSM/Setup menu** and then **My menu.** Press the multi-selector right button. You'll see a list of menus you can modify, as shown in Figure 3.30.

Figure 3.30
Choose which menu to modify.

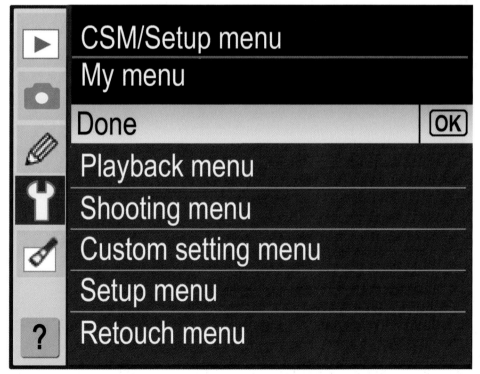

2. Choose the menu you'd like to change, and press the multi-selector right button. All the available menu entries for that menu that can be modified are shown, next to check boxes, as you can see in Figure 3.31.

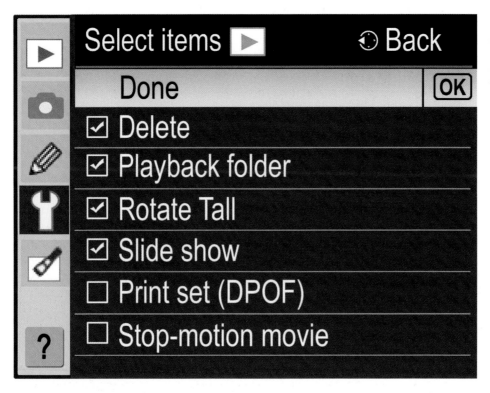

Figure 3.31
Mark or unmark menu items to show or hide them.

3. Use the multi-selector up/down buttons to choose an item you'd like to hide/reveal. Press the multi-selector right button to mark or unmark the check box.

4. When finished, highlight **Done** and press the OK button to return to the previous screen.

5. Select additional menus if you want to modify them. Otherwise, highlight **Done** and press **OK** to return to the Setup menu.

Format Memory Card

I recommend using this menu entry to reformat your memory card after each shoot. While you can move files from the memory card to your computer, leaving behind a blank card, or delete files using the Playback menu's Delete feature, both of those options can leave behind stray files (such as those that have been marked as Protected). Format removes those files completely and beyond retrieval (unless you use a special utility program as described in Chapter 9) and establishes a spanking new fresh file system on the card, with all the file allocation table (FAT) pointers (which tell the camera and your computer's operating system where all the images reside) efficiently pointing where they are supposed to on a blank card.

To format a memory card, choose this entry from the Setup menu, highlight **Yes** on the screen that appears, and press **OK**.

Info Display Format

You can choose the format the Nikon D60 uses for its Shooting Information screen. Three formats are available, and you can specify them separately for the camera's fully automated Digital Vari-Program (DVP/Scene) modes, and for the semi-automated Program, Aperture Priority, Shutter Priority, and Manual exposure modes (collectively known as **P, S, A, M**). The available modes are as follows:

- **Classic.** This is a mostly text-based format with a few icons, as shown in Figure 3.32. You'll find this format the fastest to use once you've grown accustomed to the D60 and its features, as all the information is clustered in a no-nonsense way that is easy to read. I set both DVP and PASM mode groups to this format.

Figure 3.32
The Classic information display is clean and based mostly on text.

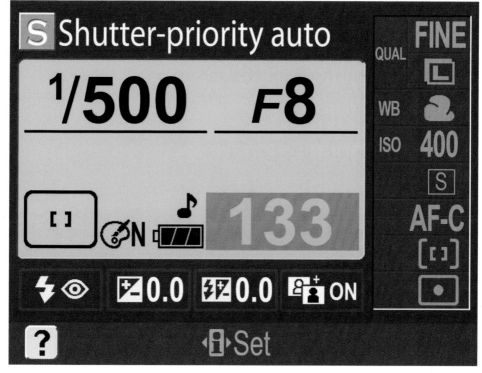

- **Graphic.** This format mixes text and graphics, and includes a facsimile of the mode dial that appears briefly on the left side of the screen as you change from one exposure mode to the other. (See Figure 3.33.) It's prettier to look at and adds a little flair to the display, because you can choose black, white, or orange backgrounds, but I find it distracting. As you gain familiarity with your D60, you might want to keep the Classic format for PASM modes that you'll be using most often, and apply the Graphic format for the DVP modes, which, I predict, will come into play only when you hand your camera to a less-experienced photographer.

- **Wallpaper.** This format allows you to apply a photograph of your choice as the background, with either black or white text and icons overlaid (see Figure 3.34). Choose your background image carefully. It should be as evenly toned as possible to avoid obscuring the informational display with clutter. I never use this option, but I imagine it will be favored by those who apply flame decals to the flanks of their cars, have transparent computer cases with blue-glowing innards, and leopard-skin wrappers for their iPods. Who says individuality is obsolete?

You can change the Shooting Information display to the format of your choice using three easy-to-understand screens:

1. Choose **Info display** format from the Setup menu.

2. Select either **Digital Vari-Program** or **P, S, A, M** and press the multi-selector right button.

3. Choose either **Classic**, **Graphic**, or **Wallpaper** and press the multi-selector right button.

4. Specify a background color and press **OK**:

    Classic: Blue, Black, or Orange

    Graphic: White, Black, or Orange

    Wallpaper: **Dark on light** or **Light on dark** fonts (your image is your background).

5. You'll be returned to the first screen you saw, where you can again choose from **Digital Vari-Program**, or **P, S, A, M**, choose a wallpaper, or press the Menu button (or tap the shutter release) to exit.

6. When you choose **Select wallpaper**, you're taken to the D60's standard image selection screen, where you can scroll though images on your memory card, or another one you insert, with the left/right multi-selector buttons, zoom in on a highlighted image with the Zoom button, or select the image of your choice by pressing **OK**.

Figure 3.33
The Graphic format spices up the display with some graphical elements.

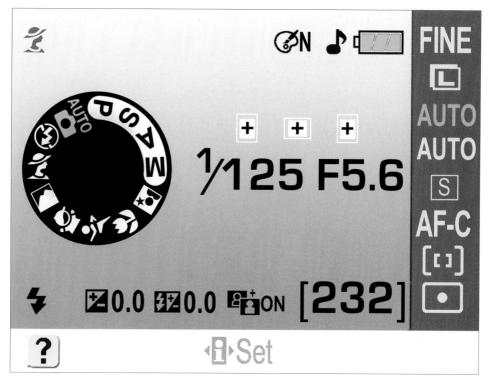

Figure 3.34
The Wallpaper format lets you use your own photograph as the background.

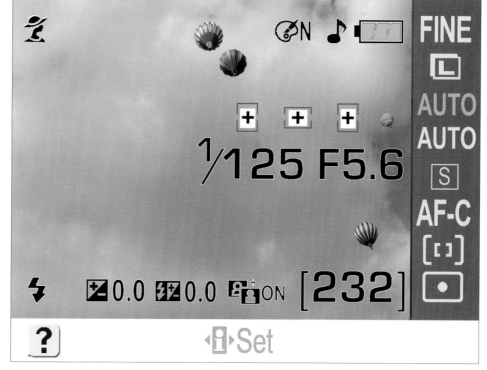

Auto Shooting Info

This setting controls when the Shooting Information display is shown on the LCD. The display is a handy tool for checking your settings as you shoot. It does use up battery power, so you might want to turn off the automatic display if you don't need to review your settings frequently, or if you especially want to conserve battery power. The Shooting Information display can be viewed any time by pressing the Info button at the lower-left side of the back of the D60. Here's how this option works:

- **On.** The D60 will display the Shooting Information screen if the shutter release button is pressed halfway and released. The screen will vanish temporarily if you bring the camera to your eye (within range of the eye sensors) and appear again when you remove your eye from the viewfinder. As always, the information display goes away when you press the shutter release halfway and hold it. If you've set Image Review to **Off** (**CSM #7**), the Shooting Information screen appears as soon as the photograph is taken. If CSM #7 is set to **On**, the Shooting Information screen appears when the shutter release is pressed halfway and released, or if the Info button is pressed.

- **Off.** The Shooting Information screen is not displayed when you press the shutter release button halfway and release it. You can activate the display by pressing the Info button.

Shooting Info Auto Off

Nikon probably gave this option a separate menu listing to avoid confusion, but new users of the Nikon D60 are likely to be confused, anyway. This particular setting controls whether the Shooting Information screen is shown or hidden when your eye or face (or any other object) is present at the viewfinder, where they can be detected by the eye sensor.

- **On.** With this default setting, the Shooting Information display vanishes from the LCD when the exposure meters are on and the eye sensor detects your face or some other object in close proximity. The informational display is shown at the bottom of the viewfinder instead. When the eye sensor no longer detects an object, the viewfinder display is turned off and the Shooting Information display on the LCD reappears.

- **Off.** The eye sensor is disabled, and both the viewfinder display and Shooting Information screen are shown when the D60's exposure meters are active. This uses more power, but can be helpful if you find the frequent on/off display on the LCD distracting.

World Time

Use this menu entry to adjust the D60's internal clock. Your options include:

■ **Time zone.** A small map will pop up on the setting screen and you can choose your local time zone. I sometimes forget to change the time zone when I travel (especially when going to Europe), so my pictures are all time-stamped incorrectly. I like to use the time stamp to recall exactly when a photo was taken, so keeping this setting correct is important.

■ **Date.** Use this setting to enter the exact year, month, day, hour, minute, and second.

■ **Date format.** Choose from **Year/month/day** (Y/M/D), **Month/day/year** (M/D/Y), or **Day/month/year** (D/M/Y) formats.

■ **Daylight saving time.** Use this to turn daylight saving time **On** or **Off**. Because the date on which DST takes effect has been changed from time to time, if you turn this feature on you may need to monitor your camera to make sure DST has been implemented correctly.

LCD Brightness

Choose this menu option and you can choose to turn **Auto dim** on or off (the default is **On**), which causes the LCD brightness to decrease gradually while shooting information is displayed, producing a slight decrease in power consumed. You can also choose to adjust the intensity of the display using the **LCD brightness** option. A grayscale strip appears on the LCD, as shown in Figure 3.35. Use the multi-selector up/down keys to adjust the brightness to a comfortable viewing level over a range of +3 to –3. Under the lighting conditions that exist when you make this adjustment, you should be able to see all 10 swatches from black to white. If the two end swatches blend together, the brightness has been set too low. If the two whitest swatches on the right end of the strip blend together, the brightness is too high. Brighter settings use more battery power, but can allow you to view an image on the LCD outdoors in bright sunlight. When you have the brightness you want, press **OK** to lock it in and return to the menu.

Video Mode

This setting is the first option on the second "page" of the Setup menu (see Figure 3.36). It controls the output of the Nikon D60 when directed to a conventional video system though the video cable when you're displaying images on a monitor or connected to a VCR through the external device's yellow video input jack. You can select either **NTSC**, used in the United States, Canada, Mexico, many Central, South American, and Caribbean countries, much of Asia, and other countries; or **PAL**, which is used in the UK, much of Europe, Africa, India, China, and parts of the Middle East.

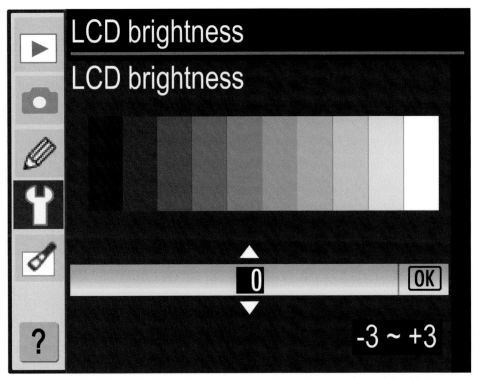

Figure 3.35
Adjust the LCD brightness so that all the grayscale strips are visible.

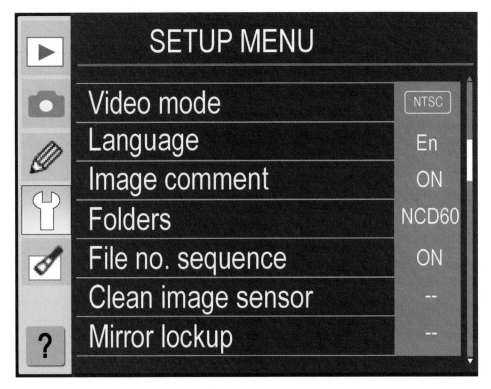

Figure 3.36
The second "page" of the Setup menu has seven more entries.

Language

Choose from 15 languages for menu display, choosing from German, English, Spanish, Finnish, French, Italian, Dutch, Polish, Portuguese, Russian, Swedish, Traditional Chinese, Simplified Chinese, Japanese, or Korean.

Image Comment

The Image Comment is your opportunity to add a copyright notice, personal information about yourself (including contact info), or even a description of where the image was taken (e.g., Seville Photos 2008), although text entry with the Nikon D60 is a bit too clumsy for doing a lot of individual annotation of your photos. (But you still might want to change the comment each time, say, you change cities during your travels.) The embedded comments can be read by many software programs, including Nikon ViewNX or Capture NX.

The standard text entry screen can be used to enter your comment, with up to 36 characters available. For the copyright symbol, embed a lowercase "c" within opening and closing parentheses: **(c)**. You can enter text by choosing **Input comment**, turn attachment of the comment On or Off using the **Attach Comment** entry, and select **Done** when you're finished working with comments. If you find typing with a cursor too tedious, you can enter your comment in Nikon Capture NX and upload it to the camera though a USB cable.

Now is a good time to master text entry, because you can use it to enter comments, rename folders, and perform other functions.

1. Press **Menu** and select the Setup menu.

2. Scroll to **Image comment** with the multi-selector up/down buttons and press the multi-selector right button.

3. Scroll down to **Input comment** and press the multi-selector right button to confirm your choice.

4. Use the multi-selector navigational buttons to scroll around within the array of alphanumerics, as shown in Figure 3.37. There is a full array of uppercase, lowercase, and symbol characters. They can't be viewed all at once, so you may need to scroll up or down to locate the one you want. Then, enter your text:

   ■ Press the multi-selector's center OK button to insert the highlighted character. The cursor will move one place to the right to accept the next character.

   ■ Rotate the command dial buttons to move the cursor within the line of characters that have been input.

- To remove a character you've already input, move the cursor with the command dial to highlight that character, and then press the Trash button.

- When you're finished entering text, press the Zoom button to confirm your entry and return to the Image comment screen.

5. In the Image comment screen, scroll down to Attach comment and press the multi-selector right button to activate the comment, or to disable it.

6. When finished, scroll up to **Done** and press **OK**.

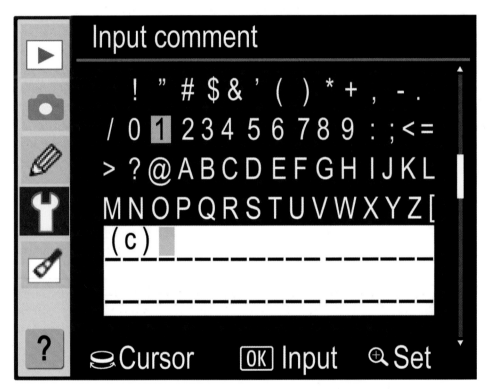

Figure 3.37
Enter a comment on this screen.

Folders

If you want to store images in a folder other than the one created and selected by the Nikon D60, you can switch among available folders on your memory card, or create your own folder. Remember that any folders you create will be deleted when you reformat your memory card.

The Nikon D60 automatically creates a folder on a newly formatted memory card with a name like 100NCD60, and when it fills with 999 images, will automatically create a new folder with a number incremented by one (such as 101NCD60). The numeric portion of the folder name is always created by the D60; your folder choice is based on the remaining five characters:

■ If there are folders on your memory card named 100NCD60 and 101NCD60, you can choose the folder name NCD60 from the folder screen. If you've specified a folder name such as SPAIN, the D60 will create a folder named 100SPAIN, and when it fills up with 999 images, it will create a new folder numbered 101SPAIN, and so forth.

■ The D60 always uses the highest numbered folder with the specified name suffix when creating new images. For example, if you select NCD60, in the example above, all images will be created in folder 101NCD60 until it fills up, and will then be deposited into a new folder 102NCD60. If you chose SPAIN as your active folder name, all images would go into 100SPAIN until it fills and then 101SPAIN is created.

To change the currently active folder:

1. Choose **Folders** in the Setup menu.

2. Scroll down to **Select folder** and press the multi-selector right button.

3. From among the available folders shown, scroll to the one that you want to become active for image storage and playback. (Handy when displaying slide shows.)

4. Press the OK button to confirm your choice, or press the multi-selector right button to return to the Setup menu.

5. You can also choose **Delete** within the Folders menu to remove all empty folders on your memory card. This option is useful when you've created a bunch of folders and decided not to use them.

Why create your own folders? Perhaps you're traveling and have a high-capacity memory card and want to store the images for each day (or for each city that you visit) in a separate folder. Maybe you'd like to separate those wedding photos you snapped at the ceremony from those taken at the reception. To create your own folder, or to rename an existing folder:

1. Choose **Folders** in the Setup menu.

2. Scroll down to **New** and press the multi-selector right button. You can also select **Rename** to apply a new name to an existing folder; you'll be asked to choose a folder before proceeding.

3. Use the text-entry screen (see Figure 3.38) to enter a name for your folder. Follow the instructions I outlined under Image Comment to enter text. The Folder text screen has only uppercase characters and the numbers 0-9, and just five letters can be entered.

4. Press the Zoom button when finished to create and activate the new or renamed folder and return to the Setup menu.

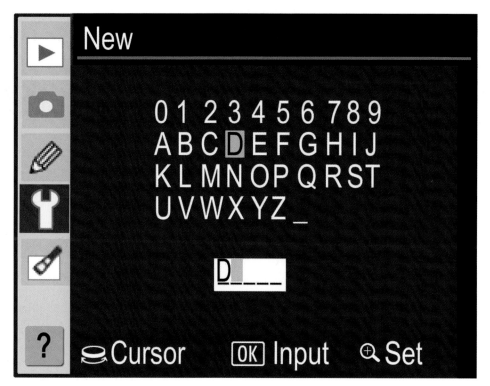

Figure 3.38
Enter a folder
name.

File Number Sequence

The Nikon D60 will automatically apply a file number to each picture you take, using consecutive numbering for all your photos over a long period of time, spanning many different memory cards, starting over from scratch when you insert a new card, or when you manually reset the numbers. Numbers are applied from 0001 to 9999, at which time the D60 "rolls over" to 0001 again.

The camera keeps track of the last number used in its internal memory and, if File Number Sequence is turned **On**, will apply a number that's one higher, or a number that's one higher than the largest number in the current folder on the memory card inserted in the camera. You can also start over each time a new folder has been created on the memory card, or reset the current counter back to 0001 at any time. Here's how it works:

- **Off.** At this default setting, if you're using a blank/reformatted memory card, or a new folder is created, the next photo taken will be numbered 0001. File number sequences will be reset every time you use or format a card, or a new folder is created (which happens when an existing folder on the card contains 999 shots).

- **On.** The Nikon D60 will apply a number one higher than the last picture taken, even if a new folder is created, a new memory card inserted, or an existing memory card formatted.

■ **Reset.** The D60 starts over with 0001, even if a folder containing images exists on the card. In that case, a new folder will be created. At this setting, new or reformatted memory cards will always have 0001 as the first file number.

HOW MANY SHOTS, REALLY?

The file numbers produced by the D60 don't provide information about the actual number of times the camera's shutter has been tripped—called actuations. For that data, you'll need a third-party software solution, such as the free Opanda iExif (www.opanda.com) for Windows or the non-free ($34.95) GraphicConverter for Macintosh (www.lemkesoft.com). These utilities can be used to extract the true number of actuations from the Exif information embedded in a JPEG file.

Clean Image Sensor

This entry gives you some control over the Nikon D60's automatic sensor cleaning feature, which removes dust through a vibration cycle that shakes the sensor until dust, presumably, falls off and is captured by a sticky surface at the bottom of the sensor area. If you happen to take a picture and notice an artifact in an area that contains little detail (such as the sky or a blank wall), you can access this menu choice, place the camera with its base downward, choose **Clean now**, and press **OK**. A message **Image sensor cleaning** appears, and the dust you noticed has probably been shaken off.

You can also tell the D60 when you'd like it to perform automatic cleaning without specific instructions from you. Choose **Clean at** and select from:

■ **ON.** Clean at startup. This allows you to start off a particular shooting session with a clean sensor.

■ **OFF.** Clean at shutdown. This removes any dust that may have accumulated since the camera has been turned on, say, from dust infiltration while changing lenses. Note that this choice does not turn off automatic cleaning; it simply moves the operation to the camera power-down sequence.

■ **ON/OFF.** Clean at both startup and shutdown. Use this setting if you're paranoid about dust and don't mind the extra battery power consumed each time the camera is turned on or off. If you only turn off the D60 when you're finished shooting, the power penalty is not large, but if you're the sort who turns off the camera every time you pause in shooting, the extra power consumed by the dust removal may exceed any savings you get from leaving the camera off.

■ **Cleaning Off.** No automatic dust removal will be performed. Use this to preserve battery power, or if you prefer to use automatic dust removal only when you explicitly want to apply it.

Mirror Lockup

You can also clean the sensor manually. Use this menu entry to raise the mirror and open the shutter so you'll have access to the sensor for cleaning with a blower, brush, or swab, as described in Chapter 9. You don't want power to fail while you're poking around inside the camera, so this option is available only when sufficient battery power (at least 60 percent) is available. Using a fully charged battery or connecting the D60 to an EH-5/EH5a AC adapter is an even better idea.

Firmware Version

You can see the current firmware release in use in this menu listing, which you must scroll to view the menu entry that provides the information (see Figure 3.39). You can learn how to update firmware in Chapter 9.

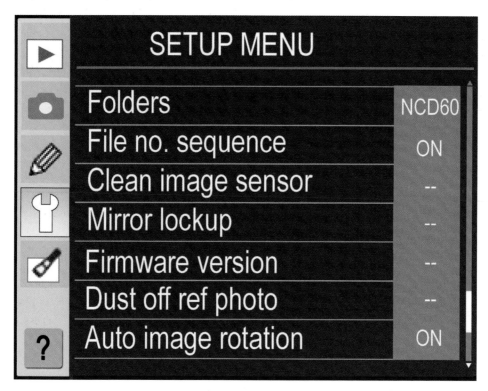

Figure 3.39
Scrolling down reveals the last few entries in the Setup menu.

Dust Off Ref Photo

This menu choice lets you "take a picture" of any dust or other particles that may be adhering to your sensor. The D60 will then append information about the location of this dust to your photos, so that the Image Dust Off option in Capture NX can be used to mask the dust in the NEF image.

To use this feature, select **Dust off ref photo,** choose either **Start** or **Clean sensor, then start**, and then press **OK**. If directed to do so, the camera will first perform a self-cleaning operation by applying ultrasonic vibration to the low-pass filter that resides on top of the sensor. Then, a screen will appear asking you to take a photo of a bright feature-less white object 10 cm from the lens. Nikon recommends using a lens with a focal length of at least 50mm. Point the D60 at a solid white card and press the shutter release. An image with the extension .ndf will be created, and can be used by Nikon Capture NX as a reference photo if the "dust off" picture is placed in the same folder as an image to be processed for dust removal.

Auto Image Rotation

Turning this setting **On** tells the Nikon D60 to include camera orientation information in the image file. The orientation can be read by many software applications, including Adobe Photoshop, Nikon ViewNX, and Capture NX, as well as the Rotate Tall setting in the Playback menu. Turn this feature **Off,** and none of the software applications or Playback's Rotate Tall will be able to determine the correct orientation for the image. Nikon notes that only the first image's orientation is used when shooting continuous bursts; subsequent photos will be assigned the same orientation, even if you rotate the camera during the sequence (which is something I have been known to do myself when shooting sports like basketball).

Retouch Menu

The Retouch menu has seven entries on its first screen (see Figure 3.40), plus three more options that you can view by scrolling down. This menu allows you to create a new copy of an existing image with trimmed or retouched characteristics. You can apply D-lighting, remove red-eye, create a monochrome image, apply filter effects, rebalance color, overlay one image on another, and compare two images side-by-side. Just select a picture during Playback mode, and then scroll down to one of the retouching options. You can also go directly to the Retouch menu, select a retouching feature, and then choose a picture from the standard D60 picture selection screen shown multiple times in Chapter 2. Your choices are:

- Quick Retouch
- D-Lighting
- Red-Eye Correction
- Trim
- Monochrome
- Filter Effects
- Small Picture
- Image Overlay
- NEF (Raw processing)
- Stop-Motion Movie
- Before and After

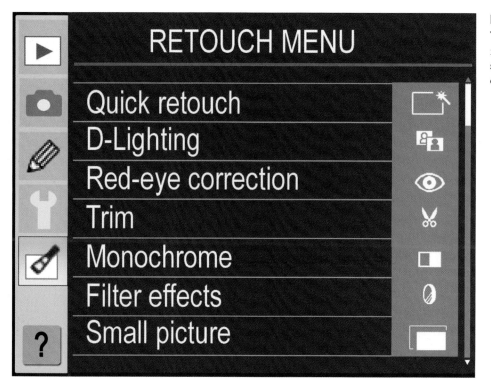

Figure 3.40
The Retouch menu allows simple in-camera editing.

The Retouch menu is most useful when you want to create a modified copy of an image on the spot, for immediate printing or e-mailing without first importing into your computer for more extensive editing. You can also use it to create a JPEG version of an image in the camera when you are shooting RAW-only photos.

While you can retouch images that have already been processed by the Retouch menu, you may notice some quality loss. Some retouching options are mutually exclusive: you can't apply Quick Retouch to images that have had D-lighting applied, and vice versa. Once you've applied a Filter effect, you can't apply a second filter effect to a copied image, except for those given the Cross Screen effect. Quick Retouch, D-Lighting, Red-Eye Correction, and Filter effects (except for Cross Screen) can't be applied to monochrome copies. Use of the Trim or Small Picture options create copies that cannot be further modified in the Retouch menu. There are quite a few additional conflicts that you may discover as you work with this menu. In real life, few of us do a lot of retouching to images in the camera; when things start to get complicated, it's a better idea to work on them in your image editor.

To create a retouched copy of an image:

1. While browsing among images in Playback mode, press **OK** when an image you want to retouch is displayed on the screen. The Retouch menu will pop up, and you can select a retouching option.

2. From the Retouch menu, select the option you want and press the multi-selector right button. The Nikon D60's standard image selection screen appears. Scroll among the images as usual with the left/right multi-selector buttons, press the Zoom button to examine a highlighted image more closely, and press OK to choose that image.

3. Work with the options available from that particular Retouch menu feature and press **OK** to create the modified copy, or **Playback** to cancel your changes.

4. The retouched image will bear a filename that reveals its origin. For example, if you make a Small Picture version of an image named DSC_0112.jpg, the reduced-size copy will be named SSC_0113.jpg. Copies incorporating other retouching features would be named CSC_0113.jpg instead.

Quick Retouch

This option brightens the shadows of pictures that have already been taken. Once you've selected your photo for processing, use the multi-selector up/down keys in the screen that pops up (see Figure 3.41). The amount of correction that you select (**High**, **Normal**, or **Low**) will be applied to the version of the image shown at right. The left-hand version of the image shows the uncorrected version. While working on your image, you can press the Zoom image to temporarily magnify the original photo.

Figure 3.41
Quick Retouch applies D-lighting, enhanced contrast, and added saturation to an image.

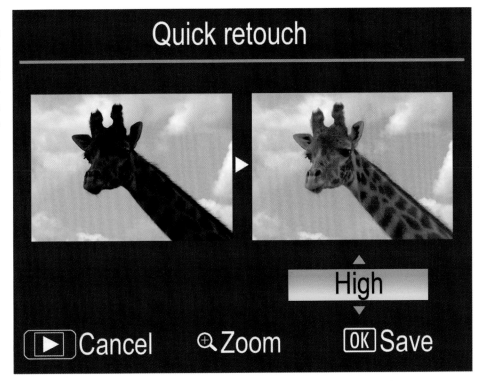

Quick Retouch brightens shadows, enhances contrast, and adds color richness (saturation) to the image. Press **OK** to create a copy on your memory card with the retouching applied.

Tip

With Quick Retouch and other Retouching menu tools, you can work with JPEG Fine, JPEG Normal, or JPEG Basic images to create a JPEG copy at the same quality level. However if you use a RAW or RAW+JPEG Basic original, the retouched copy is created at the JPEG Fine quality level.

D-Lighting

This option brightens the shadows of pictures that have already been taken, and it is a useful tool for backlit photographs or any image with deep shadows with important detail. Once you've selected your photo for modification, you'll be shown side-by-side images with the unaltered version on the left, and your adjusted version on the right.

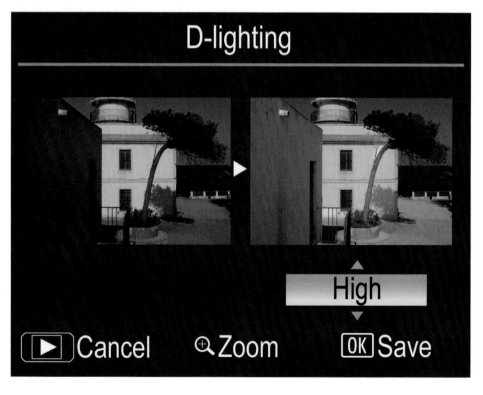

Figure 3.42
D-lighting brightens dark shadows while producing minimal changes on the highlights.

Press the multi-selector's up/down buttons to choose from **High**, **Normal**, or **Low** corrections. Press the Zoom button to magnify the image. When you're happy with the corrected image on the right, compared to the original on the left, press **OK** to save the copy to your memory card.

Red-Eye Correction

This Retouch menu tool can be used to remove the residual red-eye look that remains after applying the Nikon D60's other remedies, such as the red-eye reduction lamp. (You can use the red-eye tools found in most image editors, as well.)

Your Nikon D60 has a fairly effective red-eye reduction flash mode. Unfortunately, your camera is unable, on its own, to totally *eliminate* the red-eye effects that occur when an electronic flash (or, rarely, illumination from other sources) bounces off the retinas of the eye and into the camera lens. Animals seem to suffer from yellow or green glowing pupils, instead; the effect is equally undesirable. The effect is worst under low-light conditions (exactly when you might be using a flash) as the pupils expand to allow more light to reach the retinas. The best you can hope for is to *reduce* or minimize the red-eye effect.

The best way to truly eliminate red-eye is to raise the flash up off the camera so its illumination approaches the eye from an angle that won't reflect directly back to the retina and into the lens. The extra height of the built-in flash may not be sufficient, however. That alone is a good reason for using an external flash. If you're working with your D60's built-in flash, your only recourse may be to switch on the red-eye reduction flash mode. That causes a lamp on the front of the camera to illuminate with a half-press of the shutter release button, which may result in your subjects' pupils contracting, decreasing the amount of the red-eye effect. (You may have to ask your subject to look at the lamp to gain maximum effect.)

If your image still displays red-eye effects, you can use the Retouch menu to make a copy with red-eye reduced further. First, select a picture that was taken with flash (non-flash pictures won't be available for selection). After you've selected the picture to process, press **OK**. The image will be displayed on the LCD. You can magnify the image with the Zoom button, scroll around the zoomed image with the multi-selector buttons, and zoom out with the Zoom Out button. While zoomed, you can cancel the zoom by pressing the OK button.

When you are finished examining the image, press **OK** again. The D60 will look for red-eye, and, if detected, create a copy that has been processed to reduce the effect. If no red-eye is found, a copy is not created. Figure 3.43 shows an original image (left) and its processed copy (right).

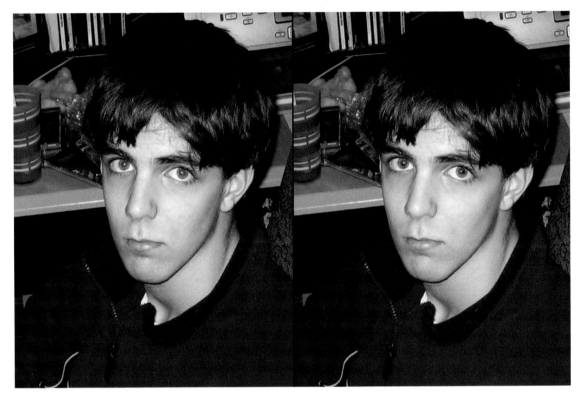

Figure 3.43 An image with red-eye (left) can be processed to produce a copy with no red-eye effects (right).

Trim

This option creates copies in specific sizes based on the final size you select, chosen from among 2560 × 1920, 1920 × 1440, 1280 × 960, 960 × 720, or 640 × 480 pixel dimensions. You can use this feature to create smaller versions of a picture for e-mailing without the need to first transfer the image to your own computer. If you're traveling, create your smaller copy here, insert the memory card in a card reader at an Internet café, your library's public computers, or some other computer, and e-mail the reduced-size version. Just follow these steps:

1. **Select your photo.** Choose Trim from the Retouch menu. You'll be shown the standard Nikon D60 image selection screen. Scroll among the photos using the multi-selector left/right buttons, and press **OK** when the image you want to trim is highlighted. While selecting, you can temporarily enlarge the highlighted image by pressing the Zoom button.

2. **Crop in on your photo.** Press the Zoom button to crop in on your picture. The pixel dimensions of the cropped image will be displayed in the upper-left corner (see Figure 3.44) as you zoom. The current framed size is outlined in yellow within an inset image in the lower-right corner.

Figure 3.44
The Trim feature of the Retouch menu allows in-camera cropping.

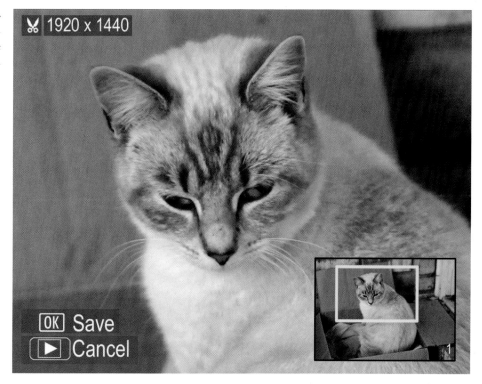

3. **Move cropped area within the image.** Use the multi-selector left/right and up/down buttons to relocate the yellow cropping border within the frame.

4. **Save the cropped image.** Press **OK** to save a copy of the image using the current crop and size, or press the Playback button to exit without creating a copy.

Monochrome

This Retouch choice allows you to produce a copy of the selected photo as a black-and-white image, sepia-toned image, or cyanotype (blue-and-white). You can fine-tune the color saturation of the previewed Sepia or Cyanotype version by pressing the multi-selector up button to increase color richness, and the down button to decrease saturation. When satisfied, press **OK** to create the monochrome duplicate.

Filter Effects

Add effects somewhat similar to photographic filters with this tool. You can choose from among seven different choices:

- **Skylight.** This option makes the image slightly less blue.

- **Warm.** Use this filter to add a rich warm cast to the duplicate.

- **Red, Green, Blue intensifiers.** These three options makes the red, green, and blue hues brighter, respectively. Use them to brighten a rose, intensify the greens of foliage, or deepen the blue of the sky.

- **Cross screen.** This option adds radiating star points to bright objects—such as the reflection of light sources on shiny surfaces. You can choose four different attributes of your stars:

  Number of points. You can select from four, six, or eight points for each star added to your image.

  Filter amount. Select from three different intensities, represented by two, three, and four stars in the menu (this doesn't reflect the actual number of stars in your image, which is determined by the number of bright areas in the photo).

  Filter angle. Select from three different angles: steep, approximately 45 degrees, and a shallower angle.

  Length of points. Three different lengths for the points can be chosen: short, medium, and long.

- **Color balance.** This option produces the screen shown in Figure 3.45, with a preview image of your photo. Use the multi-selector up/down (green/pink) and left/right buttons (blue/red) to bias the color of your image in the direction of the hues shown on the color square below the preview.

Small Picture

This Retouch menu option allows you to create small copies of full images (without cropping or trimming) at resolutions of 640 × 480, 320 × 240, or 160 × 120. All three of these optional small sizes may be useful for e-mailing, website display, or use in presentations on television screens.

To create a Small Picture copy:

1. Choose **Small picture** from the Retouch menu.

2. Select Choose size and specify your preference from among the three available sizes, 640 × 480, 320 × 240, or 160 × 120. Press **OK**.

3. Next choose **Select picture** and choose your image using the standard Nikon D60 image selection screen.

Figure 3.45
Press the multi-selector buttons to bias the color in the direction you prefer.

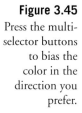

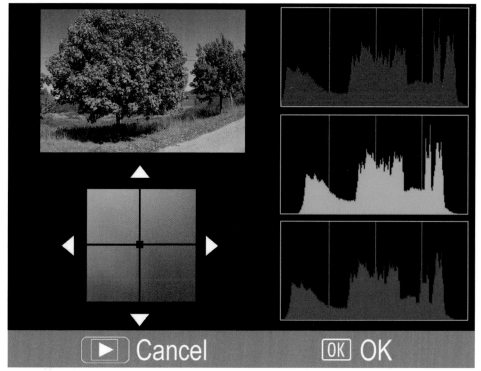

4. Press the up/down button to mark a highlighted image for reduction.

5. You can select more than one picture, marking each with the up/down button. Use the button to unmark any photos if you change your mind.

6. Press **OK.** You'll see a message: **Create small picture? 2 images.** (Or whatever number of images you have marked.)

7. Press **OK** to create the small pictures.

Image Overlay

You can access this feature by scrolling to the final three entries in the Retouch menu, as shown in Figure 3.46. This tool allows you to combine two RAW photos (only NEF files can be used) in a composite image that Nikon claims is better than a "double exposure" created in an image editing application because the overlays are made using RAW data. To produce this composite image, follow these steps:

1. Choose **Image overlay**. The screen shown in Figure 3.47 will be displayed, with the Image 1 box highlighted.

2. Press **OK** and the Nikon D60's image selection screen appears. Choose the first image for the overlay and press **OK**.

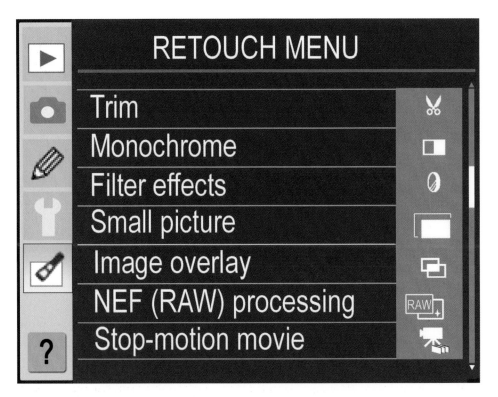

Figure 3.46
Image Overlay, NEF (RAW) Processing, and Stop-Motion Movie are the last three entries in the Retouch menu.

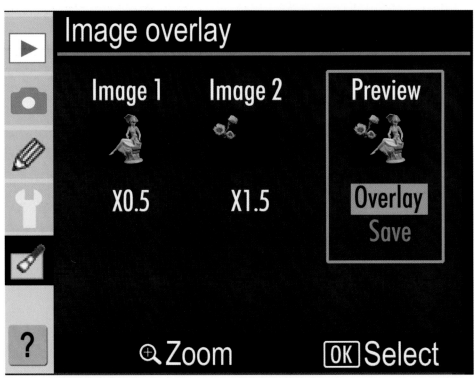

Figure 3.47
Overlay two RAW images to produce a "double exposure."

3. Press the multi-selector right button to highlight the Image 2 box, and press **OK** to produce the image selection screen. Choose the second image for the overlay.

4. By highlighting either the **Image 1** or **Image 2** boxes and pressing the multi-selector up/down buttons, you can adjust the "gain," or how much of the final image will be "exposed" from the selected picture. You can choose from X0.5 (half-exposure) to X2.0 (twice the exposure) for each image. The default value is 1.0 for each, so that each image will contribute equally to the final exposure.

5. Use the multi-selector right button to highlight the Preview box and view the combined picture. Press the Zoom button to enlarge the view.

6. When you're ready to store your composite copy, press the multi-selector down button when the Preview box is highlighted to select **Save**, and press **OK**. The combined image is stored on the memory card.

NEF (RAW) Processing

Use this tool to create a JPEG version of any image saved in either straight RAW (with no JPEG version) or RAW+Basic (with a Basic JPEG version). You can select from among several parameters to "process" your new JPEG copy right in the camera.

1. Choose a RAW image. Select NEF (RAW) processing from the Retouch menu. You'll be shown the standard Nikon D60 image selection screen. Use the left/right buttons to navigate among the RAW images displayed. Press **OK** to select the highlighted image.

2. In the NEF (RAW) processing screen, shown in Figure 3.48, you can use the multi-selector up/down keys to select from five different attributes of the RAW image information to apply to your JPEG copy. Choose **Image quality** (Fine, Normal, or Basic), **Image size** (Large, Medium, or Small), **White balance**, **Exposure compensation**, and **Optimize image** parameters.

Tip

The White Balance parameter cannot be selected for images created with the Image Overlay tool, and the Preset manual white balance setting can be fine-tuned only with images that were originally shot using the Preset white balance setting. Exposure compensation cannot be adjusted for images taken using Active D-lighting, and both white balance and optimize image settings cannot be applied to pictures taken using any of the DVP/Scene modes.

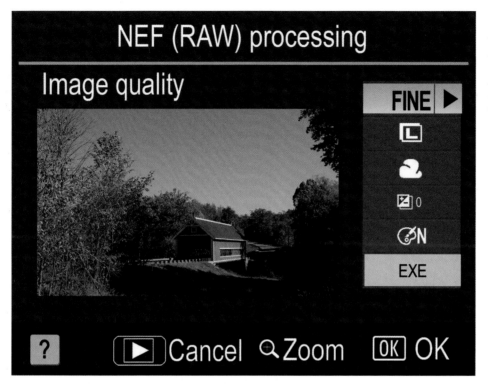

Figure 3.48
Adjust five
parameters and
then save your
JPEG copy
from a RAW
original file.

3. Press the Zoom button to magnify the image temporarily while the button is held down.

4. Press the Playback button if you change your mind, to exit from the processing screen.

5. When all parameters are set, highlight EXE (for Execute) and press **OK**. The D60 will create a JPEG file with the settings you've specified, and show an **Image saved** message on the LCD when finished.

Stop-Motion Movie

Analyze your golf swing, make flip-book movies, or create animations for your web page using this clever capability. This is one tool readily available in your Nikon D60 that ordinarily requires an image editor or standalone program in your computer. The movies aren't sophisticated, but they are surprisingly effective.

Your first step is to create a series of frames that can be assembled into a stop-motion movie. You can shoot a series of pictures at 3 fps using your D60's continuous shooting mode, if you like. Or, you can take the pictures one at a time. If you were doing clay animation, for example, you'd mount your camera firmly on a tripod, take the first picture in a series, then move your clay figures slightly, take the next picture, and repeat multiple times (a hundred times if you're ambitious!). The Nikon ML-L3 infrared remote control, and the D60 set to Quick Release mode would help you not move the camera between exposures. I'd recommend using a non-variable light source (such as lamps indoors) and setting the D60 for manual exposure to ensure that the exposure of each frame is identical.

Then, when you've collected all your shots on a single memory card, it's time to create the stop-motion movie. When you choose this option from the Retouch menu, a screen with three choices appears. Highlight any of the three and press **OK**:

■ **Create movie.** This choice leads you to a submenu where you select the actual frames that will be used to make your movie.

■ **Frame size.** Here, you choose frame sizes from 640×480 (good for full-screen movies on your computer display or a television); 320×240 (for smaller, more compact movies); and 160×120 (which produces coarse movies that are not much larger than a postage stamp on most computer screens, but which are better suited for display over the Internet, because their file size is very small).

■ **Frame rate.** The frame rate determines how many pictures are displayed each second. The standard for video display is 30 frames per second. The fastest frame rate available for these stop-motion movies is 15 frames per second, which produces a movie that displays a little jerkiness. You can also choose 10 fps, 6 fps, and 3 fps rates, which produce a little less smoothness, but allow for longer movies with a given number of frames to work with.

The **Create movie** screen is the editing and assembly portion of the stop-motion movie tool. You'll see a screen like the one shown in Figure 3.49.

1. All the images available for the movie will be shown in a continuous strip in the top half of the screen. Press the multi-selector left/right buttons to move along the strip until you have highlighted the first image in the movie sequence. Press **OK** to select it.

2. Press the multi-selector left/right buttons to locate the last image in the sequence, and press **OK** to select it. You can include 100 images, in total, between the first and last in the sequence. All selected images will be marked with a checkmark.

3. If you like, you can select **Edit** to change the **Start**, **Middle**, or **End** image in your sequence. Modify the Start and End images to change the length of the sequence. Use the Middle editing feature to remove (unmark) images.

4. When satisfied, press **Save**.

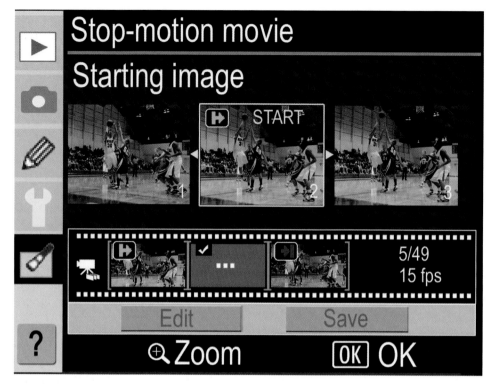

Figure 3.49
Choose first
and last frames
of your stop-
motion movie
here; then
either Edit or
Save the clip.

5. A screen will appear with options to **Save**, **Preview**, change the **Frame rate**, or **Edit** the movie. It's usually a good idea to preview your movie (it will take a few seconds to create the preview), and then make any additional editing changes.

6. When you're happy with your movie after the preview, choose **Save**.

Before and After

Use this option to compare a retouched photo side-by-side with the original from which it was derived. Don't look for the Before and After entry in the Retouch menu. It doesn't appear there. Instead, this option is shown on the pop-up menu that appears when you are viewing an image (or copy) full screen and press the OK button.

To use Before and After comparisons:

1. Press the Playback button and review images in full-frame mode until you encounter a source image or retouched copy you want to compare. The retouched copy will have the retouching icon displayed in the upper-left corner. Press **OK**.

2. The Retouch menu with **Trim**, **Monochrome**, **Filter effects**, **Small picture**, and **Before and after** appears. These are the only options that can be applied to an image that has already been retouched. Scroll down to **Before and after** and press **OK**.

3. The original and retouched image will appear next to each other, with the retouching options you've used shown as a label above the images, as you can see in Figure 3.50.

4. Highlight the original or the copy with the multi-selector left/right buttons, and press the Zoom button to magnify the image to examine it more closely.

5. If you have created more than one copy of an original image, select the retouched version shown, and press the multi-selector up/down buttons to view the other retouched copies. The up/down buttons will also let you view the other image used to create an **Image overlay** copy.

6. When done comparing, press the Playback button to exit.

Figure 3.50
You can easily compare an original image and the retouched version side-by-side.

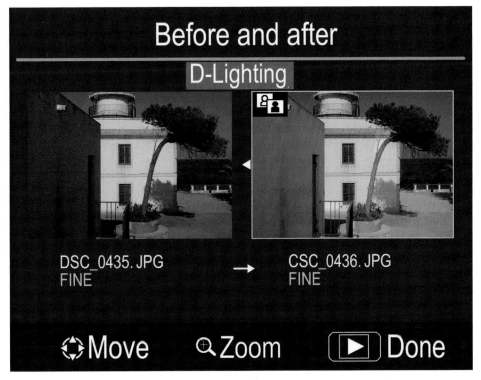

4

Getting the Right Exposure

When you bought your Nikon D60, you probably thought your days of worrying about getting the correct exposure were over. For the most part, that's an accurate assumption. The D60 is one of the smartest cameras available when it comes to calculating the right exposure for most situations. You can generally choose one of the DVP/Scene modes, or spin the mode dial to Program, Aperture Priority, or Shutter Priority and shoot away.

So, why am I including an entire chapter titled "Getting the Right Exposure?" As you learn to use your D60 creatively, you're going to find that the right settings—as determined by the camera's exposure meter and intelligence—need to be *adjusted* to account for your creative decisions or special situations.

For example, when you shoot with the main light source behind the subject, you end up with *backlighting*, which results in an overexposed background and/or an underexposed subject. The Nikon D60 recognizes backlit situations nicely, and can properly base exposure on the main subject, producing a decent photo. But what if you *want* to underexpose the subject, to produce a silhouette effect? Or, perhaps, you might want to flip up the D60's built-in flash unit to fill in the shadows on your subject. The more you know about how to use your D60, the more you'll run into situations where you want to creatively tweak the exposure to provide a different look than you'd get with a straight shot.

This chapter shows you the fundamentals of exposure, so you'll be better equipped to override the Nikon D60's default settings when you want to, or need to. After all, correct exposure is one of the foundations of good photography, along with accurate focus and sharpness, appropriate color balance, freedom from unwanted noise and excessive contrast, as well as pleasing composition.

The Nikon D60 gives you a great deal of control over all of these, although composition is entirely up to you. You must still frame the photograph to create an interesting arrangement of subject matter, but all the other parameters are basic functions of the camera. You can let your D60 set them for you automatically, you can fine-tune how the camera applies its automatic settings, or you can make them yourself, manually. The amount of control you have over exposure, sensitivity (ISO settings), color balance, focus, and image parameters like sharpness and contrast make the D60 a versatile tool for creating images.

In the next few pages I'm going to give you a grounding in one of those foundations, and explain the basics of exposure, either as an introduction or as a refresher course, depending on your current level of expertise. When you finish this chapter, you'll understand most of what you need to know to take well-exposed photographs creatively in a broad range of situations.

Getting a Handle on Exposure

Exposure can make or break your photo. Correct exposure brings out the detail in the areas you want to picture, providing the range of tones and colors you need to create the desired image. Poor exposure can cloak important details in shadow, or wash them out in glare-filled featureless expanses of white. However, getting the perfect exposure requires some intelligence—either that built into the camera, or the smarts in your head—because digital sensors can't capture all the tones we are able to see. If the range of tones in an image is extensive, embracing both inky black shadows and bright highlights, we often must settle for an exposure that renders most of those tones—but not all—in a way that best suits the photo we want to produce.

There are four things within our control that affect exposure, listed in the order of the passage of light from the subject to the sensor:

- **Light that is reflected, transmitted, or emitted.** We see and photograph objects by light that is reflected from our subjects, transmitted (say, from translucent objects that are lit from behind), or emitted (by a candle or television screen). When more or less light reaches the lens from the subject, we need to adjust the exposure. This part of the equation is under our control to the extent we can increase the amount of light falling on or passing through the subject (by adding extra light sources or using reflectors), or by pumping up the light that's emitted (by increasing the brightness of the glowing object).

- **Light that passes through the lens.** Not all the illumination that reaches the front of the lens makes it all the way through. Filters can remove some of the light before it enters the lens. Inside the lens barrel is a variable-sized opening called an *aperture* that dilates and contracts to control the amount of light that enters the lens.

You, or the D60's autoexposure system, can control exposure at this point by varying the size of the opening. The relative size of the aperture is called the *f/stop*.

■ **Light passing through the shutter.** Once light passes through the lens, the amount of time the sensor receives it is determined by the D60's shutter, a pair of window-shade-like curtains that pass in front of the sensor. The gap between them exposes the sensor to light, and allows shutter speeds as long as 30 seconds (or even longer if you use the Bulb setting) or as brief as 1/4,000th second.

■ **Light captured by the sensor.** Not all the light falling onto the sensor is captured and recorded. If the number of photons reaching a particular photosensitive site, or pixel, doesn't pass a certain threshold, no information is recorded. Similarly, if too much light illuminates a pixel in the sensor, then the excess isn't recorded or, worse, spills over to contaminate adjacent pixels. We can modify the minimum and maximum number of pixels that contribute to image detail by adjusting the ISO setting. At higher ISOs, the incoming light is amplified to boost the effective sensitivity of the sensor.

These four factors—quantity of light, light passed by the lens, the amount of time the shutter is open, and the sensitivity of the sensor—all work proportionately and reciprocally to produce an exposure. That is, if you double the amount of light, increase the aperture by one stop, make the shutter speed twice as long, or boost the ISO setting 2X, you'll get twice as much exposure. Similarly, you can increase any of these factors while decreasing one of the others by a similar amount to keep the same exposure.

F/STOPS AND SHUTTER SPEEDS

If you're *really* new to more advanced cameras (and I realize that many soon-to-be-ambitious photographers do purchase the D60 as their first digital SLR), you might need to know that the lens aperture, or f/stop, is a ratio, much like a fraction, which is why f/2 is larger than f/4, just as 1/2 is larger than 1/4. However, f/2 is actually *four times* as large as f/4. (If you remember your high school geometry, you'll know that to double the area of a circle, you multiply its diameter by the square root of two: 1.4.)

Lenses are usually marked with intermediate f/stops that represent a size that's twice as much/half as much as the previous aperture. So, a lens might be marked: f/2, f/2.8, f/4, f/5.6, f/8, f/11, f/16, f/22, with each larger number representing an aperture that admits half as much light as the one before, as shown in Figure 4.1.

Shutter speeds are actual fractions (of a second), but the numerator is omitted, so that 60, 125, 250, 500, 1,000, and so forth represent 1/60th, 1/125th, 1/250th, 1/500th, and 1/1,000th second. To avoid confusion, Nikon uses quotation marks to signify longer exposures: 2", 2"5, 4", and so forth representing 2.0, 2.5, and 4.0-second exposures, respectively.

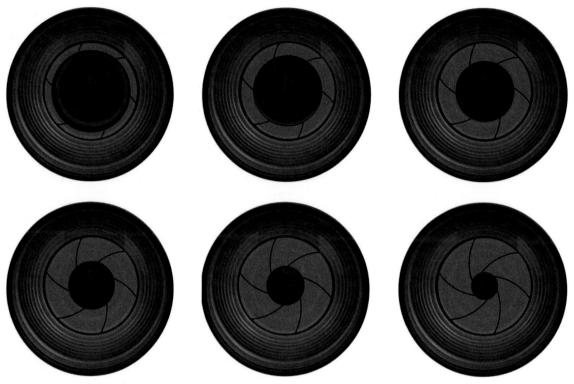

Figure 4.1 Top row (left to right): f/2, f/2.8, f/4; bottom row, f/5.6, f/8, f11.

Most commonly, exposure settings are made using the aperture and shutter speed, followed by adjusting the ISO sensitivity if it's not possible to get the preferred exposure (that is, the one that uses the "best" f/stop or shutter speed for the depth-of-field or action stopping we want). Table 4.1 shows equivalent exposure settings using various shutter speeds and f/stops.

Table 4.1 Equivalent Exposures			
Shutter speed	**f/stop**	**Shutter speed**	**f/stop**
1/30th second	f/22	1/500th second	f/5.6
1/60th second	f/16	1/1,000th second	f/4
1/125th second	f/11	1/2,000th second	f/2.8
1/250th second	f/8	1/4,000th second	f/2

When the D60 is set for P mode, the metering system selects the correct exposure for you automatically, but you can change quickly to an equivalent exposure by holding down the shutter release button halfway ("locking" the current exposure), and then spinning the command dial until the desired *equivalent* exposure combination is displayed. You can use this Flexible Program feature more easily if you remember that you need to rotate the command dial towards the left when you want to increase the amount of depth-of-field or use a slower shutter speed; rotate to the right when you want to reduce the depth-of-field or use a faster shutter speed. The need for more/less DOF and slower/faster shutter speed are the primary reasons you'd want to use the Flexible Program. This program shift mode does not work when you're using flash, or if the light level is very low.

In Aperture Priority (A) and Shutter Priority (S) modes, you can change to an equivalent exposure using a different combination of shutter speed and aperture, but only by either adjusting the aperture in Aperture Priority mode (the camera then chooses the shutter speed) or shutter speed in Shutter Priority mode (the camera then selects the aperture). I'll cover all these exposure modes later in the chapter.

How the D60 Calculates Exposure

Your Nikon D60 calculates exposure by measuring the light that passes through the lens and is bounced up by the mirror to a 420-segment RGB sensor located near the focusing surface, using a pattern you can select (more on that later) and based on the assumption that each area being measured reflects about the same amount of light as a neutral gray card with 18 percent reflectance. That assumption is necessary, because different subjects reflect different amounts of light.

In a photo containing a white cat and a dark gray cat, the white cat might reflect five times as much light as the gray cat. An exposure based on the white cat will cause the gray cat to appear to be black, while an exposure based only on the gray cat will make the white cat washed out. Light-measuring devices handle this by assuming that the areas measured average a standard value of 18 percent gray, a figure that's been used as a rough standard (not all vendors calibrate their metering for exactly 18 percent gray) for many years. Black, white, and gray cats have been a standard metaphor for many years, as well, so I'm going to explain this concept using a different, and more cooperative, life form: peppers.

Figure 4.2 shows three peppers. The yellow pepper at upper right represents a white cat, or any object that is very light but which contains detail that we want to see in the light areas. The red pepper in the lower center is a stand-in for a gray cat, because it has most of its details in the middle tones. The green pepper serves as our black cat, because it is a dark object with detail in its shadows.

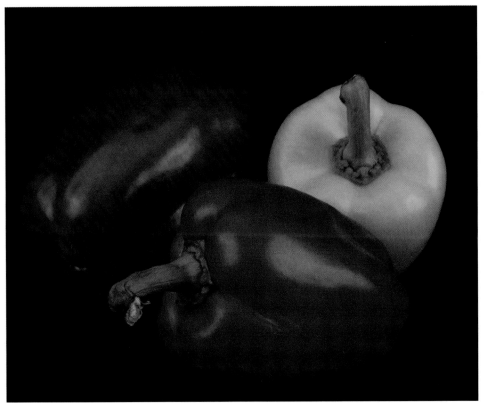

Figure 4.2
The yellow pepper, red pepper, and green pepper represent light, middle, and dark tones.

The colors confuse the issue, so I'm going to convert our color peppers to black-and-white. For the version shown in Figure 4.3, the exposure was optimized for the white (yellow) pepper, changing its tonal value to a medium, 18-percent gray. The dark (green) and medium-toned (red) peppers are now *too* dark. For Figure 4.4, the exposure was optimized for the dark (green) pepper, making most of its surface, now, fall into the middle-tone, 18-percent gray range. The yellow (light) and midtone (red) peppers are now too light.

The solution, of course, is to measure exposure from the object with the middle tones that most closely correspond to the 18 percent gray "standard." Do that, and you wind up with a picture that more closely resembles the original tonality of the red, yellow, and green papers, and which looks, in black-and-white, like Figure 4.5.

In the real world, you could calculate exposure the hard way, and arrive at accurate settings by pointing your D60 at an evenly lit object, such as an actual gray card or the palm of your hand (the backside of the hand is too variable). You'll need to increase the exposure by one stop in the latter case, because the human palm—of any ethnic group—reflects about twice as much light as a gray card. As you'll see, however, it's more practical though, to use your D60's system to meter the actual scene.

Figure 4.3
Exposing for the light-colored pepper (upper right) renders the other two excessively dark.

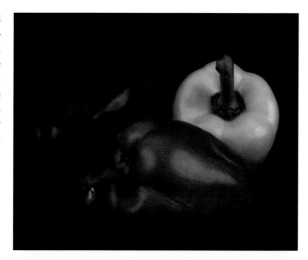

Figure 4.4
Exposing for the dark pepper (upper left) causes the two vegetables in the right half of the picture to become too light.

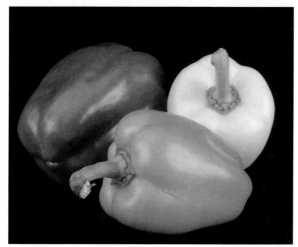

Figure 4.5
Exposing for the middle-toned red pepper produces an image in which the tones of all three subjects appear accurately.

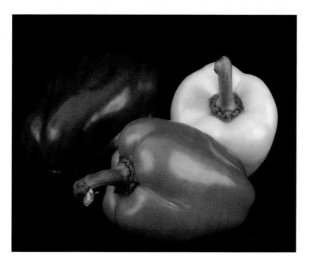

F/STOPS VERSUS STOPS

In photography parlance, *f/stop* always means the aperture or lens opening. However, for lack of a current commonly used word for one exposure increment, the term *stop* is often used. (In the past, EV served this purpose, but Exposure Value and its abbreviation has been inextricably intertwined with its use in describing Exposure Compensation.) In this book, when I say "stop" by itself (no *f*), I mean one whole unit of exposure, and am not necessarily referring to an actual f/stop or lens aperture. So, adjusting the exposure by "one stop" can mean both changing to the next shutter speed increment (say, from 1/125th second to 1/250th second) or the next aperture (such as f/4 to f/5.6). Similarly, 1/3 stop or 1/2 stop increments can mean either shutter speed or aperture changes, depending on the context. Be forewarned.

In most cases, your camera's light meter will do a good job of calculating the right exposure, especially if you use the exposure tips in the next section. But if you want to double-check, or feel that exposure is especially critical, take the light reading off an object of known reflectance. Photographers sometimes carry around an 18 percent gray card (available from any camera store) and, for critical exposures, actually use that card, placed in the subject area, to measure exposure (or to set a custom white balance if needed). You can even take one shot with the card in the photo to provide a reference color and tone when image editing.

To meter properly, you'll want to choose both the *metering method* (how light is evaluated) and *exposure method* (how the appropriate shutter speeds and apertures are chosen based on the metered information). I'll describe both in the following sections.

MODES, MODES, AND MORE MODES

Call them modes or methods, the Nikon D60 seems to have a lot of different sets of options that are described using similar terms. Here's how to sort them out:

- **Metering method.** These modes determine the *parts of the image* within the 420-sensor array that are examined in order to calculate exposure. The D60 may look at many different points within the image, segregating them by zone (Matrix metering), examine the same number of points, but give greater weight to those located in the middle of the frame (Center-Weighted metering), or evaluate only a limited number of points in a limited area (Spot metering).

- **Exposure method.** These modes determine *which* settings are used to expose the image. The D60 may adjust the shutter speed, the aperture, or both, depending on the method you choose.

Choosing a Metering Method

The D60 has three different schemes for evaluating the light received by its exposure sensors, Matrix (with several variations, depending on what lens you have attached); Center-Weighted; and Spot metering. Matrix metering is always used when you select one of the DVP/Scene modes; you can't change to Center-Weighted or Spot metering when using Auto, Auto/No Flash, Portrait, Landscape, Child, Sports, Close-up, or Night Portrait modes. Exposure will generally be calculated well in one of these Scene modes, but the ability to choose an alternate metering method is one of the major reasons to select Program, Aperture Priority, Shutter Priority, or Manual exposure instead.

In P, A, S, and M exposure modes, select the metering mode you want to use (Matrix, Center-Weighted, or Spot) by rotating the metering method dial immediately to the right of the viewfinder window. Here is what you need to know about each metering method:

Matrix Metering

For its Matrix metering mode, the D60 slices up the frame into 420 different zones, arrayed in 10 rows of 42 columns that cover most of the sensor area, shown in Figure 4.6. When Matrix metering is active, its icon (shown as an overlay at the upper-right corner of the figure) appears in the right column of the Shooting Information display.

In all cases, the D60 evaluates the differences between the zones, and compares them with a built-in database of several hundred thousand images to make an educated guess about what kind of picture you're taking. For example, if the top sections of a picture are much lighter than the bottom portions, the algorithm can assume that the scene is a landscape photo with lots of sky. An image that includes most of the lighter portions in the center area may be a portrait. The Nikon D60 also uses information other than brightness to make its evaluation:

- **3D Color Matrix metering II.** This metering mode is used by default when the D60 is equipped with a lens that has a type G or type D designator in its name, such as the AF-S DX Nikkor 16-85mm f/3.5-5.6G ED VR lens. The G after the f/5.6 is the giveaway. (More on lens nomenclature in Chapter 6.) The camera calculates exposure based on brightness, colors of the subject matter (that is, blue pixels in the upper part of the image are probably sky; green pixels in the lower half probably foliage), focus point, and distance information. The D60 is able to use that additional distance data to better calculate what kind of scene you have framed. For example, if you're shooting a portrait with a longer focal-length lens focused to about 5 to 12 feet from the camera, and the upper half of the scene is very bright, the camera assumes you would prefer to meter for the rest of the image, and discount the bright area. However, if the camera has a wide-angle lens attached and is focused at infinity, the D60 can assume you're taking a landscape photo and take the bright upper area into account to produce better looking sky and clouds.

■ **Color Matrix metering II.** If you have a non-G or non-D lens equipped with a CPU chip (these are generally older lenses, although chips can be added to optics which lack them), the distance range is not used. Instead, only focus, brightness, and color information is taken into account to calculate an appropriate exposure.

Matrix metering is best for most general subjects, because it is able to intelligently analyze a scene and make an excellent guess of what kind of subject you're shooting a great deal of the time. The camera can tell the difference between low-contrast and high-contrast subjects by looking at the range of differences in brightness across the scene. Because the D60 has a fairly good idea about what kind of subject matter you are shooting, it can underexpose slightly when appropriate to preserve highlight detail when image contrast is high. (It's often possible to pull detail out of shadows that are too dark using an image editor, but once highlights are blown out to white pixels, they are gone forever.)

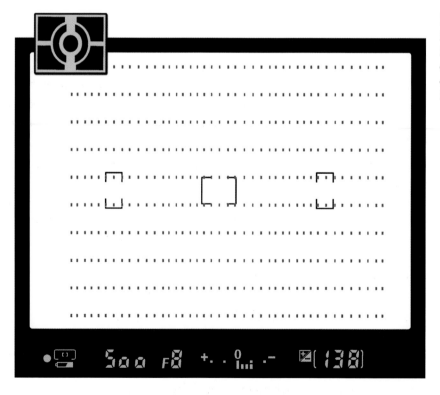

Figure 4.6

Matrix metering calculates exposure based on 420 points in the frame.

Center-Weighted Metering

In this mode, the exposure meter emphasizes a zone in the center of the frame to calculate exposure, as shown in Figure 4.7. About 75 percent of the exposure is based on that central area, and the remaining exposure is based on the rest of the frame. The theory, here, is that, for most pictures, the main subject will be located in the center. So, if the D60 reads the center portion and determines that the exposure for that region should be f/8 at 1/250 second, while the outer area, which is a bit darker, calls for f/4 at 1/125 second, the camera will give the center portion the most weight and arrive at a final exposure of f/5.6 at 1/250 second.

Center-Weighting works best for portraits, architectural photos, backlit subjects with extra-bright backgrounds (such as snow or sand), and other pictures in which the most important subject is located in the middle of the frame. As the name suggests, the light reading is *weighted* towards the central portion, but information is also used from the rest of the frame. If your main subject is surrounded by very bright or very dark areas, the exposure might not be exactly right. However, this scheme works well in many situations if you don't want to use one of the other modes. This mode can be useful for close-ups of subjects like flowers, or for portraits.

Spot Metering

Spot metering is favored by those of us who used to work with a hand-held light meter to measure exposure at various points (such as metering highlights and shadows separately). However, you can use Spot metering in any situation where you want to individually measure the light reflecting from light, midtone, or dark areas of your subject—or any combination of areas.

This mode confines the reading to a limited area in the center of the viewfinder, making up only 2.5 percent of the image, as shown in Figure 4.8. The circle is centered on the current focus point when you're using Closest Subject as your AF-Area mode, as described in Chapter 3. Otherwise, the center focus zone is used. However, the metering circle *is larger than the focus zone*, so don't fall into the trap of believing that exposure is being measured only within the brackets that represent the active focus point. This is the only metering method you can use to tell the D60 exactly where to measure exposure.

You'll find spot metering useful when you want to base exposure on a small area in the frame. If that area is in the center of the frame, so much the better. If not, you'll have to make your meter reading for an off-center subject and then lock exposure by pressing the shutter release halfway, or by pressing the AE-Lock button. This mode is best for subjects where the background is significantly brighter or darker.

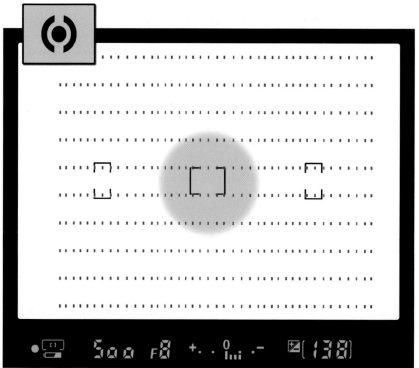

Figure 4.7
Center-Weighted metering calculates exposure based on the full frame, but gives 75 percent of the weight to the approximate center area shown; the remaining 25 percent of the exposure is determined by the rest of the image area.

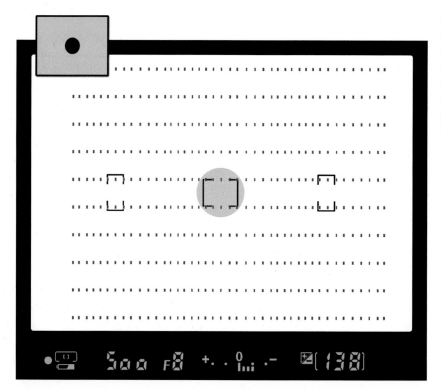

Figure 4.8
Spot metering calculates exposure based on a center spot that's only 2.5 percent of the image area.

Choosing an Exposure Method

The Nikon D60's DVP/Scene modes choose an exposure method for you. But there are three semi-automated methods (plus manual) that you can use to choose the appropriate shutter speed and aperture. You can choose among them by rotating the mode dial until the one you want is selected. Your choice of which is best for a given shooting situation will depend on things like your need for lots of (or less) depth-of-field, a desire to freeze action or allow motion blur, or how much noise you find acceptable in an image. Each of the D60's exposure methods emphasizes one aspect of image capture or another. This section introduces you to all four.

Aperture Priority

In A mode (don't confuse this with Auto; some point-and-shoot cameras use the letter A to represent automatic mode), you specify the lens opening used, and the D60 selects the shutter speed. Aperture Priority is especially good when you want to use a particular lens opening to achieve a desired effect. Perhaps you'd like to use the smallest f/stop possible to maximize depth-of-field in a close-up picture. Or, you might want to use a large f/stop to throw everything except your main subject out of focus, as in Figure 4.9. Maybe you'd just like to "lock in" a particular f/stop because it's the sharpest available aperture with that lens. Or, you might prefer to use, say, f/2.8 on a lens with a maximum aperture of f/1.4, because you want the best compromise between speed and sharpness.

Aperture Priority can even be used to specify a *range* of shutter speeds you want to use under varying lighting conditions, which seems almost contradictory. But think about it. You're shooting a soccer game outdoors with a telephoto lens and want a relatively high shutter speed, but you don't care if the speed changes a little should the sun duck behind a cloud. Set your D60 to A, and adjust the aperture until a shutter speed of, say, 1/1,000th second is selected at your current ISO setting. (In bright sunlight at ISO 400, that aperture is likely to be around f/11.) Then, go ahead and shoot, knowing that your D60 will maintain that f/11 aperture (for sufficient DOF as the soccer players move about the field), but will drop down to 1/750th or 1/500th second if necessary should the lighting change a little.

A **Lo** or **HI** indicator in the viewfinder and Shooting Information display, accompanied by a **Subject is too dark** or **Subject is too bright warning** on the LCD indicates that the D60 is unable to select an appropriate shutter speed at the selected aperture and that over- and underexposure will occur at the current ISO setting. That's the major pitfall of using A: you might select an f/stop that is too small or too large to allow an optimal exposure with the available shutter speeds. For example, if you choose f/2.8 as your aperture and the illumination is quite bright (say, at the beach or in snow), even your camera's fastest shutter speed might not be able to cut down the amount of light

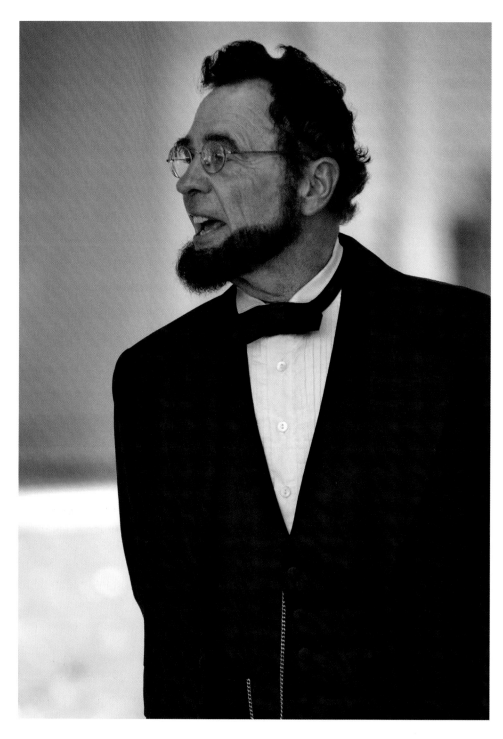

Figure 4.9
Use Aperture Priority to "lock in" a large f/stop when you want to blur the background.

reaching the sensor to provide the right exposure. Or, if you select f/8 in a dimly lit room, you might find yourself shooting with a very slow shutter speed that can cause blurring from subject movement or camera shake. Aperture Priority is best used by those with a bit of experience in choosing settings. Many seasoned photographers leave their D60 set on A all the time.

Shutter Priority

Shutter Priority (S) is the inverse of Aperture Priority: you choose the shutter speed you'd like to use, and the camera's metering system selects the appropriate f/stop. Perhaps you're shooting action photos and you want to use the absolute fastest shutter speed available with your camera ; in other cases you might want to use a slow shutter speed to add some blur to a sports photo that would be mundane if the action were completely frozen (see Figure 4.10.). Shutter Priority mode gives you some control over how much action-freezing capability your digital camera brings to bear in a particular situation.

You'll also encounter the same problem as with Aperture Priority when you select a shutter speed that's too long or too short for correct exposure under some conditions. I've shot outdoor soccer games on sunny Fall evenings and used Shutter Priority mode to lock in a 1/1,000th second shutter speed, only to find my D60 refused to shoot when the sun dipped behind some trees and there was no longer enough light to shoot at that speed, even with the lens wide open.

Like A mode, it's possible to choose an inappropriate shutter speed. If that's the case, the maximum aperture of your lens (to indicate underexposure) or the minimum aperture (to indicate overexposure) will blink.

Program Mode

Program mode (P) uses the D60's built-in smarts to select the correct f/stop and shutter speed using a database of picture information that tells it which combination of shutter speed and aperture will work best for a particular photo. If the correct exposure cannot be achieved at the current ISO setting, the **Lo** or **HI** indicator in the viewfinder and LCD will appear, along with the **Subject is too dark** or **Subject is too bright** warnings. You can then boost or reduce the ISO to increase or decrease sensitivity.

The D60's recommended exposure can be overridden if you want. Use the EV setting feature (described later, because it also applies to S and A modes) to add or subtract exposure from the metered value. And, as I mentioned earlier in this chapter, in Program mode you can rotate the command dial to change from the recommended setting to an equivalent setting (as shown in Table 4.1) that produces the same exposure, but using a different combination of f/stop and shutter speed.

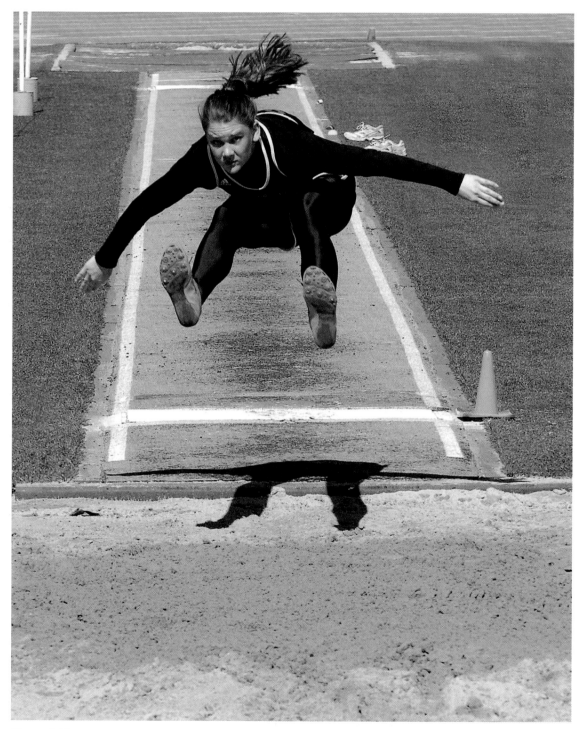

Figure 4.10 Lock the shutter at a high speed to freeze action.

This is called "Flexible Program" by Nikon. Rotate the command dial counterclockwise to reduce the size of the aperture (going from, say, f/4 to f/5.6), so that the D60 will automatically use a slower shutter speed (going from, say, 1/250 second to 1/125 second). Rotate the command dial clockwise to use a larger f/stop, while automatically producing a shorter shutter speed that provides the same equivalent exposure as metered in P mode. An asterisk appears next to the P in the LCD and viewfinder so you'll know you've overridden the D60's default program setting. Your adjustment remains in force until you rotate the command dial until the asterisk disappears, or you switch to a different exposure mode, or turn the D60 off.

MAKING EV CHANGES

Sometimes you'll want more or less exposure than indicated by the D60's metering system. Perhaps you want to underexpose to create a silhouette effect, or overexpose to produce a high key look. It's easy to use the D60's exposure compensation system to override the exposure recommendations. Press the EV button on the top of the camera (just southeast of the shutter release). Then rotate the command dial counterclockwise to add exposure, and clockwise to subtract exposure. The EV change you've made remains for the exposures that follow, until you manually zero out the EV setting. The EV plus/minus icon appears in the viewfinder and monochrome status panel to warn you that an exposure compensation change has been entered.

Manual Exposure

Part of being an experienced photographer comes from knowing when to rely on your D60's automation (with DVP/Scene modes or P mode), when to go semiautomatic (with S or A), and when to set exposure manually (using M). Some photographers actually prefer to set their exposure manually, as the D60 will be happy to provide an indication of when its metering system judges your manual settings provide the proper exposure, using the analog exposure scale at the bottom of the viewfinder and on the status LCD.

Manual exposure can come in handy in some situations. You might be taking a silhouette photo and find that none of the exposure modes or EV correction features give you exactly the effect you want. Set the exposure manually to use the exact shutter speed and f/stop you need. Or, you might be working in a studio environment using multiple flash units. The additional flash are triggered by slave devices (gadgets that set off the flash when they sense the light from another flash, or, perhaps from a radio or infrared remote control). Your camera's exposure meter doesn't compensate for the extra illumination, so you need to set the aperture manually.

Although, depending on your proclivities, you might not need to set exposure manually very often, you should still make sure you understand how it works. Fortunately, the D60 makes setting exposure manually very easy. Just rotate the mode dial to change to Manual mode, and then turn the command dial to set the shutter speed, and the sub-command dial to adjust the aperture. Press the shutter release halfway or press the AE-Lock button, and the exposure scale in the viewfinder shows you how far your chosen setting diverges from the metered exposure.

Adjusting Exposure with ISO Settings

Another way of adjusting exposures is by changing the ISO sensitivity setting. Sometimes photographers forget about this option, because the common practice is to set the ISO once for a particular shooting session (say, at ISO 200 for bright sunlight outdoors, or ISO 800 when shooting indoors) and then forget about ISO. The reason for that is that ISOs higher than ISO 200 or 400 are seen as "bad" or "necessary evils." However, changing the ISO is a valid way of adjusting exposure settings, particularly with the Nikon D60, which produces good results at ISO settings that create grainy, unusable pictures with some other camera models.

Indeed, I find myself using ISO adjustment as a convenient alternate way of adding or subtracting exposure when shooting in Manual mode, and as a quick way of choosing equivalent exposures when in Program or Shutter Priority or Aperture Priority modes. For example, I've selected a Manual exposure with both f/stop and shutter speed suitable for my image using, say, ISO 200. I can change the exposure in one-stop increments by using the Quick Settings screen to change the ISO to 400 (for one additional stop) or to 100 (for one less stop's worth of exposure). I keep my preferred f/stop and shutter speed in either case, but still adjust the exposure.

Or, perhaps, I am using S mode and the metered exposure at ISO 200 is 1/500th second at f/11. If I decide on the spur of the moment I'd rather use 1/500th second at f/8, I can change the ISO to 100. Of course, it's a good idea to monitor your ISO changes, so you don't end up at H1 (ISO 3200) accidentally. An ISO indicator appears on the Shooting Information screen to remind you what sensitivity setting has been dialed in.

ISO settings can, of course, also be used to boost or reduce sensitivity in particular shooting situations. The D60 can use ISO settings from ISO 100 up to H 1.0 (3,200 equivalent). The camera can also adjust the ISO automatically as appropriate for various lighting conditions. When you choose the Auto ISO setting in the Shooting menu, as described in Chapter 3, the D60 adjusts the sensitivity dynamically to suit the subject matter, based on minimum shutter speed and ISO limits you have prescribed. As I noted in Chapter 3, you should use Auto ISO cautiously if you don't want the D60 to use an ISO higher than you might otherwise have selected.

Fixing Exposures with Histograms

While you can often recover poorly exposed photos in your image editor, your best bet is to arrive at the correct exposure in the camera, minimizing the tweaks that you have to make in post-processing. However, you can't always judge exposure just by viewing the image on your D60's LCD after the shot is made. Instead, you can use a histogram, which is a chart displayed on the D60's LCD that shows the number of tones being captured at each brightness level. You can use the information to provide correction for the next shot you take.

You can view a histogram for an image displayed during playback by pressing the multi-selector up/down buttons to switch to the histogram overlay, as shown in Figure 4.11. This screen provides a large histogram at the bottom of the image that displays the distribution of luminance or brightness.

Figure 4.11
A histogram shows the relationship of tones in an image.

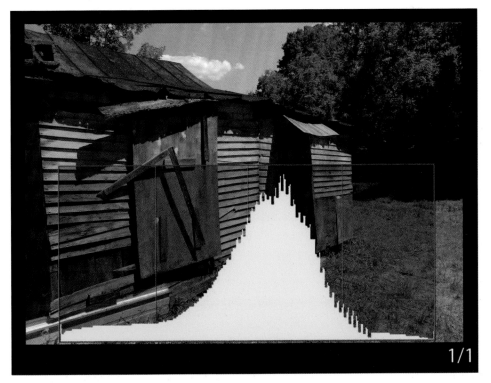

This histogram, called a brightness or *luminance* histogram, is a chart that includes a representation of up to 256 vertical lines on a horizontal axis that show the number of pixels in the image at each brightness level, from 0 (black) on the left side to 255 (white) on the right. (The LCD doesn't have enough pixels to show each and every one of the 256 lines, but, instead provides a representation of the shape of the curve formed.) The more pixels at a given level, the taller the bar at that position. If no bar appears at a particular position on the scale from left to right, there are no pixels at that particular brightness level.

As you can see, a typical histogram produces a mountain-like shape, with most of the pixels bunched in the middle tones, with fewer pixels at the dark and light ends of the scale. Ideally, though, there will be at least some pixels at either extreme, so that your image has both a true black and a true white representing some details. Learn to spot histograms that represent over- and underexposure, and add or subtract exposure using an EV modification to compensate.

For example, Figure 4.12 shows the histogram for an image that is badly underexposed. You can guess from the shape of the histogram that many of the dark tones to the left of the graph have been clipped off. There's plenty of room on the right side for additional pixels to reside without having them become overexposed. Or, a histogram might look like Figure 4.13, which is overexposed. In either case, you can increase or decrease the exposure (either by changing the f/stop or shutter speed in Manual mode or by adding or subtracting an EV value in A or S modes) to produce the corrected histogram shown in Figure 4.11, earlier, in which the tones "hug" the right side of the histogram to produce as many highlight details as possible. See "Making EV Changes" above for information on dialing in exposure compensation.

The histogram can also be used to aid in fixing the contrast of an image, although gauging incorrect contrast is more difficult. For example, if the histogram shows all the tones bunched up in one place in the image, the photo will be low in contrast. If the tones are spread out more or less evenly, the image is probably high in contrast. In either case, your best bet may be to switch to RAW (if you're not already using that format) so you can adjust contrast in post processing. However, you can also change to a user-defined Optimize Image setting with contrast set lower (–1 to –2) or higher (+1 to +2) as required. You'll find instructions for creating a Custom Optimize Image setting in Chapter 3.

One useful, but often overlooked tool in evaluating histograms is the Highlight display (available by pressing the up/down multi-selector buttons during image review), which shows blown out highlights in the image with a black blinking border. Highlights can give you a better picture of what information is being lost to overexposure.

Figure 4.12
This histogram shows an underexposed image.

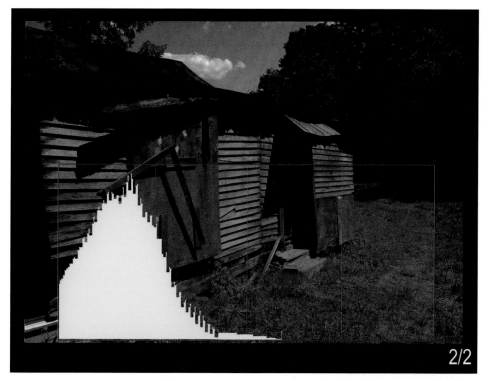

Figure 4.13
This histogram reveals that the image is over-exposed.

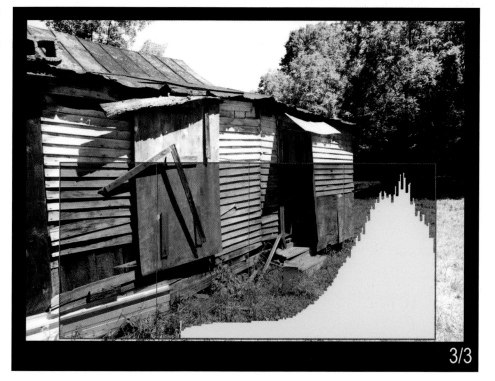

In working with histograms, your goal should be to have all the tones in an image spread out between the edges, with none clipped off at the left and right sides. Underexposing (to preserve highlights) should be done only as a last resort, because retrieving the under-exposed shadows in your image editor will frequently increase the noise, even if you're working with RAW files. A better course of action is to expose for the highlights, but, when the subject matter makes it practical, fill in the shadows with additional light, using reflectors, fill flash, or other techniques rather than allowing them to be seriously underexposed.

5

Advanced Shooting Tips for Your Nikon D60

Getting the right exposure is one of the foundations of a great photograph, but a lot more goes into a compelling shot than good tonal values. A sharp image, proper white balance, good color, and other factors all can help elevate your image from good to exceptional. So, now that you've got a good understanding of exposure tucked away, you'll want to learn how to work with additional exposure options available with the Nikon D60, and explore some of the intricacies of automatic focus.

This chapter is a bit of a grab-bag, because I'm including some specific advanced shooting techniques that didn't quite fit into the other chapters. If you master these concepts, you can be confident that you're well on your way towards mastering your Nikon D60. In fact, you'll be ready for the discussions of using lenses (Chapter 6) and working with light (Chapter 7).

A Tiny Slice of Time

Exposures that seem impossibly brief can reveal a world we didn't know existed. In the 1930s, Dr. Harold Edgerton, a professor of electrical engineering at MIT, pioneered high-speed photography using a repeating electronic flash unit he patented called the *stroboscope*. As the inventor of the electronic flash, he popularized its use to freeze objects in motion, and you've probably seen his photographs of bullets piercing balloons and drops of milk forming a coronet-shaped splash.

Electronic flash freezes action by virtue of its extremely short duration—as brief as 1/50,000th second or less. Although the D60's built-in flash unit can give you these ultra-quick glimpses of moving subjects, an external flash, such as one of the Nikon Speedlights, offers even more versatility. You can read more about using electronic flash to stop action in Chapter 7.

Of course, the D60 is fully capable of immobilizing all but the fastest movement using only its shutter speeds, which range all the way up to a respectably quick 1/4,000th second. Indeed, you'll rarely have need for such a brief shutter speed in ordinary shooting. If you wanted to use an aperture of f/1.8 at ISO 200 outdoors in bright sunlight, for some reason, a shutter speed of 1/4,000th second would more than do the job. You'd need a faster shutter speed only if you moved the ISO setting to a higher sensitivity, say, to compensate for a polarizing filter you attached to your lens. Under less than full sunlight, 1/4,000th second is more than fast enough for any conditions you're likely to encounter.

Most sports action can be frozen at 1/2,000th second or slower, and for many sports a slower shutter speed is actually preferable—for example, to allow the wheels of a racing automobile or motorcycle, or the propeller on a classic aircraft to blur realistically. Other times, freezing a moment in time concentrates the focus of the picture on the interaction of the subjects. Figure 5.1 is example. The 1/1000 second shutter speed effectively stopped the football players in mid-stride, creating a tableau in which each athlete pictured had a role.

If you want to do some exotic action-freezing photography, you can use the Nikon D60's faster shutter speeds, or resort to an electronic flash (internal or external), which, as you'll learn in Chapter 7, provides the effect of a high shutter speed because of its short duration.

Of course, you'll need a lot of light. High shutter speeds cut very fine slices of time and sharply reduce the amount of illumination that reaches your sensor. To use 1/4,000th second at an aperture of f/6.3, you'd need an ISO setting of 800—even in full daylight. To use an f/stop smaller than f/6.3 or an ISO setting lower than 1,600, you'd need more light than full daylight provides. (That's why electronic flash units work so well for high-speed photography when used as the sole illumination; they provide both the effect of a brief shutter speed and the high levels of illumination needed.)

High shutter speeds with electronic flash comes with a penalty: you have to use a shutter speed slower than 1/200th second. Perhaps you want to stop some action in daylight with a brief shutter speed and use electronic flash only as supplemental illumination to fill in the shadows. Unfortunately, under most conditions you can't use flash with your D60 at any shutter speed faster than 1/200th second. That's the fastest speed at which the camera's focal plane shutter is fully open: at shorter speeds, the "slit" (described in more detail in Chapter 7) comes into play, so that the flash will expose only the small portion of the sensor exposed by the slit during its duration.

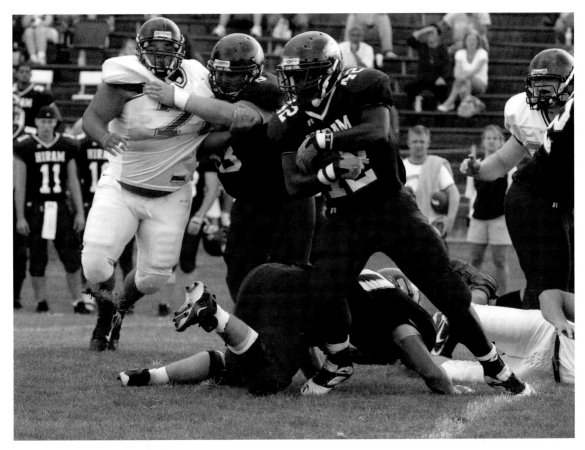

Figure 5.1 An action-stopping shutter speed froze these players in place.

Working with Short Exposures

You can have a lot of fun exploring the kinds of pictures you can take using very brief exposure times, whether you decide to take advantage of the action-stopping capabilities of your built-in or external electronic flash or work with the Nikon D60's faster shutter speeds. Here are a few ideas to get you started:

■ **Take revealing images.** Fast shutter speeds can help you reveal the real subject behind the façade, by freezing constant motion to capture an enlightening moment in time. Legendary fashion/portrait photographer Philippe Halsman used leaping photos of famous people, such as the Duke and Duchess of Windsor, Richard Nixon, and Salvador Dali to illuminate their real selves. Halsman said, "*When you ask a person to jump, his attention is mostly directed toward the act of jumping and the mask falls so that the real person appears.*" Try some high-speed portraits of people you know in motion to see how they appear when concentrating on something other than the portrait.

■ **Create unreal images.** High-speed photography can also produce photographs that show your subjects in ways that are quite unreal. A helicopter in mid-air with its rotors frozen or a motocross cyclist leaping over a ramp, but with all motion stopped so that the rider and machine look as if they were frozen in mid-air, make for an unusual picture. When we're accustomed to seeing subjects in motion, seeing them stopped in time can verge on the surreal.

■ **Capture unseen perspectives.** Some things are *never* seen in real life, except when viewed in a stop-action photograph. Edgerton's balloon bursts were only a starting point. Freeze a hummingbird in flight for a view of wings that never seem to stop. Or, capture the splashes as liquid falls into a bowl, as shown in Figure 5.2. No electronic flash was required for this image (and wouldn't have illuminated the water in the bowl as evenly). Instead, a clutch of high intensity lamps and an ISO setting of 1,600 allowed the D60 to capture this image at 1/2,000th second.

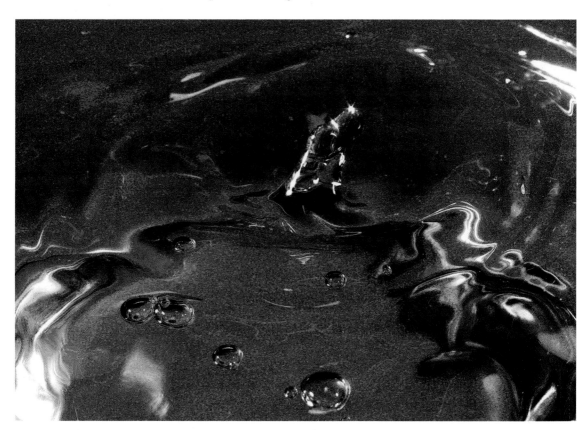

Figure 5.2 A large amount of artificial illumination and an ISO 1,600 sensitivity setting allowed capturing this shot at 1/2,000th second without use of an electronic flash.

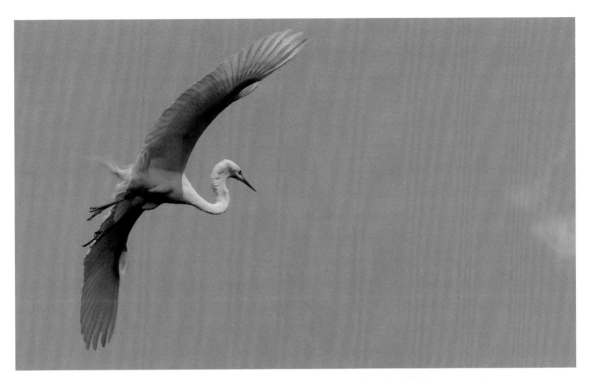

Figure 5.3 Outdoors, you may need a shutter speed of 1/2,000th second to hand-hold a 500mm lens to capture distant wildlife.

- **Vanquish camera shake and gain new angles.** Here's an idea that's so obvious it isn't always explored to its fullest extent. A high enough shutter speed can free you from the tyranny of a tripod, making it easier to capture new angles, or to shoot quickly while moving around, especially with longer lenses. I tend to use a mono-pod or tripod for almost everything when I'm not using an image-stabilized lens, and I end up missing some shots because of a reluctance to adjust my camera sup-port to get a higher, lower, or different angle. If you have enough light and can use an f/stop wide enough to permit a high shutter speed, you'll find a new freedom to choose your shots (see Figure 5.3). I have a favored 170mm-500mm lens that I use for sports and wildlife photography, almost invariably with a tripod, as I don't find the "reciprocal of the focal length" rule particularly helpful in most cases. I would *not* hand-hold this hefty lens at its 500mm setting with a 1/500th second shutter speed under most circumstances. Nor, if you want to account for the crop factor, would I use 1/750 second. However, at 1/2,000th second or faster, it's entirely pos-sible for a steady hand to use this lens without a tripod or monopod's extra support, and I've found that my whole approach to shooting animals and other elusive sub-jects changes in high-speed mode. Selective focus allows dramatically isolating my prey wide open at f/6.3, too.

Long Exposures

Longer exposures are a doorway into another world, showing us how even familiar scenes can look much different when photographed over periods measured in seconds. At night, long exposures produce streaks of light from moving, illuminated subjects like automobiles or amusement park rides. Extra-long exposures of seemingly pitch-dark subjects can reveal interesting views using light levels barely bright enough to see by. At any time of day, including daytime (in which case you'll often need the help of neutral density filters to make the long exposure practical), long exposures can cause moving objects to vanish entirely, because they don't remain stationary long enough to register in a photograph.

Three Ways to Take Long Exposures

There are actually three common types of lengthy exposures: *timed exposures, bulb exposures*, and *time exposures*. The Nikon D60 offers only the first two. Because of the length of the exposure, all shots with very slow shutter speeds should be taken with a tripod to hold the camera steady.

- **Timed exposures.** These are long exposures from 1 second to 30 seconds, measured by the camera itself. To take a picture in this range, simply use Manual or S modes and use the main command dial to set the shutter speed to the length of time you want, choosing from preset speeds of 1.0, 1.3, 1.6, 2.0, 2.5, 3.2, 4.0, 5.0, 6.0, 8.0, 10.0, 13.0, 15.0, 20.0, 25.0, and 30.0 seconds (because the D60 uses 1/3 stop increments). The advantage of timed exposures is that the camera does all the calculating for you. There's no need for a stop-watch. If you review your image on the LCD and decide to try again with the exposure doubled or halved, you can dial in the correct exposure with precision. The disadvantage of timed exposures is that you can't take a photo for longer than 30 seconds.

- **Bulb exposures.** This type of exposure is so-called because in the olden days the photographer squeezed and held an air bulb attached to a tube that provided the force necessary to keep the shutter open. Traditionally, a bulb exposure is one that lasts as long as the shutter release button is pressed; when you release the button, the exposure ends. To make a bulb exposure with the D60, set the camera on Manual mode, set the f/stop, and then use the main command dial to select the shutter speed immediately after 30 seconds—Bulb. Then, press the shutter to start the exposure, and release it again to close the shutter.

- **Time exposures.** This is a setting found on some cameras to produce longer exposures. With cameras that implement this option, the shutter opens when you press the shutter release button, and remains open until you press the button again. With the Nikon D60, you can't get this exact effect; the best you can do is use a Bulb exposure.

Working with Long Exposures

Because the D60 produces such good images at longer exposures, and there are so many creative things you can do with long-exposure techniques, you'll want to do some experimenting. Get yourself a tripod or another firm support and take some test shots with long exposure noise reduction both enabled and disabled (to see whether you prefer low noise or high detail) and get started. Here are some things to try:

- **Make people invisible.** One very cool thing about long exposures is that objects that move rapidly enough won't register at all in a photograph, while the subjects that remain stationary are portrayed in the normal way. That makes it easy to produce people-free landscape photos and architectural photos at night or, even, in full daylight if you use a plain gray neutral density filter (or two or three) to allow an exposure of at least a few seconds. At ISO 100, f/22, and a pair of ND8 neutral density filters (which each remove three stops' worth of light—giving you, in effect, the equivalent of ISO 1.5!) you can use exposures of nearly two seconds; overcast days and/or even more neutral density filtration would work even better if daylight people-vanishing is your goal. They'll have to be walking *very* briskly and across the field of view (rather than directly toward the camera) for this to work. At night, it's much easier to achieve this effect with the 20- to 30-second exposures that are possible, as you can see in Figure 5.4.

Figure 5.4

This European alleyway is thronged with people, but with the camera on a tripod, a 30-second exposure rendered the passersby almost invisible.

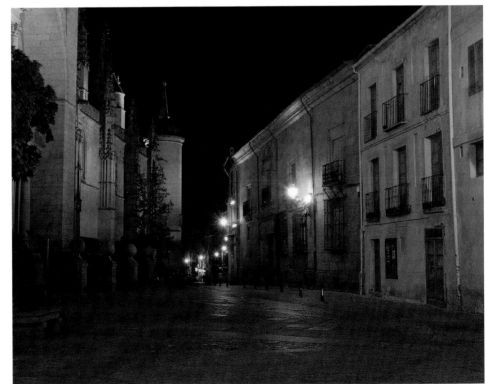

- **Create streaks.** If you aren't shooting for total invisibility, long exposures with the camera on a tripod can produce some interesting streaky effects. Even a single ND8 filter will let you shoot at f/22 and 1/6th second in daylight.

- **Produce light trails.** At night, car headlights and taillights and other moving sources of illumination can generate interesting light trails. If the lights aren't moving, you can make them move by zooming or jiggling the camera during a long exposure. Your camera doesn't even need to be mounted on a tripod; hand-holding the D60 for longer exposures adds movement and patterns to your trails, as shown in Figure 5.5. If you're shooting fireworks, a longer exposure may allow you to combine several bursts into one picture.

- **Blur waterfalls, etc.** You'll find that waterfalls and other sources of moving liquid produce a special type of long-exposure blur, because the water merges into a fantasy-like veil that looks different at different exposure times, and with different waterfalls. Cascades with turbulent flow produce a rougher look at a given longer exposure than falls that flow smoothly. Although blurred waterfalls have become almost a cliché, there are still plenty of variations for a creative photographer to explore.

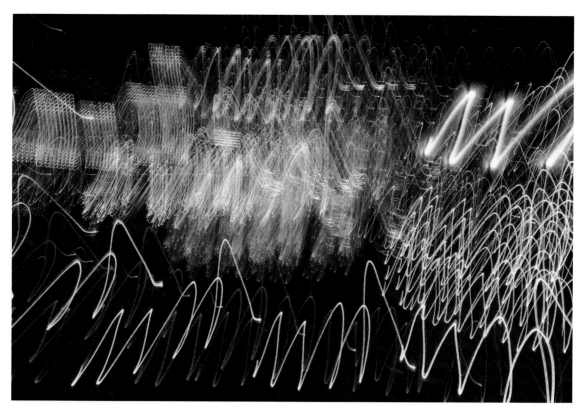

Figure 5.5 Long exposures can transform the most mundane nighttime subjects, such as these holiday lights, into an interesting light-trails display.

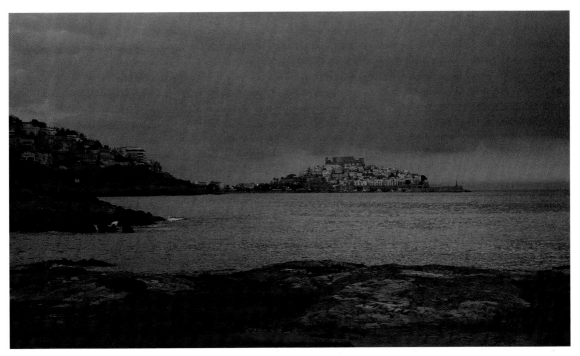

Figure 5.6 A 20-second exposure on a dark night revealed this Mediterranean scene, illuminated only by moonlight that penetrated the cloud cover.

■ **Show total darkness in new ways.** Even on the darkest, moonless nights, there is enough starlight or glow from distant illumination sources to see by, and, if you use a long exposure, there is enough light to take a picture, too. It was after midnight when I photographed the scene in Figure 5.6, but there was enough light for a 20-second exposure with the camera mounted on a tripod. The lengthy shutter speed also served to smooth out the waves in the sea, which was a bit choppier than pictured.

How Focus Works

Although Nikon added autofocus capabilities to its cameras in the 1980s, back in the day of film, prior to that focusing was always done manually. Honest. Even though viewfinders were bigger and brighter than they are today, special focusing screens, magnifiers, and other gadgets were often used to help the photographer achieve correct focus. Imagine what it must have been like to focus manually under demanding, fast-moving conditions such as sports photography.

Focusing was problematic because our eyes and brains have poor memory for correct focus, which is why your eye doctor must shift back and forth between sets of lenses and ask "Does that look sharper—or was it sharper before?" in determining your correct prescription. Similarly, manual focusing involves jogging the focus ring back and forth as you go from almost in focus, to sharp focus, to almost focused again. The little clockwise and counterclockwise arcs decrease in size until you've zeroed in on the point of correct focus. What you're looking for is the image with the most contrast between the edges of elements in the image.

The camera also looks for these contrast differences among pixels to determine relative sharpness. There are two ways that sharp focus is determined. The Nikon D60 uses a method called *phase detection.* In this mode, each autofocus sampling area, or focus zone, is divided into two halves by a lens in each of the three autofocus sensor areas in the camera (represented by the three sets of brackets in the viewfinder). The two halves are compared, much like (actually, exactly like) a two-window rangefinder used in surveying, weaponry, and in non-SLR cameras like the venerable Leica M film models. The contrast between the two images changes as focus is moved in or out, until sharp focus is achieved when the images are "in phase," or lined up. Figure 5.7 shows the contrast difference between an image that is out of focus and one that is in sharp focus.

Phase detection is used by the D60. As with any rangefinder-like function, accuracy is better when the "base length" between the two images is larger. (Think back to your high school trigonometry; you could calculate a distance more accurately when the separation between the two points where the angles were measured was greater.) For that reason, phase detection autofocus is more accurate with larger (wider) lens openings than with smaller lens openings, and may not work at all when the f/stop is smaller than f/5.6. (Of course, the greater amount of light makes the contrast difference easier to *see*, too, but that's an additional factor.) The D60 is able to perform these comparisons very quickly.

The other method of autofocusing is used by point-and-shoot cameras (and also by Nikon cameras which have a Live View feature with a Tripod Mode option). It's called *contrast detection.* This is a slower mode, suitable for static subjects and with point-and-shoot cameras where the sensor can be exposed to the actual image that will be captured for long periods. (With the typical dSLR like the D60, the sensor "hides" behind the shutter and flip-up mirror and doesn't "see" the image until the moment of exposure.) When such an image is viewed by the sensor, out-of-focus areas are soft and blurred. When the image is brought into focus, the transitions between edges are sharp and clear.

The D60's autofocus mechanism, like all such systems found in SLR cameras, evaluates the degree of focus, but, unlike the human eye, it is able to remember the progression perfectly, so that autofocus can lock in much more quickly and, with an image that has sufficient contrast, more precisely. Unfortunately, while the D60's focus system finds it easy to measure degrees of apparent focus at each of the focus points in the viewfinder,

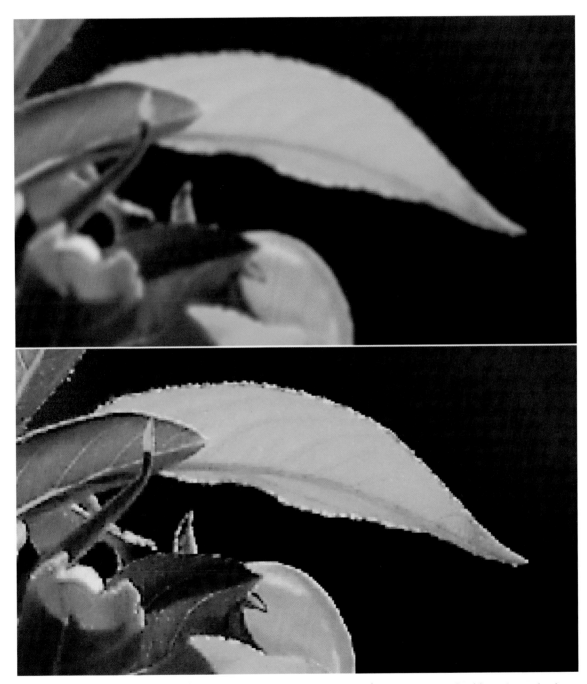

Figure 5.7 Focus sensors detect the increase in contrast in the edges of subjects, starting with a blurry image (top) and producing a sharp, contrasty image (bottom).

it doesn't really know with any certainty *which* object should be in sharpest focus. Is it the closest object? The subject in the center? Something lurking *behind* the closest subject? A person standing over at the side of the picture? Many of the techniques for using autofocus effectively involve telling the D60 exactly what it should be focusing on, by choosing a focus zone or by allowing the camera to choose a focus zone for you. I'll address that topic shortly. But first, some confusion…

Adding Circles of Confusion

There are other factors in play, as well. You know that increased depth-of-field brings more of your subject into focus. But more depth-of-field also makes autofocusing (or manual focusing) more difficult because the contrast is lower between objects at different distances. So, autofocus with a 200mm lens (or zoom setting) may be easier than at a 28mm focal length (or zoom setting) because the longer lens has less apparent depth-of-field. By the same token, a lens with a maximum aperture of f/1.8 will be easier to autofocus (or manually focus) than one of the same focal length with an f/4 maximum aperture, because the f/4 lens has more depth-of-field *and* a dimmer view. That's the other reason why lenses with a maximum aperture smaller than f/5.6 can give your D60's autofocus system fits. (Take heart; I'll explain all the intricacies of working with lenses in Chapter 6.)

To make things even more interesting, many subjects aren't polite enough to remain still. They move around in the frame, so that even if the D60 is sharply focused on your main subject, it may change position and require refocusing. An intervening subject may pop into the frame and pass between you and the subject you meant to photograph. You (or the D60) have to decide whether to lock focus on this new subject, or remain focused on the original subject.

Finally, there are some kinds of subjects that are difficult to bring into sharp focus because they lack enough contrast to allow the D60's AF system (or our eyes) to lock in. Blank walls, a clear blue sky, or other subject matter may make focusing difficult. If you encounter such a subject, try locking in focus on some other object at an equivalent distance, press the AE-L/AF-L button, and then reframe with your original composition.

If you find all these focus factors confusing, you're on the right track. Focus is, in fact, measured using something called a *circle of confusion*. An ideal image consists of zillions of tiny little points, which, like all points, theoretically have no height or width. There is perfect contrast between the point and its surroundings. You can think of each point as a pinpoint of light in a darkened room. When a given point is out of focus, its edges decrease in contrast and it changes from a perfect point to a tiny disc with blurry edges (remember, blur is the lack of contrast between boundaries in an image). (See Figure 5.8.)

Figure 5.8

When a pin-point of light (left) goes out of focus, its blurry edges form a circle of confusion (center and right).

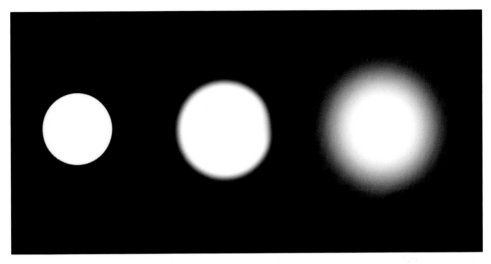

If this blurry disc—the circle of confusion—is small enough, our eye still perceives it as a point. It's only when the disc grows large enough that we can see it as a blur rather than a sharp point that a given point is viewed as out of focus. You can see, then, that enlarging an image, either by displaying it larger on your computer monitor or by making a large print, also enlarges the size of each circle of confusion. Moving closer to the image does the same thing. So, parts of an image that may look perfectly sharp in a 5 × 7-inch print viewed at arm's length, might appear blurry when blown up to 11 × 14 and examined at the same distance. Take a few steps back, however, and it may look sharp again.

To a lesser extent, the viewer also affects the apparent size of these circles of confusion. Some people see details better at a given distance and may perceive smaller circles of confusion than someone standing next to them. For the most part, however, such differences are small. Truly blurry images will look blurry to just about everyone under the same conditions.

Technically, there is just one plane within your picture area, parallel to the back of the camera (or sensor, in the case of a digital camera), that is in sharp focus. That's the plane in which the points of the image are rendered as precise points. At every other plane in front of or behind the focus plane, the points show up as discs that range from slightly blurry to extremely blurry (see Figure 5.9). In practice, the discs in many of these planes will still be so small that we see them as points, and that's where we get depth-of-field. Depth-of-field is just the range of planes that include discs that we *perceive* as points, rather than as blurred splotches, even though they might actually be very slightly out of focus. The size of this range increases as the aperture is reduced in size (remember that the larger numbers, such as f/11, f/16, and f/22, represent smaller apertures) and is allocated roughly one-third in front of the plane of sharpest focus, and two-thirds behind it. Although this "rule" isn't precisely true most of the time, in practice, the range of sharp focus is always greater behind your subject than in front of it.

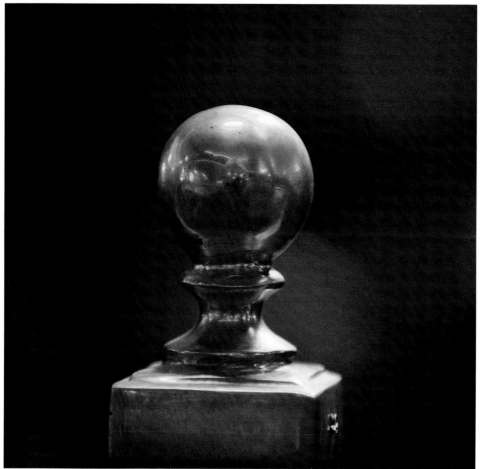

Figure 5.9
Only the subject in the foreground is in focus—the area behind it appears blurry because the depth-of-field is limited.

Using Autofocus with the Nikon D60

Autofocus can sometimes be frustrating for the new digital SLR photographer, especially those coming from the point-and-shoot world. That's because correct focus plays a greater role among your creative options with a dSLR, even when photographing the same subjects. Most non-dSLR digital cameras have sensors that are much tinier than the (approximately) 24mm × 16mm (about 1 × .67 inches) sensor in the D60. Those smaller sensors require shorter focal lengths, which (as you'll learn in Chapter 6) have, effectively, more depth-of-field.

The bottom line is that with the average point-and-shoot camera, *everything* is in focus from about one foot to infinity and at virtually every f/stop. Unless you're shooting close-up photos a few inches from the camera, the depth-of-field is prodigious, and autofocus is almost a non-factor. The D60, on the other hand, uses longer focal length lenses to achieve the same field of view with its larger sensor, so there is less depth-of-field.

That's a *good* thing, creatively, because you have the choice to use selective focus to isolate subjects. But it does make the correct use of autofocus more critical. To maintain the most creative control, you have to choose three attributes:

■ **How much is in focus.** Generally, by choosing the f/stop used, you'll determine the *range* of sharpness/amount of depth-of-field. The larger the DOF, the "easier" it is for the autofocus system's locked-in focus point to be appropriate (even though, strictly speaking, there is only one actual plane of sharp focus). With less depth-of-field, the accuracy of the focus point becomes more critical, because even a small error will result in an out-of-focus shot.

■ **What subject is in focus.** The portion of your subject that is zeroed in for autofocus is determined by the autofocus zone that is active, and which is chosen either by you or by the Nikon D60 (as described next). For example, when shooting portraits, it's actually okay for part of the subject—or even part of the subject's face—to be slightly out of focus as long as the eyes (or even just the *nearest* eye) appear sharp. (See Figure 5.10.)

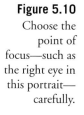

Figure 5.10
Choose the point of focus—such as the right eye in this portrait—carefully.

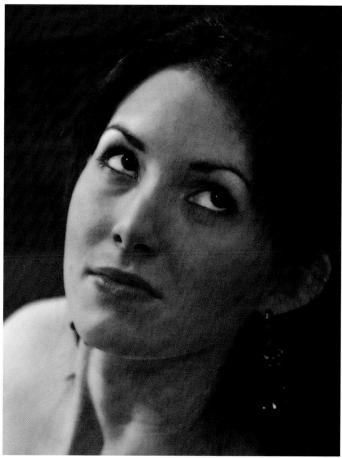

■ **When focus is applied.** For static shots of objects that aren't moving, *when* focus is applied doesn't matter much. But when you're shooting sports, or birds in flight, or children, the subject may move within the viewfinder as you're framing the image. Whether that movement is across the frame or headed right towards you, timing the instant when autofocus is applied can be important.

Choosing Autofocus Area Mode

The Nikon D60's autofocus area mode determines how the camera selects the point used to evaluate focus. The camera can select the closest object to the camera, work with an area you specify—but depart from that area if the subject moves—or use a single focus point you specify. I explained how to choose from among the three AF-area modes (described next) in Chapter 1. Just use the Quick Setting screen (accessed by pressing the Info button when the Shooting Information display is on the LCD), then navigate to the AF-Area Mode icon (seventh from the top of the right-hand column), press **OK**, choose **Closest Subject, Dynamic Area,** or **Single Point** and press **OK** again to confirm.

The three modes are as follows:

■ **Closest Subject.** This is the mode to use if you know your subject is always going to be the closest thing seen through the viewfinder, as the focus point is always selected by the camera, and cannot be chosen by you. A friend or relative posing in front of the Eiffel Tower, or even a flower in the foreground that you're capturing with close-focusing would be typical scenes suitable for this mode. The Nikon D60 evaluates the scene and selects the focus point containing the subject that is nearest to the camera. It is the default mode for Program, Shutter Priority, Aperture Priority, and Manual exposure modes, and is used automatically in Auto, Auto (Flash Off), Portrait, Landscape, Child, and Night Portrait scene modes.

■ **Dynamic area.** You'd want to use this mode when photographing subjects that are moving unpredictably, but want the flexibility of being able to choose one of the three focus zones yourself. Once you've specified the focus bracket you want using the multi-selector's left/right buttons, the D60 will use that area exclusively in Single-Servo autofocus mode (AF-S, described next). If you've chosen Continuous-Servo autofocus mode (AF-C) or automatic autofocus mode (AF-A), if the subject begins moving after autofocus is activated, the D60 will focus based on information from one of the other two focus zones. Well suited for sports photography, this mode is applied automatically with the Sports scene setting, and can be used with other types of moving subjects, such as active children.

■ **Single point.** You choose which of the three focus points are used, and the Nikon D60 sticks with that focus bracket, no matter what. This mode is best for stationary subjects, and is used automatically in Close-up scene mode. In this mode, you always select the focus point manually, using the multi-selector button (which responds to your thumb-presses only in the left/right directions). The D60 evaluates focus based solely on the point you select, making this a good choice for subjects that don't move much.

Autofocus Mode

Choosing the right autofocus mode (AF-S, AF-C, or Manual) is another key to focusing success. To save battery power, your D60 doesn't start to focus the lens until you partially depress the shutter release or the AE-L/AF-L button if you've programmed it to serve as an AF-ON button using **CSM #12**. But, autofocus isn't some mindless beast out there snapping your pictures in and out of focus with no feedback from you after you press the relevant button. Your first decision should be whether you set the D60 to AF-S, AF-C, AF-A, or Manual focus mode.

The focus mode determines when the Nikon D60 starts to evaluate and lock in focus prior to pressing the shutter release down all the way as you take the picture. As I described in Chapter 1, the focus mode is chosen using the Quick Settings screen (or, optionally, from the Custom Setting menu as outlined in Chapter 3). The fastest way is to press the Info button when the Shooting Information screen is displayed, navigating to the focus mode icon (sixth from the top in the right-hand column), pressing **OK**, and then choosing **AF-A, AF-C, AF-S,** or **M** (manual focusing).

The four focus modes are as follows:

Single-Servo Autofocus (AF-S)

In this mode, also called *AF-S*, focus is set once and remains at that setting until the button is fully depressed, taking the picture, or until you release the shutter button without taking a shot. For non-action photography, this setting is usually your best choice, as it minimizes out-of-focus pictures (at the expense of spontaneity). The drawback here is that you might not be able to take a picture at all while the camera is seeking focus; you're locked out until the autofocus mechanism is happy with the current setting.

When sharp focus is achieved, the selected focus point will flash red in the viewfinder, and the focus confirmation light at the lower left will remain at a steady glow. If you're using Matrix metering, the exposure will be locked at the same time. By keeping the shutter button depressed halfway, you'll find you can reframe the image while retaining the focus (and exposure) that's been set. You can also use the AE-L/AF-L button, as described in Chapter 3, if you've set that button to lock focus when pressed. Because of the small delay while the camera zeroes in on correct focus, you might experience slightly more shutter lag. This mode uses less battery power.

Continuous-Servo Autofocus (AF-C)

This mode, also known as *AF-C*, is the mode to use for sports and other fast-moving subjects. In this mode, once the shutter release is partially depressed, the camera sets the focus but continues to monitor the subject, so that if it moves or you move, the lens will be refocused to suit. Focus and exposure aren't really locked until you press the shutter release down all the way to take the picture. You'll find that AF-C produces the least amount of shutter lag of any autofocus mode when set to release priority: press the button and the camera fires. It also uses the most battery power, because the autofocus system operates as long as the shutter release button is partially depressed.

Continuous-Servo autofocus uses a technology called *predictive AF*, which allows the D60 to calculate the correct focus if the subject is moving toward or away from the camera at a constant rate. It uses either the automatically selected AF point or the point you select manually to set focus. You can also temporarily lock the focus point by partially depressing the shutter release, or pressing the AE-L/AF-L button (unless you've redefined this behavior to some other controls in the Custom Setting menu).

Automatic Autofocus (AF-A)

This mode begins to set autofocus as if it were AF-S, but, if the subject begins to move, the D60 shifts into AF-C mode. The camera automatically chooses the right mode for your subject, based on movement.

Manual Focus

In this mode, or when you've set the lens autofocus switch to Manual (or when you're using a non AF-S lens), the D60 always focuses manually using the rotating focus ring on the lens barrel. However, if you are using a lens with a maximum aperture of at least f/5.6, the focus confirmation light will confirm when focus is set properly. You can also use the Rangefinder, described in Chapter 3 under the description of Custom Setting menu option **CSM #19**.

Continuous Shooting

The Nikon D60's three frames-per-second continuous shooting release mode reminds me how far digital photography has brought us. The first accessory I purchased when I worked as a newspaper sports photographer some years ago was a motor drive for my film SLR. It enabled me to snap off a series of shots in rapid succession, which came in very handy when a fullback broke through the line and headed for the end zone. Even a seasoned action photographer can miss the decisive instant when a crucial block is made, or a baseball superstar's bat shatters and pieces of cork fly out. Continuous shooting simplifies taking a series of pictures, either to ensure that one has more or less the exact moment you want to capture or to capture a sequence that is interesting as a collection of successive images.

The D60's "motor drive" capabilities are, in many ways, much superior to what you get with a film camera. For one thing, a motor-driven film camera can eat up film at an incredible pace, which is why many of them were used with cassettes that held hundreds of feet of film stock. At three frames per second (typical of film cameras), a short burst of a few seconds can burn up as much as half of an ordinary 36 exposure roll of film. The Nikon D60, which fires off bursts at the same frame rate, has reusable "film," so if you waste a few dozen shots on non-decisive moments, you can erase them and shoot more.

The increased capacity of digital film cards gives you a prodigious number of frames to work with. At a basketball game I covered earlier this year, I took more than 1,000 images in a couple hours. Yet, even shooting JPEG Fine, I could fit more than 560 images on a single 4GB memory card. Given an average burst of about six frames per sequence (nobody really takes 15-20 shots or more at one stretch in a basketball game), I was able to capture almost 100 different sequences before I needed to swap cards. (See Figure 5.11.)

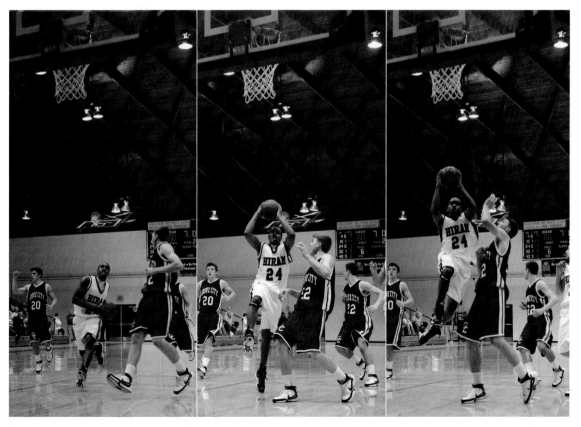

Figure 5.11 Continuous shooting allows you to capture an entire sequence of exciting moments as they unfold.

To use the D60's continuous shooting modes, press the Info button twice to summon the Quick Settings screen, navigate to the Release Mode icon, press OK, and select the continuous shooting option, represented by an icon that looks like a stack of photos. When you partially depress the shutter button, the viewfinder will display at the right side a number representing the maximum number of shots you can take at the current quality settings. As a practical matter, the buffer in the Nikon D60 will generally allow you to take several dozen JPEG shots in a single burst, but only six RAW photos.

To get the maximum number of shots, reduce the image-quality setting by switching to JPEG only (from RAW+Basic), to a lower JPEG quality setting, or by reducing the D60's resolution from L to M or S. The reason the size of your bursts is limited is that continuous images are first shuttled into the D60's internal memory buffer, then doled out to the memory card as quickly as they can be written to the card. Technically, the D60 takes the RAW data received from the digital image processor and converts it to the output format you've selected—either .jpg or .nef (raw)—and deposits it in the buffer ready to store on the card.

This internal "smart" buffer can suck up photos much more quickly than the memory card and, indeed, some memory cards are significantly faster or slower than others. When the buffer fills, you can't take any more continuous shots until the D60 has written some of them to the card, making more room in the buffer. (You should keep in mind that faster memory cards write images more quickly, freeing up buffer space faster.)

6

Working with Lenses

If Nikon has one advantage over many of the other vendors of digital SLRs (other than making great, affordable cameras), it's the mind-bending assortment of high-quality lenses available to enhance the capabilities of cameras like the Nikon D60. You can use thousands of current and older lenses introduced by Nikon and third-party vendors since 1959 (although lenses made before 1977 may need an inexpensive modification for use with cameras *other* than the Nikon D60, D40, and D40x—more on this later). These can give you a wider view, bring distant subjects closer, let you focus closer, shoot under lower light conditions, or provide a more detailed, sharper image for critical work. Other than the sensor itself, the lens you choose for your dSLR is the most important component in determining image quality and perspective of your images.

This chapter explains how to select the best lenses for the kinds of photography you want to do.

But First, a Word from Our Sensor

One pervasive consideration that will trip us up in this chapter (and throughout this book) is the omnipresent *lens crop factor*. If the sensor is smaller than the standard 35mm film frame (24mm × 36mm), then any given lens will produce a field of view that's *cropped* from that full frame. To express the "real" field of view in 35mm terms, you must multiply a lens's focal length by the crop factor, which in the case of the Nikon D60 is 1.5X. Nikon also sells dSLRs with 1X (full-frame) sensors (currently only the Nikon D3), which provide the field of view shown in Figure 6.1.

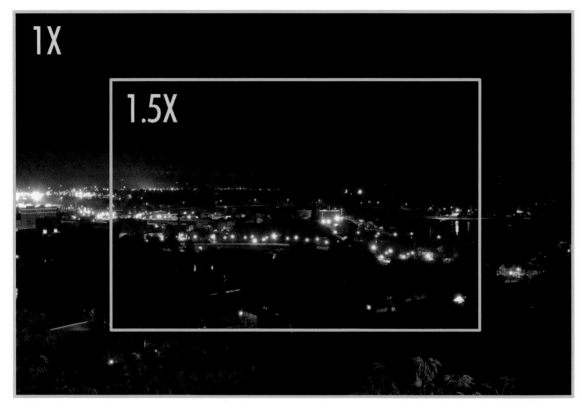

Figure 6.1 Most Nikon digital SLRs offer a 1.5X crop like the D60, but the company has begun offering full-frame (1X crop) cameras such as the Nikon D3.

If you're accustomed to using full-frame film cameras, you might find it helpful to use the crop factor "multiplier" to translate a lens's real focal length into the full-frame equivalent, even though nothing is actually being multiplied. Throughout most of this book, I've been using actual focal lengths and not equivalents, except when referring to specific wide-angle or telephoto focal length ranges and their fields of view.

Your First Lens

Some Nikon dSLRs are almost always purchased with a lens. The entry- and mid-level Nikon dSLRs, like the Nikon D40 and D60, are often bought by those new to digital photography, frequently by first-time SLR or dSLR owners who find the AF-S DX Zoom-Nikkor 18-55mm f/3.5-5.6G ED II VR autofocus lens with vibration reduction an irresistible bargain. Other Nikon models, including the Nikon D300, D2xs, and D3, are generally purchased without a lens by veteran Nikon photographers who already have a complement of optics to use with their cameras.

I bought my D60 with the 18-55 VR lens, even though I already had a (large) collection of lenses, because the VR was an attractive feature, and the lens is perfect to mount on the camera when I loan it to family members who have little photographic experience. Depending on which category of photographer you fall into, you'll need to make a decision about what kit lens to buy, or decide what other kind of lenses you need to fill out your complement of Nikon optics. This section will cover "first lens" concerns, while later in the chapter we'll look at "add-on lens" considerations.

When deciding on a first lens, there are several factors you'll want to consider:

- **Cost.** You might have stretched your budget a bit to purchase your Nikon D60, so the 18-55 VR kit lens helps you keep the cost of your first lens fairly low. In addition, there are excellent moderately priced lenses available that will add from $100 to $300 to the price of your camera if purchased at the same time.

- **Zoom range.** If you have only one lens, you'll want a fairly long zoom range to provide as much flexibility as possible. Fortunately, the several popular basic lenses for the D60 have 3X to 5X zoom ranges, extending from moderate wide-angle/normal out to medium telephoto. Either is fine for everyday shooting, portraits, and some types of sports.

- **Adequate maximum aperture.** You'll want an f/stop of at least f/3.5 to f/4 for shooting under fairly low light conditions. The thing to watch for is the maximum aperture when the lens is zoomed to its telephoto end. You may end up with no better than an f/5.6 maximum aperture. That's not great, but you can often live with it, particularly with a lens having vibration reduction (VR) capabilities, because you can often shoot at lower shutter speeds to compensate for the limited maximum aperture.

- **Image quality.** Your starter lens should have good image quality, because that's one of the primary factors that will be used to judge your photos. Even at a low price, several of the different lenses that can be used with the D60 kit include extra-low dispersion glass and aspherical elements that minimize distortion and chromatic aberration; they are sharp enough for most applications. If you read the user evaluations in the online photography forums, you know that owners of the kit lenses have been very pleased with its image quality.

- **Size matters.** A good walking-around lens is compact in size and light in weight.

- **Fast/close focusing.** Your first lens should have a speedy autofocus system, which is where the Silent Wave motor found in all but the bargain basement lenses, older, non-AF-S models is an advantage. Close focusing (to 12 inches or closer) will let you use your basic lens for some types of macro photography.

You can find comparisons of the lenses discussed in the next section, as well as third-party lenses from Sigma, Tokina, Tamron, and other vendors, in online groups and websites. I'll provide my recommendations, but more information is always helpful.

Buy Now, Expand Later

When the Nikon D60 was introduced, it was available only in kit form with the 18-55 VR lens. By the time this book is published, I expect to see it offered packaged with other lenses—all good, basic lenses that can serve you well as a "walk-around" lens (one you keep on the camera most of the time, especially when you're out and about without your camera bag). The number of options available to you is actually quite amazing, even if your budget is limited to about $100-$350 for your first lens. One other vendor, for example, offers only 18mm-70mm and 18mm-55mm kit lenses in that price range, plus a 24mm-85mm zoom. Here's a list of Nikon's best-bet "first" lenses. Don't worry about sorting out the alphabet soup right now; I provide a complete list of Nikon lens "codes" later in the chapter.

- **AF-S DX Nikkor 18-55mm f/3.5-5.6G VR.** This new VR version of the 18-55 is a better choice than the basic 18-55 optic, which remains available from many stores. That's because the vibration reduction ("anti-shake") feature of this lens partially offsets the relatively slow maximum aperture of the lens at the telephoto position. It can be mated with Nikon's AF-S DX VR Zoom-Nikkor 55-200mm f/4-5.6G IF-ED to give you a two-lens VR pair that will handle everything from 18mm to 200mm, at a relatively low price. (See Figure 6.2.)

- **AF-S DX Zoom-Nikkor 18-55mm f/3.5-5.6G ED II.** This is the least expensive basic zoom Nikon offers, and suitable for the D60 if you're really pinching pennies. You can always upgrade to better lenses in the near future.

- **AF-S DX Nikkor 16-85mm f/3.5-5.6G ED VR.** The new 16-85mm VR lens is the zoom that would make the most sense as a kit lens for the D60 if price were no object. It costs almost as much as the D60 itself! If you really want to use just a single lens with your camera, this one provides an excellent combination of focal lengths, image quality, and features. Its zoom range extends from a true wide-angle (equivalent to a 24mm lens on a full-frame camera) to useful medium telephoto (about 128mm equivalent), and so can be used for everything from architecture to portraiture to sports. If you think vibration reduction is useful only with longer telephoto lenses, you may be surprised at how much it helps you hand-hold your D60 even at the widest focal lengths. The only disadvantage to this lens is its relatively slow speed (f/5.6) when you crank it out to the telephoto end. (See Figure 6.3.)

- **AF-S DX Zoom-Nikkor 18-70mm f/3.5-4.5G IF-ED.** If you don't plan on getting a longer zoom-range basic lens and can't afford the 16-85 zoom, I highly recommend this aging, but impressive lens, if you can find one in stock. Originally introduced as the kit lens for the venerable Nikon D70, the 18-70mm zoom quickly gained a reputation as a very sharp lens at a bargain price. It doesn't provide a view that's as long or as wide as the 16-85, but it's a half-stop faster at its maximum zoom position. You may have to hunt around to find one of these, but they are available for $250-$300 and well worth it.

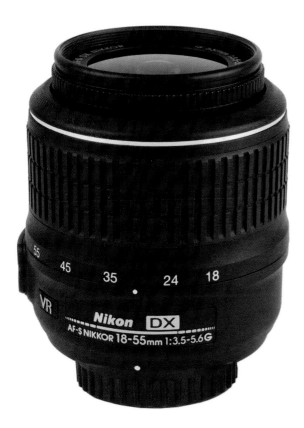

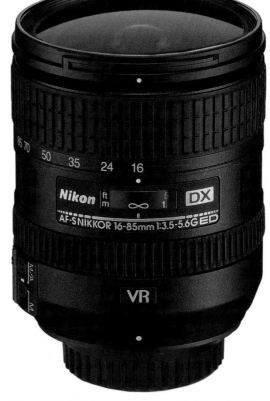

Figure 6.2 The AF-S DX Nikkor 18-55mm f/3.5-5.6G VR is the basic kit lens sold with the Nikon D60.

Figure 6.3 The AF-S DX Nikkor 16-85mm f/3.5-5.6G ED VR has extra wide-angle perspective and longer telephoto reach.

■ **AF-S DX Zoom-Nikkor 18-135mm f/3.5-5.6G IF-ED.** This lens has been sold as a kit lens for intermediate amateur-level Nikons, and is being packaged with the D60 as well. While decent, it's really best suited for the crowd who buy one do-everything lens and then never purchase another. Available for less than $300, you won't tie up a lot of money in this lens.

■ **AF-S DX VR Zoom-Nikkor 18-200mm f/3.5-5.6G IF-ED.** I owned this lens for about three months, and decided it really didn't meet my needs. It was introduced as an ideal "kit" lens for the Nikon D200 a few years back, and, at the time had almost everything you might want. It's a holdover, more upscale kit lens for the D60. Its stunning 11X zoom range covers everything from the equivalent of 27mm to 300mm when the 1.5X crop factor is figured in, and its VR capabilities plus light weight let you use it without a tripod most of the time. However, I found the image quality to be good, but not outstanding, and the slow maximum aperture at 200mm to be limiting when a fast shutter speed is required to stop action. The "zoom creep" (a tendency for the lens to zoom when the camera is tilted up or down) found in many examples will drive you nuts after awhile. (See Figure 6.4.)

■ **AF-S VR Zoom-Nikkor 24-120mm f/3.5-5.6G IF-ED.** I felt I had to mention this lens because I see a large number of them available used at low prices. There are two versions, an older non-VR lens, and this model, which added vibration reduction, internal focusing, and some extra low dispersion (ED) elements to improve image quality. Unfortunately, while image quality is very good at the maximum 120mm, the lens softens quite a bit at shorter focal lengths and at larger apertures, making it less suitable as an all-around tool.

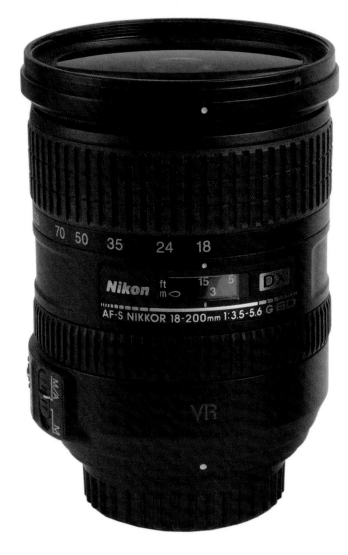

Figure 6.4
The AF-S DX VR Zoom-Nikkor 18-200mm f/3.5-5.6G IF-ED is a light-weight "walking around" lens.

What Lenses Can You Use?

The previous section helped you sort out what basic lens you need to buy with your Nikon D60. Now, you're probably wondering what lenses can be added to your growing collection (trust me, it will grow). You need to know which lenses are suitable and, most importantly, which lenses are fully compatible with your Nikon D60.

With the Nikon D60, the compatibility issue is a simple one: It can use any Nikon lens with the AF-S designation, with full availability of all autofocus, auto aperture, auto-exposure, and image-stabilization features (if present). With lenses having the AF designation, all features *except* autofocus are available. You can also use any Nikon AI, AI-S, or AI-P lens, which are manual focus lenses produced starting in 1977 and effectively through the present day, because Nikon continues to offer a limited number of manual focus lenses for those who need them.

If you own a Nikon camera in addition to the Nikon D60, D40, or D40x, Nikon lenses produced prior to 1977 must have a minor conversion done to be used safely, because cameras other than the Nikon entry-level trio I mentioned have a pin on the lens mount that can be damaged by an older, unmodified lens. John White at www.aiconversions.com will do the work for about $35 to allow these older lenses to be safely used on any Nikon digital camera. However, if you don't own any other Nikon digital camera, and promise not to loan an older lens to someone who does have a camera that might be damaged, you can pick up these ancient optics for a song and use them safely with your D60.

As far as third-party (non-Nikon) lenses go, your D60 will accept virtually all modern lenses produced by Tokina, Tamron, Sigma, and other vendors, but will autofocus only with those that contain an internal focusing motor. Vendors have different designators to indicate these lenses, such as HSM (for hyper-sonic motor). You'll have to check with the manufacturer of non-Nikon lenses to see if they are compatible with the D60, particularly since some vendors have been gradually introducing revamped versions of their existing lenses with the addition of an internal motor.

Today, in addition to its traditional full-frame lenses, Nikon offers lenses with the DX designation, which is intended for use only on DX-format cameras (currently every Nikon digital camera except for the D3). While the lens mounting system is the same, DX lenses have a coverage area that fills only the smaller frame, allowing the design of more compact, less-expensive lenses especially for non-full-frame cameras.

Ingredients of Nikon's Alphanumeric Soup

Nikon has always been fond of appending cryptic letters and descriptors onto the names of its lenses. Here's an alphabetical list of lens terms you're likely to encounter, either as part of the lens name, or in reference to the lens's capabilities. Not all of these are used as parts of a lens's name; but you may come across some of these terms in discussions of particular Nikon optics:

- **AF, AF-D, AF-I, AF-S.** In all cases, AF stands for *autofocus* when appended to the name of a Nikon lens. An extra letter is added to provide additional information. A plain-old **AF** lens is an autofocus lens that uses a slot-drive motor in the camera body to provide autofocus functions (and so cannot be used in AF mode on the Nikon D40, D40x, or D60, which lack the camera body motor). The **D** means that it's a D-type lens (described later in this listing); the **I** indicates that focus is through a motor inside the lens; and the **S** means that a super-special (Silent Wave) motor in the lens provides focusing. (Don't confuse a Nikon AF-S lens with the AF-S [Single-Servo Autofocus mode]). Nikon is currently upgrading its older AF lenses with AF-S versions, but it's not safe to assume that all newer Nikkors are AF-S, or even offer autofocus. For example, the brand-new PC-E Nikkor 24mm f/3.5D ED perspective control lens must be focused manually, and Nikon offers a surprising collection of other manual focus lenses to meet specialized needs.

- **AI, AI-S.** All Nikkor lenses produced after 1977 have either automatic aperture indexing (AI) or automatic indexing-shutter (AI-S) features that eliminate the previous requirement to manually align the aperture ring on the camera when mounting a lens. Within a few years, all Nikkors had this automatic aperture indexing feature (except for G-type lenses, which have no aperture ring at all), including Nikon's budget-priced Series E lenses, so the designation was dropped at the time the first autofocus (AF) lenses were introduced.

- **E.** The E designation was used for Nikon's budget-priced E Series optics, five prime and three zoom manual focus lenses built using aluminum or plastic parts rather than the preferred brass, so they were less rugged. All are effectively AI-S lenses. They do have good image quality, which makes them a bargain for those who treat their lenses gently and don't need the latest autofocus features. They were available in 28mm f/2.8, 35mm f/2.5, 50mm f/1.8, 100mm f/2.8, and 135mm f/2.8 focal lengths, plus 36-72mm f/3.5, 75mm-150mm f/3.5, and 70-210mm f/4 zooms. (All these would be considered fairly "fast" today.)

- **D.** Appended to the maximum f/stop of the lens (as in f/2.8D), a D Series lens is able to send focus distance data to the camera, which uses the information for flash exposure calculation and 3D Color Matrix II matrix metering.

- **DC.** The DC stands for defocus control, which allows managing the out-of-focus parts of an image to produce better-looking portraits and close-ups.

- **DX.** The DX lenses are designed for use with digital cameras using the APS-C–sized sensor having the 1.5X crop factor. The image circle they produce isn't large enough to fill up a full 35mm frame at all focal lengths, but they can be used on Nikon's full-frame D3 model using the automatic/manual DX crop mode.

- **ED (or LD/UD).** The ED (extra low dispersion) designation indicates that some lens elements are made of a special hard and scratch-resistant glass that minimizes the divergence of the different colors of light as they pass through, thus reducing chromatic aberration (color "fringing") and other image defects. A gold band around the front of the lens indicates an optic with ED elements. You sometimes find LD (low dispersion) or UD (ultra-low dispersion) designations.

- **FX.** When Nikon introduced the Nikon D3 full-frame camera, it coined the term "FX," representing the 23.9 × 36mm sensor format as a counterpart to "DX," which was used for its 15.8 × 23.6mm APS-C-sized sensors. Although FX hasn't been officially applied to any Nikon lenses so far, expect to see the designation used more often to differentiate between lenses that are compatible with any Nikon digital SLR (FX) and those that operate only on DX-format cameras, or in DX mode when used on an FX camera like the D3.

- **G.** G-type lenses have no aperture ring, and you can use them at other than the maximum aperture only with electronic cameras like the D60 that set the aperture automatically or by using the command dial while the Exposure Compensation/ Aperture button is depressed. This includes all Nikon digital dSLRs.

- **IF.** Nikon's *internal focusing* lenses change focus by shifting only small internal lens groups with no change required in the lens's physical length, unlike conventional double helicoid focusing systems that move all lens groups toward the front or rear during focusing. IF lenses are more compact and lighter in weight, provide better balance, focus more closely, and can be focused more quickly.

- **IX.** These lenses were produced for Nikon's long-discontinued Pronea 6i and S APS film cameras. While the Pronea could use many standard Nikon lenses, IX lenses cannot be mounted on any Nikon digital SLR.

- **Micro.** Nikon uses the term *micro* to designate its close-up lenses. Most other vendors use *macro* instead.

- **PC (Perspective Control).** A PC lens is capable of shifting the lens from side to side (and up/down) to provide a more realistic perspective when photographing architecture and other subjects that otherwise require tilting the camera so that the sensor plane is not parallel to the subject. Older Nikkor PC lenses offered shifting only, but more modern models, such as the PC-E Nikkor 24mm f/3.5D ED lens introduced early in 2008 allow both shifting and tilting.

- **UV.** This term is applied to special (and expensive) lenses designed to pass ultra-violet light.

- **UW.** Lenses with this designation are designed for underwater photography with Nikonos camera bodies, and cannot be used with Nikon digital SLRs.

- **VR.** Nikon has an expanding line of vibration reduction (VR) lenses, including several very affordable models and the new AF-S DX Nikkor 16-85mm f/3.5-5.6G ED VR lens, which shifts lens elements internally to counteract camera shake. The VR feature allows using a shutter speed up to four stops slower than would be possible without vibration reduction.

What Lenses Can Do for You

No one can afford to buy even a percentage of the lenses available. The sanest approach to expanding your lens collection is to consider what each of your options can do for you and then choosing the type of lens and specific model that will really boost your creative opportunities. So, in the sections that follow, I'm going to provide a general guide to the sort of capabilities you can gain for your D60 by adding a lens to your repertoire.

- **Wider perspective.** Your 18-55mm f/3.5-5.6 or 16-85mm f/4-5.6 lens has served you well for moderate wide-angle shots. Now you find your back is up against a wall and you *can't* take a step backwards to take in more subject matter. Perhaps you're standing on the rim of the Grand Canyon, and you want to take in as much of the breathtaking view as you can. You might find yourself just behind the baseline at a high school basketball game and want an interesting shot with a little perspective distortion tossed in the mix.

- **Bring objects closer.** A long lens brings distant subjects closer to you, offers better control over depth-of-field, and avoids the perspective distortion that wide-angle lenses provide. They compress the apparent distance between objects in your frame. Don't forget that the Nikon D60's crop factor narrows the field of view of all these lenses, so your 70-300mm lens looks more like a 105mm-450mm zoom through the viewfinder. The image shown in Figure 6.5 was taken using a wide 16mm lens, while the images in Figures 6.6 and 6.7 were taken from the same position as Figure 6.5, but with focal lengths of 40mm and 85mm, respectively.

- **Bring your camera closer.** Macro lenses allow you to focus to within an inch or two of your subject. Nikon's best close-up lenses are all fixed focal length optics in the 60mm to 200mm range, but you'll find good macro zooms available from Sigma and others. They don't tend to focus quite as close, but they provide a bit of flexibility when you want to vary your subject distance (say, to avoid spooking a skittish creature).

Figure 6.5
An ultra-wide-angle lens provided this view of an 8th century castle.

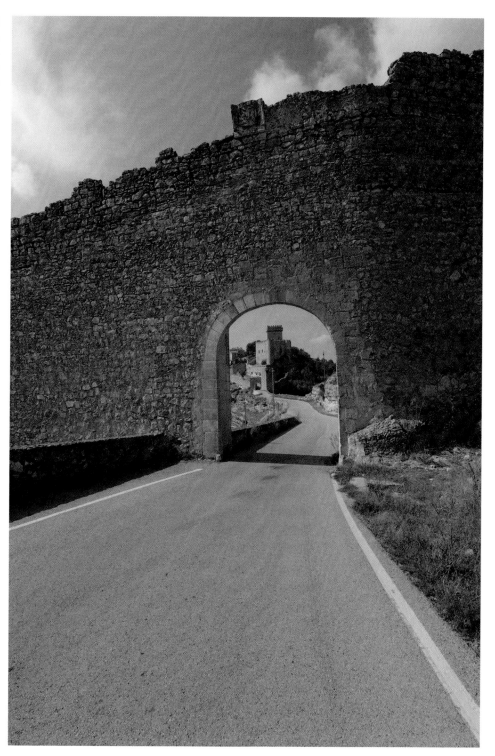

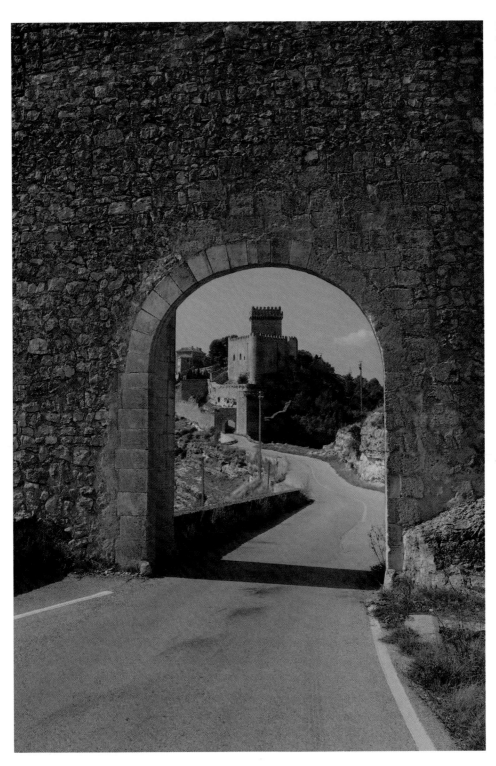

Figure 6.6
This photo, taken from roughly the same distance shows the view using a "normal" lens.

Figure 6.7
A medium tele-
photo lens cap-
tured this
close-up view
of the castle
from approxi-
mately the
same shooting
position.

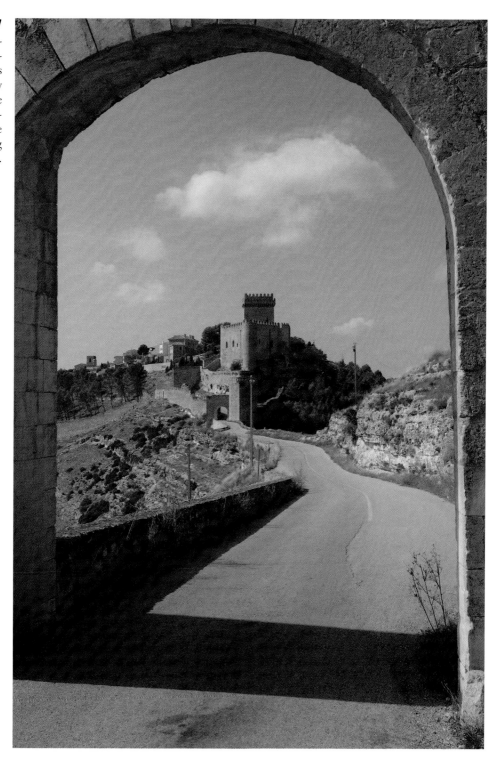

- **Look sharp.** Many lenses are prized for their sharpness and overall image quality. While your run-of-the-mill lens is likely to be plenty sharp for most applications, the very best optics are even better over their entire field of view (which means no fuzzy corners), are sharper at a wider range of focal lengths (in the case of zooms), and have better correction for various types of distortion.

- **More speed.** Your Nikon 70-300mm f/4.5-5.6 telephoto zoom lens might have the perfect focal length and sharpness for sports photography, but the maximum aperture won't cut it for night baseball or football games, or, even, any sports shooting in daylight if the weather is cloudy or you need to use some ungodly fast shutter speed, such as 1/4,000th second. You might be happier to gain a full f/stop with an AF-S Nikkor 300mm f/4D IF-ED for a little more than $1,000, mated to a 1.4x teleconverter (giving you a 420mm f/5.6 lens). Or, maybe you just need the speed and can benefit from an f/1.8 or f/1.4 prime lens. They're all available in Nikon mounts (there's even an 85mm f/1.4 and 50mm f/1.4 for the real speed demons, if you're willing to give up autofocus). With any of these lenses you can continue photographing under the dimmest of lighting conditions without the need for a tripod or flash.

- **Special features.** Accessory lenses give you special features, such as tilt/shift capabilities to correct for perspective distortion in architectural shots. You'll also find macro lenses, including the new AF-S Micro-Nikkor 60mm f/2.8G ED. Fisheye lenses like the AF DX Fisheye-Nikkor 10.5mm f/2.8G ED, and all other VR (vibration reduction) lenses also count as special-feature optics.

Zoom or Prime?

Zoom lenses have changed the way serious photographers take pictures. One of the reasons that I own 12 SLR film bodies dating back to the pre-zoom days is that in ancient times it was common to mount a different fixed focal length prime lens on various cameras and take pictures with two or three cameras around your neck (or tucked in a camera case) so you'd be ready to take a long shot or an intimate close-up or wide-angle view on a moment's notice, without the need to switch lenses. It made sense (at the time) to have a half-dozen or so bodies (two to use, one in the shop, one in transit, and a couple backups). Zoom lenses of the time had a limited zoom range, were heavy, and not very sharp (especially when you tried to wield one of those monsters hand-held). That's all changed today. Smaller, longer, sharper zoom lenses, many with VR features, are available.

When selecting between zoom and prime lenses, there are several considerations to ponder. Here's a checklist of the most important factors. I already mentioned image quality and maximum aperture earlier, but those aspects take on additional meaning when comparing zooms and primes.

- **Logistics.** As prime lenses offer just a single focal length, you'll need more of them to encompass the full range offered by a single zoom. More lenses mean additional slots in your camera bag, and extra weight to carry. Just within Nikon's line alone you can choose from a good selection of general purpose (if you can count lenses that won't autofocus with the D60 as "general purpose") prime lenses in 28mm, 35mm, 50mm, 85mm, 100mm, 135mm, and 200mm focal lengths, all of which are overlapped by the 18-200mm zoom I mentioned earlier. Even so, you might be willing to carry an extra prime lens or two in order to gain the speed or image quality that lens offers.

- **Image quality.** Prime lenses usually produce better image quality at their focal length than even the most sophisticated zoom lenses at the same magnification. Zoom lenses, with their shifting elements and f/stops that can vary from zoom position to zoom position, are in general more complex to design than fixed focal length lenses. That's not to say that the very best prime lenses can't be complicated as well. However, the exotic designs, aspheric elements, and low-dispersion glass can be applied to improving the quality of the lens, rather than wasting a lot of it on compensating for problems caused by the zoom process itself.

- **Maximum aperture.** Because of the same design constraints, zoom lenses usually have smaller maximum apertures than prime lenses, and the most affordable zooms have a lens opening that grows effectively smaller as you zoom in. The difference in lens speed verges on the ridiculous at some focal lengths. For example, the 18mm-55mm basic zoom gives you a 55mm f/5.6 lens when zoomed all the way out, while prime lenses in that focal length commonly have f/1.8 or faster maximum apertures. Indeed, the fastest f/2, f/1.8, f1/4, and f/1.2 lenses are all manual focus primes (at least on the D60), and if you require speed, a fixed focal length lens is what you should rely on. Figure 6.8 shows an image taken with a Nikon 85mm f /1.8 lens.

- **Speed.** Using prime lenses takes time and slows you down. It takes a few seconds to remove your current lens and mount a new one, and the more often you need to do that, the more time is wasted. If you choose not to swap lenses, when using a fixed focal length lens you'll still have to move closer or farther away from your subject to get the field of view you want. A zoom lens allows you to change magnifications and focal lengths with the twist of a ring and generally saves a great deal of time.

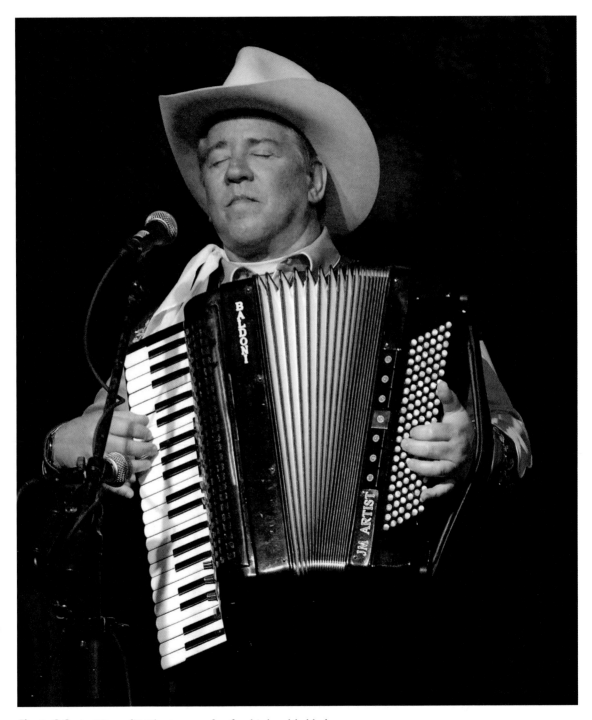

Figure 6.8 An 85mm f/1.8 lens was perfect for this hand-held photo at a concert.

Categories of Lenses

Lenses can be categorized by their intended purpose—general photography, macro photography, and so forth—or by their focal length. The range of available focal lengths is usually divided into three main groups: wide-angle, normal, and telephoto. Prime lenses fall neatly into one of these classifications. Zooms can overlap designations, with a significant number falling into the catch-all wide-to-telephoto zoom range. This section provides more information about focal length ranges, and how they are used.

When the 1.5X crop factor (mentioned at the beginning of this chapter) is figured in, any lens with an equivalent focal length of 10mm to 16mm is said to be an *ultra-wide-angle lens*; from about 16mm to 30mm is said to be a *wide-angle lens*. *Normal lenses* have a focal length roughly equivalent to the diagonal of the film or sensor, in millimeters, and so fall into the range of about 30mm to 40 on a D60. *Short telephoto lenses* start at about 40mm to 70mm, with anything from 70mm to 250 mm qualifying as a conventional *telephoto*. For the Nikon D60, anything from about 300mm-400mm or longer can be considered a *super-telephoto*.

Using Wide-Angle and Wide-Zoom Lenses

To use wide-angle prime lenses and wide zooms, you need to understand how they affect your photography. Here's a quick summary of the things you need to know.

- **More depth-of-field.** Practically speaking, wide-angle lenses offer more depth-of-field at a particular subject distance and aperture. (But see the sidebar below for an important note.) You'll find that helpful when you want to maximize sharpness of a large zone, but not very useful when you'd rather isolate your subject using selective focus (telephoto lenses are better for that).

- **Stepping back.** Wide-angle lenses have the effect of making it seem that you are standing farther from your subject than you really are. They're helpful when you don't want to back up, or can't because there are impediments in your way.

- **Wider field of view.** While making your subject seem farther away, as implied above, a wide-angle lens also provides a larger field of view, including more of the subject in your photos.

- **More foreground.** As background objects retreat, more of the foreground is brought into view by a wide-angle lens. That gives you extra emphasis on the area that's closest to the camera. Photograph your home with a normal lens/normal zoom setting, and the front yard probably looks fairly conventional in your photo (that's why they're called "normal" lenses). Switch to a wider lens and you'll discover that your lawn now makes up much more of the photo. So, wide-angle lenses are great when you want to emphasize that lake in the foreground, but problematic when your intended subject is located farther in the distance.

■ **Super-sized subjects.** The tendency of a wide-angle lens to emphasize objects in the foreground, while de-emphasizing objects in the background can lead to a kind of size distortion that may be more objectionable for some types of subjects than others. Shoot a bed of flowers up close with a wide angle, and you might like the distorted effect of the larger blossoms nearer the lens. Take a photo of a family member with the same lens from the same distance, and you're likely to get some complaints about that gigantic nose in the foreground.

■ **Perspective distortion.** When you tilt the camera so the plane of the sensor is no longer perpendicular to the vertical plane of your subject, some parts of the subject are now closer to the sensor than they were before, while other parts are farther away. So, buildings, flagpoles, or NBA players appear to be falling backwards, as you can see in Figure 6.9. While this kind of apparent distortion (it's not caused by a defect in the lens) can happen with any lens, it's most apparent when a wide angle is used.

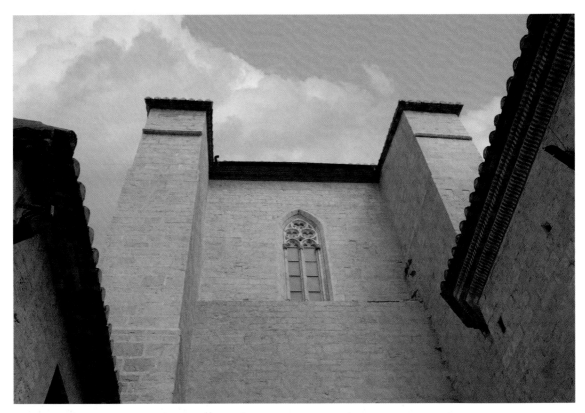

Figure 6.9 Tilting the camera back produces this "falling back" look in architectural photos.

- **Steady cam.** You'll find that you can hand-hold a wide-angle lens at slower shutter speeds, without need for vibration reduction, than you can with a telephoto lens. The reduced magnification of the wide-lens or wide-zoom setting doesn't emphasize camera shake like a telephoto lens does.

- **Interesting angles.** Many of the factors already listed combine to produce more interesting angles when shooting with wide-angle lenses. Raising or lowering a telephoto lens a few feet probably will have little effect on the appearance of the distant subjects you're shooting. The same change in elevation can produce a dramatic effect for the much-closer subjects typically captured with a wide-angle lens or wide-zoom setting.

DOF IN DEPTH

The DOF advantage of wide-angle lenses is diminished when you enlarge your picture; believe it or not, a wide-angle image enlarged and cropped to provide the same subject size as a telephoto shot would have the *same* depth-of-field. Try it: take a wide-angle photo of a friend from a fair distance, and then zoom in to duplicate the picture in a telephoto image. Then, enlarge the wide shot so your friend is the same size in both. The wide photo will have the same depth-of-field (and will have much less detail, too).

Avoiding Potential Wide-Angle Problems

Wide-angle lenses have a few quirks that you'll want to keep in mind when shooting so you can avoid falling into some common traps. Here's a checklist of tips for avoiding common problems:

- **Symptom: converging lines.** Unless you want to use wildly diverging lines as a creative effect, it's a good idea to keep horizontal and vertical lines in landscapes, architecture, and other subjects carefully aligned with the sides, top, and bottom of the frame. That will help you avoid undesired perspective distortion. Sometimes it helps to shoot from a slightly elevated position so you don't have to tilt the camera up or down.

- **Symptom: color fringes around objects.** Lenses are often plagued with fringes of color around backlit objects, produced by *chromatic aberration*, which is produced when all the colors of light don't focus in the same plane or same lateral position (that is the colors are offset to one side). Some kinds of chromatic aberration can be reduced by stopping down the lens, while all sorts can be reduced by using lenses with low diffraction index glass (or ED elements, in Nikon nomenclature) and by incorporating elements that cancel the chromatic aberration of other glass in the lens.

■ **Symptom: lines that bow outward.** Some wide-angle lenses cause straight lines to bow outwards, with the strongest effect at the edges. In fisheye (or *curvilinear*) lenses, this defect is a feature, as you can see in Figure 6.10. When distortion is not desired, you'll need to use a lens that has corrected barrel distortion. Manufacturers like Nikon do their best to minimize or eliminate it (producing a *rectilinear* lens), often using *aspherical* lens elements (which are not cross-sections of a sphere). You can also minimize barrel distortion simply by framing your photo with some extra space all around, so the edges where the defect is most obvious can be cropped out of the picture. Some image editors, such as Photoshop and Photoshop Elements have a lens distortion correction feature.

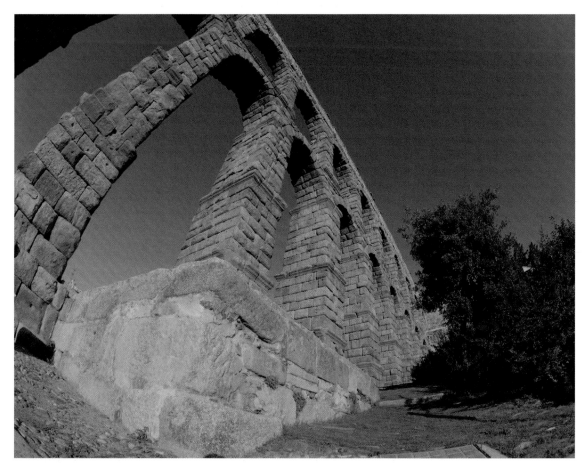

Figure 6.10 Many wide-angle lenses cause lines to bow outwards towards the edges of the image; with a fisheye lens, this tendency is considered an interesting feature.

■ **Symptom: dark corners and shadows in flash photos.** The Nikon D60's built-in electronic flash is designed to provide even coverage for lenses as wide as 17mm. If you use a wider lens, you can expect darkening, or *vignetting*, in the corners of the frame. At wider focal lengths, the lens hood of some lenses (my 18mm-70mm lens is a prime offender) can cast a semi-circular shadow in the lower portion of the frame when using the built-in flash. Sometimes removing the lens hood or zooming in a bit can eliminate the shadow. Mounting an external flash unit, such as the mighty Nikon SB-800 can solve both problems, as this high-end flash unit (it costs almost half as much as the D60 camera) has zoomable coverage up to as wide as the field of view of a 14mm lens when used with the included adapter. Its higher vantage point eliminates the problem of lens-hood shadow, too.

Using Telephoto and Tele-Zoom Lenses

Telephoto lenses also can have a dramatic effect on your photography, and Nikon is especially strong in the long-lens arena, with lots of choices in many focal lengths and zoom ranges. You should be able to find an affordable telephoto or tele-zoom to enhance your photography in several different ways. Here are the most important things you need to know. In the next section, I'll concentrate on telephoto considerations that can be problematic—and how to avoid those problems.

■ **Selective focus.** Long lenses have reduced depth-of-field within the frame, allowing you to use selective focus to isolate your subject. You can open the lens up wide to create shallow depth-of-field, or close it down a bit to allow more to be in focus. The flip side of the coin is that when you *want* to make a range of objects sharp, you'll need to use a smaller f/stop to get the depth-of-field you need. Like fire, the depth-of-field of a telephoto lens can be friend or foe. Figure 6.11 shows a photo of several blossoms of a plant photographed using a telephoto macro lens (a 105mm f/2.8 Micro-Nikkor) and wider f/stop to de-emphasize the other portions of the background.

■ **Getting closer.** Telephoto lenses bring you closer to wildlife, sports action, and candid subjects. No one wants to get a reputation as a surreptitious or "sneaky" photographer (except for paparazzi), but when applied to candids in an open and honest way, a long lens can help you capture memorable moments while retaining enough distance to stay out of the way of events as they transpire.

■ **Reduced foreground/increased compression.** Telephoto lenses have the opposite effect of wide angles: they reduce the importance of things in the foreground by squeezing everything together. This compression even makes distant objects appear to be closer to subjects in the foreground and middle ranges. You can use this effect as a creative tool to squeeze subjects together.

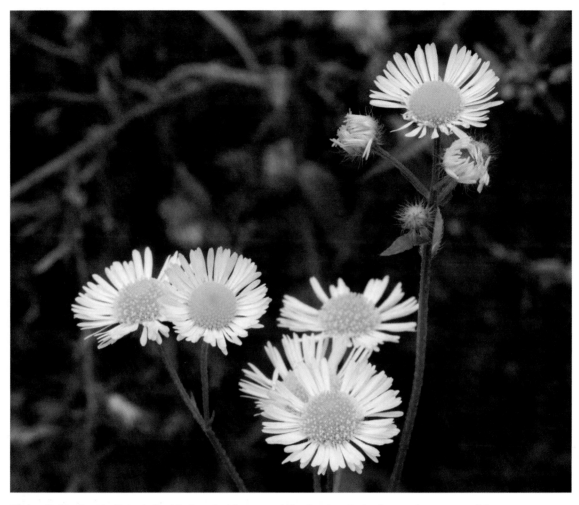

Figure 6.11 A wide f/stop helped isolate the blossoms while allowing the background to go out of focus.

- **Accentuates camera shakiness.** Telephoto focal lengths hit you with a double-whammy in terms of camera/photographer shake. The lenses themselves are bulkier, more difficult to hold steady, and may even produce a barely perceptible see-saw rocking effect when you support them with one hand halfway down the lens barrel. Telephotos also magnify any camera shake. It's no wonder that vibration reduction is popular in longer lenses.

- **Interesting angles require creativity.** Telephoto lenses require more imagination in selecting interesting angles, because the "angle" you do get on your subjects is so narrow. Moving from side to side or a bit higher or lower can make a dramatic difference in a wide-angle shot, but raising or lowering a telephoto lens a few feet probably will have little effect on the appearance of the distant subjects you're shooting.

Avoiding Telephoto Lens Problems

Many of the "problems" that telephoto lenses pose are really just challenges and not that difficult to overcome. Here is a list of the seven most common picture maladies and suggested solutions.

- **Symptom: flat faces in portraits.** Head-and-shoulders portraits of humans tend to be more flattering when a focal length of 50mm to 85mm is used. Longer focal lengths compress the distance between features like noses and ears, making the face look wider and flat. A wide angle might make noses look huge and ears tiny when you fill the frame with a face. So stick with 50mm to 85mm focal lengths, going longer only when you're forced to shoot from a greater distance, and wider only when shooting three-quarters/full-length portraits, or group shots.

- **Symptom: blur due to camera shake.** Use a higher shutter speed (boosting ISO if necessary), consider an image-stabilized lens, or mount your camera on a tripod, monopod, or brace it with some other support. Of those three solutions, only the first will reduce blur caused by *subject* motion; a VR lens or tripod won't help you freeze a racecar in mid-lap.

- **Symptom: color fringes.** Chromatic aberration is the most pernicious optical problem found in telephoto lenses. There are others, including spherical aberration, astigmatism, coma, curvature of field, and similarly scary-sounding phenomena. The best solution for any of these is to use a better lens that offers the proper degree of correction, or stop down the lens to minimize the problem. But that's not always possible. Your second-best choice may be to correct the fringing in your favorite RAW conversion tool or image editor. Photoshop's Lens Correction filter (found in the Filter menu's Distort submenu) offers sliders that minimize both red/cyan and blue/yellow fringing.

- **Symptom: lines that curve inwards.** Pincushion distortion is found in many telephoto lenses. You might find after a bit of testing that it is worse at certain focal lengths with your particular zoom lens. Like chromatic aberration, it can be partially corrected using tools like the correction tools built into Photoshop and Photoshop Elements. You can see an exaggerated example in Figure 6.12; pincushion distortion isn't always this obvious.

- **Symptom: low contrast from haze or fog.** When you're photographing distant objects, a long lens shoots through a lot more atmosphere, which generally is muddied up with extra haze and fog. That dirt or moisture in the atmosphere can reduce contrast and mute colors. Some feel that a skylight or UV filter can help, but this practice is mostly a holdover from the film days. Digital sensors are not sensitive enough to UV light for a UV filter to have much effect. So you should be prepared to boost contrast and color saturation in your image editor if necessary.

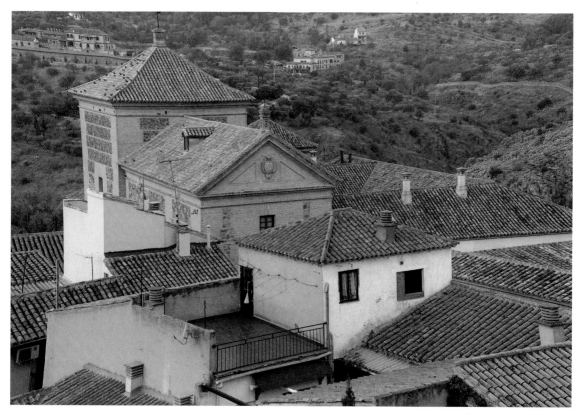

Figure 6.12 Pincushion distortion in telephoto lenses causes lines to bow inwards from the edges.

- **Symptom: low contrast from flare.** Lenses are furnished with lens hoods for a good reason: to reduce flare from bright light sources at the periphery of the picture area, or completely outside it. Because telephoto lenses often create images that are lower in contrast in the first place, you'll want to be especially careful to use a lens hood to prevent further effects on your image (or shade the front of the lens with your hand).

- **Symptom: dark flash photos.** Edge-to-edge flash coverage isn't a problem with telephoto lenses as it is with wide angles. The shooting distance is. A long lens might make a subject that's 50 feet away look as if it's right next to you, but your camera's flash isn't fooled. You'll need extra power for distant flash shots, and probably more power than your D60's built-in flash provides. The Nikon SB-800 speedlight, for example, can automatically zoom its coverage down to that of a 105mm medium telephoto lens, providing a theoretical full-power shooting aperture of about f/11 at 30 feet and ISO 400. (Try *that* with the built-in flash!)

Telephotos and Bokeh

Bokeh describes the aesthetic qualities of the out-of-focus parts of an image and whether out-of-focus points of light—circles of confusion—are rendered as distracting fuzzy discs or smoothly fade into the background. *Boke* is a Japanese word for "blur," and the h was added to keep English speakers from rendering it monosyllabically to rhyme with *broke.* Although bokeh is visible in blurry portions of any image, it's of particular concern with telephoto lenses, which, thanks to the magic of reduced depth-of-field, produce more obviously out-of-focus areas.

Bokeh can vary from lens to lens, or even within a given lens depending on the f/stop in use. Bokeh becomes objectionable when the circles of confusion are evenly illuminated, making them stand out as distinct discs, or, worse, when these circles are darker in the center, producing an ugly "doughnut" effect. A lens defect called spherical aberration may produce out-of-focus discs that are brighter on the edges and darker in the center, because the lens doesn't focus light passing through the edges of the lens exactly as it does light going through the center. (Mirror or *catadioptric* lenses also produce this effect.)

Other kinds of spherical aberration generate circles of confusion that are brightest in the center and fade out at the edges, producing a smooth blending effect, as you can see at bottom in Figure 6.13. Ironically, when no spherical aberration is present at all, the discs are a uniform shade, which, while better than the doughnut effect, is not as pleasing as the bright center/dark edge rendition. The shape of the disc also comes into play, with round smooth circles considered the best, and nonagonal or some other polygon (determined by the shape of the lens diaphragm) considered less desirable.

If you plan to use selective focus a lot, you should investigate the bokeh characteristics of a particular lens before you buy. Nikon user groups and forums will usually be full of comments and questions about bokeh, so the research is fairly easy.

Add-ons and Special Features

Once you've purchased your telephoto lens, you'll want to think about some appropriate accessories for it. There are some handy add-ons available that can be valuable. Here are a couple of them to think about.

Lens Hoods

Lens hoods are an important accessory for all lenses, but they're especially valuable with telephotos. As I mentioned earlier, lens hoods do a good job of preserving image contrast by keeping bright light sources outside the field of view from striking the lens and, potentially, bouncing around inside that long tube to generate flare that, when coupled with atmospheric haze, can rob your image of detail and snap. In addition, lens hoods

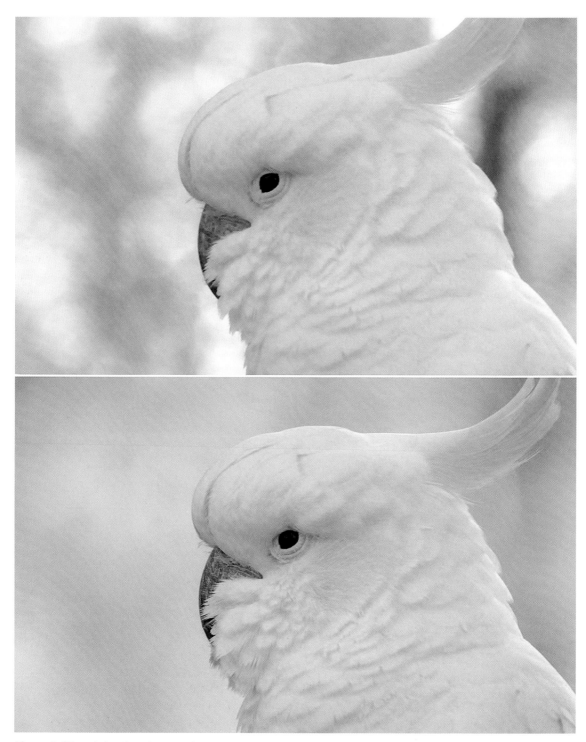

Figure 6.13 Bokeh is less pleasing when the discs are prominent (top), and less obtrusive when they blend into the background (bottom).

serve as valuable protection for that large, vulnerable, front lens element. It's easy to forget that you've got that long tube sticking out in front of your camera and accidentally whack the front of your lens into something. It's cheaper to replace a lens hood than it is to have a lens repaired, so you might find that a good hood is valuable protection for your prized optics.

When choosing a lens hood, it's important to have the right hood for the lens, usually the one offered for that lens by Nikon or the third-party manufacturer. You want a hood that blocks precisely the right amount of light: neither too much light nor too little. A hood with a front diameter that is too small can show up in your pictures as vignetting. A hood that has a front diameter that's too large isn't stopping all the light it should. Generic lens hoods may not do the job.

When your telephoto is a zoom lens, it's even more important to get the right hood, because you need one that does what it is supposed to at both the wide-angle and telephoto ends of the zoom range. Lens hoods may be cylindrical, rectangular (shaped like the image frame), or petal shaped (that is, cylindrical, but with cut-out areas at the corners which correspond to the actual image area). Lens hoods should be mounted in the correct orientation (a bayonet mount for the hood usually takes care of this).

Telephoto Converters

Teleconverters (often called telephoto extenders outside the Nikon world) multiply the actual focal length of your lens, giving you a longer telephoto for much less than the price of a lens with that actual focal length. These converters fit between the lens and your camera and contain optical elements that magnify the image produced by the lens. Available in 1.4X, 1.7X, and 2.0X configurations from Nikon, a teleconverter transforms, say, a 200mm lens into a 280mm, 340mm, or 400mm optic, respectively. Given the D60's crop factor, your 200mm lens now has the same field of view as a 420mm, 510, or 600mm lens on a full-frame camera. At around $300-$400 each, converters are quite a bargain, aren't they?

Actually, there are some downsides. While extenders retain the closest focusing distance of your original lens, autofocus is maintained only if the lens's original maximum aperture is f/4 or larger (for the 1.4X extender) or f/2.8 or larger (for the 2X extender). The components reduce the effective aperture of any lens they are used with, by one f/stop with the 1.4X converter, 1.5 f/stops with the 1.7X converter, and 2 f/stops with the 2X extender. So, your 200mm f/2.8 lens becomes a 280mm f/4 or 400mm f/5.6 lens. Although Nikon converters are precision optical devices, they do cost you a little sharpness, but that improves when you reduce the aperture by a stop or two. Each of the converters is compatible only with a particular set of lenses greater, so you'll want to check Nikon's compatibility chart to see if the component can be used with the lens you want to attach to it.

If your lenses are compatible and you're shooting under bright lighting conditions, the Nikon extenders make handy accessories. I recommend the 1.4X version because it robs you of very little sharpness and only one f/stop. The 1.7X version also works well, too, but I've found the 2X teleconverter to exact too much of a sharpness and speed penalty to be of much use.

Macro Focusing

Some telephotos and telephoto zooms available for the Nikon D60 have particularly close focusing capabilities, making them *macro* lenses. Of course, the object is not necessarily to get close (get too close and you'll find it difficult to light your subject). What you're really looking for in a macro lens is to magnify the apparent size of the subject in the final image. Camera-to-subject distance is most important when you want to back up farther from your subject (say, to avoid spooking skittish insects or small animals). In that case, you'll want a macro lens with a longer focal length to allow that distance while retaining the desired magnification.

Nikon makes five lenses that are officially designated as macro lenses. They include:

- **AF-S Micro-Nikkor 60mm f/2.8G ED.** This new type-G lens supposedly replaces the type-D lens listed next, adding an internal Silent Wave autofocus motor that should operate faster, and which is also compatible with cameras lacking a body motor, such as the Nikon D40/D40x and D60. It also has ED lens elements for improved image quality. However, because it lacks an aperture ring, you can control the f/stop only when the lens is mounted directly on the camera or used with automatic extension tubes. Should you want to reverse a macro lens using a special adapter (the Nikon BR2-A ring) to improve image quality or mount it on a bellows, you're better off with a lens having an aperture ring.

- **AF Micro-Nikkor 60mm f/2.8D.** This non-AF-S lens won't autofocus on the Nikon D60, but, then, you might be manually focusing most of the time when shooting close-ups, and may appreciate the lower cost of an "obsolete" lens.

- **AF-S VR Micro-Nikkor 105mm f/2.8G IF-ED.** This G-series lens did replace a similar D-type, non-AF-S version that also lacked VR. I own the older lens, too, and am keeping it because I find VR a rather specialized tool for macro work. Some 99 percent of the time, I shoot close-ups with my D60 mounted on a tripod or, at the very least, on a monopod, so camera vibration is not much of a concern. Indeed, *subject* movement is a more serious problem, especially when shooting plant life outdoors on days plagued with even slight breezes. Because my outdoor subjects are likely to move while I am composing my photo, I find both VR and autofocus not very useful. I end up focusing manually most of the time, too. This lens provides a little extra camera-to-subject distance, so you'll find it very useful, but consider the older non-G, non-VR version, too, if you're in the market and don't mind losing autofocus features.

- **AF Micro-Nikkor 200mm f/4D IF-ED.** With a price tag of about $1,300, you'd probably want this lens only if you planned a great deal of close-up shooting at greater distances. It focuses down to 1.6 feet, and is manual-focus only with the D60, but provides enough magnification to allow interesting close-ups of subjects that are farther away. A specialized tool for specialized shooting.

- **PC Micro-Nikkor 85mm f/2.8D.** Priced about the same as the 200mm Micro-Nikkor, this is a manual focus lens (on *any* camera; it doesn't offer autofocus features) that has both tilt and shift capabilities, so you can adjust the perspective of the subject as you shoot. The tilt feature lets you "tilt" the plane of focus, providing the illusion of greater depth-of-field, while the shift capabilities make it possible to shoot down on a subject from an angle and still maintain its correct proportions. If you need one of these for perspective control, you already know it; if you're still wondering how you'd use one, you probably have no need for these specialized capabilities. However, I have recently watched some very creative fashion and wedding photographers use this lens for portraits, applying the tilting features to throw parts of the image wildly out of focus to concentrate interest on faces, and so forth. None of these are likely pursuits of the average Nikon D60 photographer, but I couldn't resist mentioning this interesting lens.

You'll also find macro lenses, macro zooms, and other close-focusing lenses available from Sigma, Tamron, and Tokina. If you want to focus closer with a macro lens, or any other lens, you can add an accessory called an *extension tube*, like the one shown in Figure 6.14, or a *bellows extension*. These add-ons move the lens farther from the focal plane, allowing it to focus more closely. Nikon also sells add-on close-up lenses, which look like filters, and allow lenses to focus more closely.

Figure 6.14
Extension tubes enable any lens to focus more closely to the subject.

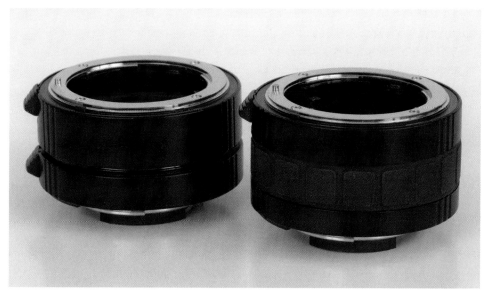

Vibration Reduction

Nikon has a burgeoning line of more than 14 lenses with built-in vibration reduction (VR) capabilities. I probably shouldn't have mentioned a specific number, because I expect another half dozen or so new VR lenses to be introduced rather early in the life of this book.

The VR feature uses lens elements that are shifted internally in response to vertical or horizontal motion of the lens, which compensates for any camera shake in those directions. Vibration reduction is particularly effective when used with telephoto lenses, which magnify the effects of camera and photographer motion. However, VR can be useful for lenses of shorter focal lengths, such as Nikon's 16-85mm and 18-55mm VR lenses. Other Nikon VR lenses provide stabilization with zooms that are as wide as 24mm.

Vibration reduction offers two to three shutter speed increments' worth of shake reduction. (Nikon claims a four-stop gain, which I feel may be optimistic.) This extra margin can be invaluable when you're shooting under dim lighting conditions or hand-holding a lens for, say, wildlife photography. Perhaps that shot of a foraging deer would require a shutter speed of 1/2,000 second at f/5.6 with your AF-S VR Zoom-Nikkor 200-400mm f/4G IF-ED lens. Relax. You can shoot at 1/250 second at f/11 and get a photo that is just as sharp, as long as the deer doesn't decide to bound off. Or, perhaps you're shooting indoors and would prefer to shoot at 1/15 second at f/4. Your 16mm-85mm VR lens can grab the shot for you at its wide-angle position. However, consider these facts:

- **VR doesn't freeze subject motion.** Vibration reduction won't freeze moving subjects in their tracks, because it is effective only at compensating for *camera* motion. It's best used in reduced illumination, to steady the up-down swaying of telephoto lenses, and to improve close-up photography. If your subject is in motion, you'll still need a shutter speed that's fast enough to stop the action.

- **VR adds to shutter lag.** The process of adjusting the lens elements, like autofocus, takes time, so vibration reduction may contribute to a slight increase in shutter lag. If you're shooting sports, that delay may be annoying, but I still use my VR lenses for sports all the time!

- **Use when appropriate.** You may find that your results are worse when using VR while panning, although newer Nikon VR lenses work fine when the camera is deliberately moved from side to side during exposure. Older lenses can confuse the panning motion with camera wobble and provide too much compensation. You might want to switch off VR when panning or when your camera is mounted on a tripod.

■ **Do you need VR at all?** Remember that an inexpensive monopod might be able to provide the same additional steadiness as a VR lens, at a much lower cost. If you're out in the field shooting wild animals or flowers and think a tripod isn't practical, try a monopod first.

The AF-S VR Zoom-Nikkor 70-200mm f/2.8G IF-ED, though atypical for the average D60 owner, is typical of the VR lenses Nikon offers, so I'll use it as an example. It has the basic controls shown in Figure 6.15, to adjust focus range (full, or limited to infinity down to 2.5 meters); VR On/Off; and Normal VR/Active VR (the latter an aggressive mode used in extreme situations, such as a moving car). Not visible (it's over the horizon, so to speak) is the M/A-M focus mode switch, which allows changing from autofocus (with manual override) to manual focus.

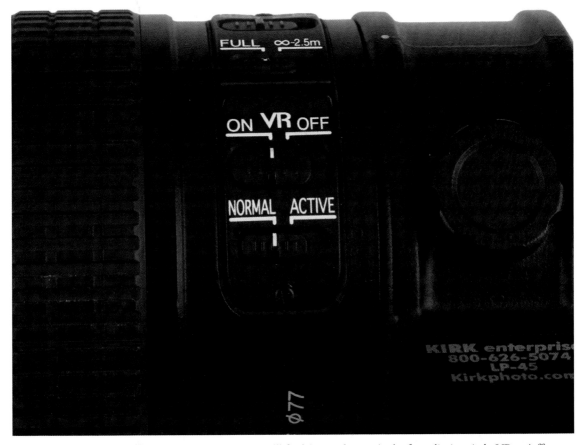

Figure 6.15 On the Nikon 70-200mm VR zoom you'll find (top to bottom): the focus limit switch, VR on/off switch, and Normal/Active VR adjustment.

VIBRATION REDUCTION: IN THE CAMERA OR IN THE LENS?

Sony's acquisition of Konica Minolta's dSLR assets and the introduction of an improved in-camera image-stabilization system has revised an old debate about whether VR belongs in the camera or in the lens. Perhaps it's my Nikon bias showing, but I am quite happy not to have vibration reduction available in the body itself. Here are some reasons:

- Should in-camera VR fail, you have to send the whole camera in for repair, and camera repairs are generally more expensive than lens repairs. I like being able to simply switch to another lens if I have a VR problem.

- VR in the camera doesn't steady your view in the viewfinder, whereas a VR lens shows you a steadied image as you shoot.

- You're stuck with the VR system built into your camera. If an improved system is incorporated into a lens and the improvements are important to you, just trade in your old lens for the new one.

- When building VR in the camera, a compromise system that works with all lenses must be designed. VR in the lens, however, can be custom-tailored to each specific lens's needs.

7

Making Light Work for You

Light is the basic tool of anyone working with a Nikon D60. All forms of visual art use light to shape the finished product. Sculptors don't have control over the light used to illuminate their finished work, so they must create shapes using planes and curved surfaces so that the form envisioned by the artist comes to life from a variety of viewing and lighting angles. Painters, in contrast, have absolute control over both shape and light in their work, as well as the viewing angle, so they can use both the contours of their two-dimensional subjects and the qualities of the "light" they use to illuminate those subjects to evoke the image they want to produce.

Photography is a third form of art. The photographer may have little or no control over the subject (other than posing human subjects) but can often adjust both viewing angle *and* the nature of the light source to create a particular compelling image. The direction and intensity of the light sources create the shapes and textures that we see. The distribution and proportions determine the contrast and tonal values: whether the image is stark or high key, or muted and low in contrast. The colors of the light (because even "white" light has a color balance that the sensor can detect), and how much of those colors the subject reflects or absorbs, paint the hues visible in the image.

As a Nikon D60 photographer, you must learn to be a painter and sculptor of light if you want to move from *taking* a picture to *making* a photograph. This chapter provides an introduction to using the two main types of illumination: *continuous* lighting (such as daylight, incandescent, or fluorescent sources) and the brief, but brilliant snippets of light we call *electronic flash*.

Continuous Illumination versus Electronic Flash

Continuous lighting is exactly what you might think: uninterrupted illumination that is available all the time during a shooting session. Daylight, moonlight, and the artificial lighting encountered both indoors and outdoors count as continuous light sources (although all of them can be "interrupted" by passing clouds, solar eclipses, a blown fuse, or simply by switching a lamp off). Indoor continuous illumination includes both the lights that are there already (such as incandescent lamps or overhead fluorescent lights indoors) and fixtures you supply yourself, including photoflood lamps or reflectors used to bounce existing light onto your subject.

The surge of light we call electronic flash is produced by a burst of photons generated by an electrical charge that is accumulated in a component called a *capacitor* and then directed through a glass tube containing xenon gas, which absorbs the energy and emits the brief flash. Electronic flash is notable because it can be much more intense than continuous lighting, lasts only a brief moment, and can be much more portable than supplementary incandescent sources. It's a light source you can carry with you and use anywhere.

Indeed, your Nikon D60 has a flip-up electronic flash unit built in, as shown in Figure 7.1. But you can also use an external flash, either mounted on the D60's accessory shoe or used off-camera and linked with a cable. Studio flash units are electronic flash, too, and aren't limited to "professional" shooters, as there are economical "monolight" (one-piece flash/power supply) units available in the $200 price range. Anyone can buy a

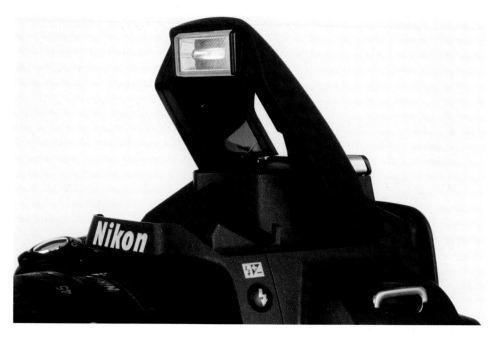

Figure 7.1

One form of light that's always available is the flip-up flash on your Nikon D60.

couple to store in a closet and use to set up a home studio, or use as supplementary lighting when traveling away from home.

There are advantages and disadvantages to each type of illumination. Here's a quick checklist of pros and cons:

- **Lighting preview—Pro: continuous lighting.** With continuous lighting, you always know exactly what kind of lighting effect you're going to get and, if multiple lights are used, how they will interact with each other. With electronic flash, the general effect you're going to see may be a mystery until you've built some experience, and you may need to review a shot on the LCD, make some adjustments, and then reshoot to get the look you want. (In this sense, a digital camera's review capabilities replace the Polaroid test shots pro photographers relied on in decades past. Today, many would use a laptop if the camera's LCD display wasn't detailed enough.)

- **Lighting preview—Con: electronic flash.** While the external units like the Nikon SB-800 have a modeling light function (consisting of a series of low-powered bursts that flash for a period of time), this feature is no substitute for continuous illumination, or an always-on modeling lamp like that found in studio flash. As the number of flash units increases, lighting previews, especially if you want to see the proportions of illumination provided by each flash, grows more complex.

- **Exposure calculation—Pro: continuous lighting.** Your D60 has no problem calculating exposure for continuous lighting, because it remains constant and can be measured through the 420-segment sensor that interprets the light reaching the viewfinder. The amount of light available just before the exposure will, in almost all cases, be the same amount of light present when the shutter is released.

- **Exposure calculation—Con: electronic flash.** Electronic flash illumination doesn't exist until the flash fires and so can't be measured by the D60's 420-segment sensor when the mirror is flipped up during the exposure. Instead, the light must be measured by metering the intensity of a *preflash* which is triggered an instant before the main flash, and then reflected back to the camera and through the lens. An alternative is to use a sensor built into the flash itself (which is an option for the Nikon SB-800 unit) and measure reflected light that has not traveled through the lens.

- **Action stopping—Con: continuous lighting.** Action stopping with continuous light sources is completely dependent on the shutter speed you've dialed in on the camera. And the speeds you can use depend on the amount of light available and your ISO sensitivity setting. Outdoors in daylight, there will probably be enough sunlight to let you shoot at 1/2000 second and f/6.3 with a non-grainy sensitivity setting of ISO 400. But inside, the reduced illumination quickly has you pushing your Nikon D60 to its limits. For example, if you're shooting indoor sports, there probably won't be enough available light to allow you to use shutter speeds faster than 1/500 second.

- **Action stopping—Pro: electronic flash.** When it comes to the ability to freeze moving objects in their tracks, the advantage goes to electronic flash. The brief duration of electronic flash serves as a very high "shutter speed" when the flash is the main or only source of illumination for the photo. Your Nikon D60's shutter speed may be set for 1/200th second during a flash exposure, but if the flash illumination predominates, the *effective* exposure time will be the 1/1,000 to 1/50,000 second or less duration of the flash, as you can see in Figure 7.2, because the flash unit reduces the amount of light released by cutting short the duration of the flash. The only fly in the ointment is that, if the ambient light is strong enough, it may produce a secondary "ghost" exposure, as I'll explain later in this chapter.

- **Cost—Pro: continuous lighting.** Incandescent or fluorescent lamps are generally much less expensive than electronic flash units, which can easily cost several hundred dollars. I've used everything from desktop hi-intensity lamps to reflector floodlights for continuous illumination at very little cost. There are lamps made especially for photographic purposes, too, priced up to $50 or so. Maintenance is economical, too: many incandescent or fluorescents use bulbs that cost only a few dollars.

- **Cost—Con: electronic flash.** Electronic flash units aren't particularly cheap. The lowest-cost dedicated flash designed specifically for the Nikon dSLRs is the Nikon SB-400 (about $110, plus about $18 for the almost-mandatory diffuser dome). If you want a more capable flash, the powerful and versatile SB-800 costs about $315 including the light-softening diffuser dome and some filters to modify the color of the flash illumination. Studio flash are priced at $200-$500 and up, and you can also purchase third-party shoe-mount units at prices comparable to the Nikon brand. Plan on spending some money to get the features that external electronic flash offers.

- **Flexibility—Con: continuous lighting.** Because incandescent and fluorescent lamps are not as bright as electronic flash, the slower shutter speeds required (see Action stopping, above) mean that you may have to use a tripod more often, especially when shooting portraits. The incandescent variety of continuous lighting can get hot, and the side effects range from discomfort (for your human subjects) to disintegration (if you happen to be shooting perishable foods like ice cream). The heat also makes it more difficult to add filtration to incandescent sources. That's why photographers who use continuous lighting often turn to daylight-equivalent fluorescents.

- **Flexibility—Pro: electronic flash.** Electronic flash's action-freezing power allows you to work without a tripod, adding flexibility and speed when choosing angles and positions. Flash units can be easily filtered, and, because the filtration is placed over the light source rather than the lens, you don't need to use high quality filter material. For example, Roscoe or Lee lighting gels, which may be too flimsy to use in front of the lens, can be mounted or taped in front of your flash with ease.

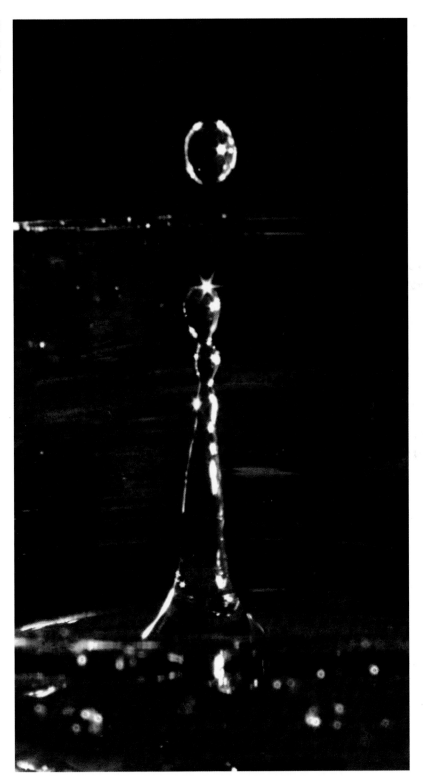

Continuous Lighting Basics

While continuous lighting and its effects are generally much easier to visualize and use than electronic flash, there are some factors you need to take into account, particularly the color temperature of the light. (Color temperature concerns aren't exclusive to continuous light sources, of course, but the variations tend to be more extreme and less predictable than those of electronic flash, which output relatively consistent daylight-like illumination.)

Color temperature, in practical terms, is how "bluish" or how "reddish" the light appears to be to the digital camera's sensor. Indoor illumination is quite warm, comparatively, and appears reddish to the sensor. Daylight, in contrast, seems much bluer to the sensor. Our eyes (our brains, actually) are quite adaptable to these variations, so white objects don't appear to have an orange tinge when viewed indoors, nor do they seem excessively blue outdoors in full daylight. Yet, these color temperature variations are real and the sensor is not fooled. To capture the most accurate colors, we need to take the color temperature into account in setting the color balance (or *white balance*) of the D60—either automatically using the camera's smarts or manually using our own knowledge and experience.

When using the Nikon D60, you don't need to think in terms of actual color temperature, because the camera won't let you set white balance using color temperature values, which are measured in *degrees Kelvin*. But it is useful to know that warmer (more reddish) color temperatures (measured in degrees Kelvin) are the *lower* numbers, while cooler (bluer) color temperatures are *higher* numbers. It might not make sense to say that 3,400K is warmer than 6,000K, but that's the way it is. If it helps, think of a glowing red ember contrasted with a white-hot welder's torch, rather than fire and ice.

You can set white balance by type of illumination, and then fine-tune it in the D60 using the Shooting menu's White Balance option, as described in Chapter 3. In most cases, however, the Nikon D60 will do an acceptable job of calculating white balance for you, so Auto can be used as your choice most of the time. Use the preset values or set a custom white balance that matches the current shooting conditions when you need to. The only really problematic light sources are likely to be fluorescents. Vendors, such as GE and Sylvania, may actually provide a figure known as the *color rendering index* (or CRI), which is a measure of how accurately a particular light source represents standard colors, using a scale of 0 (some sodium-vapor lamps) to 100 (daylight and most incandescent lamps). Daylight fluorescents and deluxe cool white fluorescents might have a CRI of about 79 to 95, which is perfectly acceptable for most photographic applications. Warm white fluorescents might have a CRI of 55. White deluxe mercury vapor lights are less suitable with a CRI of 45, while low-pressure sodium lamps can vary from CRI 0-18.

Remember that if you shoot RAW, you can specify the white balance of your image when you import it into Photoshop, Photoshop Elements, or another image editor using Nikon Capture NX, Adobe Camera RAW, or your preferred RAW converter. While color-balancing filters that fit on the front of the lens exist, they are primarily useful for film cameras, because film's color balance can't be tweaked as extensively as that of a sensor.

Daylight

Daylight is produced by the sun, and so is moonlight (which is just reflected sunlight). Daylight is present, of course, even when you can't see the sun. When sunlight is direct, it can be bright and harsh. If daylight is diffused by clouds, softened by bouncing off objects such as walls or your photo reflectors, or filtered by shade, it can be much dimmer and less contrasty.

Daylight's color temperature can vary quite widely. It is highest in temperature (most blue) at noon when the sun is directly overhead, because the light is traveling through a minimum amount of the filtering layer we call the atmosphere. The color temperature at high noon may be 6,000K. At other times of day, the sun is lower in the sky and the particles in the air provide a filtering effect that warms the illumination to about 5,500K for most of the day. Starting an hour before dusk and for an hour after sunrise, the warm appearance of the sunlight is even visible to our eyes when the color temperature may dip to 5,000-4,500K, as shown in Figure 7.3.

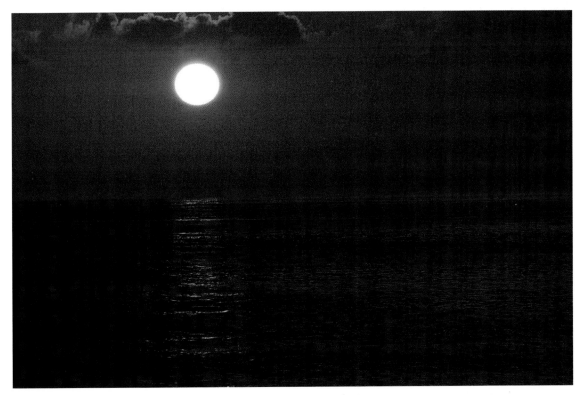

Figure 7.3 At dawn and dusk, the color temperature of daylight may dip as low as 4,500K, and at sunset can go even lower.

Incandescent/Tungsten Light

The term incandescent or tungsten illumination is usually applied to the direct descendents of Thomas Edison's original electric lamp. Such lights consist of a glass bulb that contains a vacuum, or is filled with a halogen gas, and contains a tungsten filament that is heated by an electrical current, producing photons and heat. Tungsten-halogen lamps are a variation on the basic light bulb, using a more rugged (and longer-lasting) filament that can be heated to a higher temperature, housed in a thicker glass or quartz envelope, and filled with iodine or bromine ("halogen") gases. The higher temperature allows tungsten-halogen (or quartz-halogen/quartz-iodine, depending on their construction) lamps to burn "hotter" and whiter. Although popular for automobile headlamps today, they've also been used for photographic illumination.

The other qualities of this type of lighting, such as contrast, are dependent on the distance of the lamp from the subject, type of reflectors used, and other factors that I'll explain later in this chapter.

Fluorescent Light/Other Light Sources

Fluorescent light has some advantages in terms of illumination, but some disadvantages from a photographic standpoint. This type of lamp generates light through an electro-chemical reaction that emits most of its energy as visible light, rather than heat, which is why the bulbs don't get as hot. The type of light produced varies depending on the phosphor coatings and type of gas in the tube. So, the illumination fluorescent bulbs produce can vary widely in its characteristics.

That's not great news for photographers. Different types of lamps have different "color temperatures" that can't be precisely measured in degrees Kelvin, because the light isn't produced by heating. Worse, fluorescent lamps have a discontinuous spectrum of light that can have some colors missing entirely. A particular type of tube can lack certain shades of red or other colors (see Figure 7.4), which is why fluorescent lamps and other alternative technologies such as sodium-vapor illumination can produce ghastly looking human skin tones if the white balance isn't set correctly. Their spectra can lack the reddish tones we associate with healthy skin and emphasize the blues and greens popular in horror movies.

There *is* good news, however. There are special fluorescent lamps compatible with the Spiderlites sold through dealers affiliated with the F. J. Westcott Company (www.fjwestcott.com), designed especially for photography, with the color balance and other properties required. They can be used for direct light, placed in softboxes (described later), and used in other ways.

Figure 7.4
The uncorrected fluorescent lighting in the room added a distinct greenish cast to this image when exposed with a daylight white balance setting.

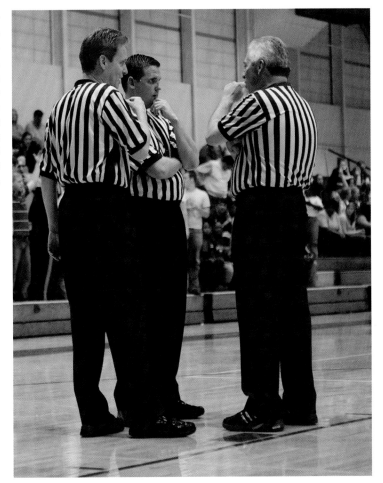

Electronic Flash Basics

You'll often hear that flash photography is less natural looking, and that the built-in flash in most cameras should never be used as the primary source of illumination because it provides a harsh, garish look. Indeed, the most advanced "pro" cameras like the Nikon D2xs and D3 don't have a built-in flash at all.

In truth, however, the bias is against *bad* flash photography. Indeed, flash has become the studio light source of choice for many pro photographers, because it's more intense (and its intensity can be varied to order by the photographer), freezes action, frees you from using a tripod (unless you want to use one to lock down a composition), and has a snappy, consistent light quality that matches daylight. The built-in flash of the Nikon D60 has some important uses as an adjunct to existing light, particularly to fill in dark shadows.

But electronic flash isn't as inherently easy to use as continuous lighting. As I noted earlier, electronic flash units are more expensive, don't show you exactly what the lighting effect will be (unless you use a second source or mode called a *modeling light* for a preview), and the exposure of electronic flash units is more difficult to calculate accurately.

For the pop-up flash built into the Nikon D60, the full burst of light lasts about 1/1,000th second and provides enough illumination to shoot a subject 10 feet away at f/5.6 using the ISO 200 setting. As you can see, the built-in flash is somewhat limited in range; you'll realize why external flash units are often a good idea later in this chapter.

An electronic flash is triggered at the instant of exposure, during a period when the sensor is fully exposed by the shutter. As I mentioned earlier in this book, the D60 has a vertically traveling shutter that consists of two curtains. The first curtain opens and moves to the opposite side of the frame, at which point the shutter is completely open. The flash can be triggered at this point (so-called *front-curtain sync*), making the flash exposure. Then, after a delay that can vary from 30 seconds to 1/200th second (with the Nikon D60; other cameras may sync at a faster or slower speed), a second curtain begins moving across the sensor plane, covering up the sensor again. If the flash is triggered just before the second curtain starts to close, then *second-curtain sync* is used. (I'll describe these in more detail later in this chapter.) In both cases, though, a shutter speed of 1/200th second is ordinarily the maximum that can be used to take a photo. If you use a faster shutter speed, you'll expose only the part of the sensor exposed by the gap between the shutter curtains when the flash fires.

Determining Exposure

Calculating the proper exposure for an electronic flash photograph is a bit more complicated than determining the settings for continuous light. The right exposure isn't simply a function of how far away your subject is (which the D60 can figure out based on the autofocus distance that's locked in just prior to taking the picture). Various objects reflect more or less light at the same distance so, obviously, the camera needs to measure the amount of light reflected back and through the lens. Yet, as the flash itself isn't available for measuring until it's triggered, the D60 has nothing to measure.

The solution is to fire the flash twice. The initial shot is a *monitor preflash* that can be analyzed, then followed virtually instantaneously by a main flash (to the eye the bursts appear to be a single flash) that's given exactly the calculated intensity needed to provide a correct exposure. As a result, the primary flash may be longer in duration for distant objects and shorter in duration for closer subjects, depending on the required intensity for exposure. This through-the-lens evaluative flash exposure system is called i-TTL (intelligent Through The Lens), and it operates whenever the pop-up internal flash is used, or you have attached a Nikon dedicated flash unit to the D60.

Guide Numbers

Guide numbers, usually abbreviated GN, are a way of specifying the power of an electronic flash in a way that can be used to determine the right f/stop to use at a particular shooting distance and ISO setting. In fact, before automatic flash units became prevalent, the GN was actually used to do just that. A GN is usually given as a pair of numbers for both feet and meters that represent the range at ISO 100. For example, the Nikon D60's built-in flash has a GN in i-TTL mode of 12/39 (meters/feet) at ISO 100. In Manual mode, the true guide number is a fraction higher: 13/43 meters/feet. To calculate the right exposure at that ISO setting, you'd divide the guide number by the distance to arrive at the appropriate f/stop.

Using the D60's built-in flash as an example, at ISO 100 with its GN of 43 in manual mode, if you wanted to shoot a subject at a distance of 10 feet, you'd use f/4.3. (43 divided by 10), or, in practice, f/4.0. At 5 feet, an f/stop of f/8 would be used. Some quick mental calculations with the GN will give you any particular electronic flash's range. You can easily see that the built-in flash would begin to peter out at about 13 feet if you stuck to the lowest ISO of 100, because you'd need an aperture of f/2.8. Of course, in the real world you'd probably bump the sensitivity up to a setting of ISO 800 so you could use a more practical f/8 at 13 feet, and the flash would be effective all the way out to 20 feet or more at wider f/stops.

Today, guide numbers are most useful for comparing the power of various flash units, rather than actually calculating what exposure to use. You don't need to be a math genius to see that an electronic flash with a GN in feet of, say, 125 at ISO 100 (like the SB-800) would be *a lot* more powerful than your built-in flash. At ISO 100, you could use f/5.6 to shoot as far as 22 feet.

Flash Metering Mode

The built-in flash in the Nikon D60, as well as external flash units attached to the camera, use the same three metering modes that are available for continuous light sources: Matrix, Center-Weighted, and Spot. You can choose a metering mode based on the same subject factors as those explained in Chapter 4 (for example, use Spot metering to measure exposure from an isolated subject within the frame). Choice of a metering mode determines how the flash reacts to balance the existing light with the light from the electronic unit:

- **iTTL Balanced Fill-in flash.** This flash mode is used when you choose Matrix or Center-Weighted exposure metering. The Nikon D60 measures the available light and then adjusts the flash output to produce a natural balance between main subject and background. This setting is useful for most photographic situations.

■ **Standard i-TTL Fill-flash.** This mode is activated when you use Spot metering or choose the standard mode with an external flash unit's controls. The flash output adjusted only for the main subject of your photograph, and the brightness of the background is not factored in. Use this mode when you want to emphasize the main subject at the expense of proper exposure for the background.

Choosing a Flash Sync Mode

The Nikon D60 has five flash sync modes, with icons resembling those shown in Figure 7.5, which determine when and how the flash is fired (as I'll explain shortly). They are selected from the Quick Settings screen, or by holding down the Flash button on the front of the camera lens housing while rotating the command dial. In both cases, the mode chosen appears in the Quick Settings screen as the selection is made.

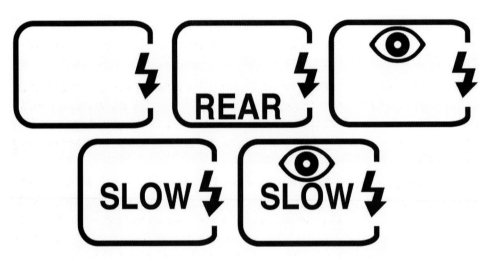

Figure 7.5
The icons representing the sync modes found in the D60 include (top row, left to right), Front-curtain sync/Auto, Rear-curtain sync, Red-eye reduction, and (bottom row, left to right), Slow sync, and Slow sync with red-eye reduction.

Not all sync modes are available with all exposure modes. Depending on whether you're using DVP/Scene modes, or Program, Aperture Priority, Shutter Priority, or Manual exposure modes, one or more of the following sync modes may not be available. I'm going to list the sync options available for each exposure mode separately, although that produces a little duplication among the options that are available with several exposure modes. However, this approach should reduce the confusion over which sync method is available with which exposure mode.

In Program and Aperture Priority modes you can select these flash modes:

- **Front-curtain sync/fill flash.** In this mode, represented by a lightning bolt symbol, the flash fires as soon as the front curtain opens completely. The shutter then remains open for the duration of the exposure, until the rear curtain closes. If the subject is moving and ambient light levels are high enough, the movement will cause a secondary "ghost" exposure that appears to be a stream of light advancing ahead of the flash exposure of the same subject. You'll find more on "ghost" exposures next.

- **Rear-curtain sync.** With this setting, the front curtain opens completely and remains open for the duration of the exposure. Then, the flash is fired and the rear curtain closes. If the subject is moving and ambient light levels are high enough, the movement will cause a secondary "ghost" exposure that appears to stream *behind* the flash exposure. In Program and Aperture Priority modes, the D60 will combine rear-curtain sync with slow shutter speeds (just like slow sync, discussed below) to balance ambient light with flash illumination. (It's best to use a tripod to avoid blur at these slow shutter speeds.)

- **Red-eye reduction.** In this mode, there is a one-second lag after pressing the shutter release before the picture is actually taken, during which the D60's red-eye reduction lamp lights, causing the subject's pupils to contract (assuming they are looking at the camera), and thus reducing potential red-eye effects. Don't use with moving subjects or when you can't abide the delay.

- **Slow sync.** This setting allows the D60 in Program and Aperture Priority modes to use shutter speeds as slow as 30 seconds with the flash to help balance a background illuminated with ambient light with your main subject, which will be lit by the electronic flash. You'll want to use a tripod at slower shutter speeds, of course. As shown in Figure 7.6, it's common that the ambient light will be incandescent illumination that's much warmer than the electronic flash's "daylight" balance, so, if you want the two sources to match, you may want to use a warming filter on the flash. That can be done with a gel if you're using an external flash like the SB-800, or by taping an appropriate warm filter over the D60's built-in flash. (That's not a convenient approach, and many find the warm/cool mismatch unobjectionable and don't bother with filtration.)

- **Red-eye reduction with slow sync.** This mode combines slow sync with the D60's red-eye reduction behavior when using Program or Aperture Priority modes.

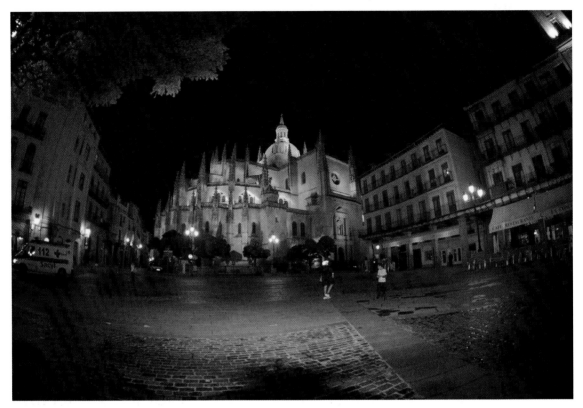

Figure 7.6 I deliberately used flash and slow sync with a scene otherwise illuminated by tungsten light to create this unconventional mixed-lighting image.

In Shutter Priority and Manual exposure modes, you can select the following three flash synchronization settings:

- **Front-curtain sync/fill flash.** This setting should be your default setting. This mode is also available in Program and Aperture priority mode, as described above, and, with high ambient light levels, can produce ghost images, as discussed below.

- **Red-eye reduction.** This mode, with its one-second lag and red-eye lamp flash, is described above.

- **Rear-curtain sync.** As noted previously, in this sync mode, the front curtain opens completely and remains open for the duration of the exposure. Then, the flash is fired and the rear curtain closes. If the subject is moving and ambient light levels are high enough, the movement will cause that "ghost" exposure that appears to be trailing the flash exposure.

In Auto, Portrait, Child, and Close-Up DVP/Scene modes, the following flash sync options are available:

- **Auto.** This setting is the same as front-curtain sync, but the flash pops up automatically in dim lighting conditions.

- **Red-eye reduction auto.** In this mode, there is a one-second lag after pressing the shutter release before the picture is actually taken, during which the D60's red-eye reduction lamp lights, causing the subject's pupils to contract (assuming they are looking at the camera), and thus reducing potential red-eye effects. Don't use with moving subjects or when you can't abide the delay.

- **Flash off.** This is not really a sync setting, although it is available from the same selection screen. It disables the flash for those situations in which you absolutely do not want it to pop up and fire.

In Night Portrait mode, only slow synchronization flash and flash off modes are available:

- **Slow sync.** This setting allows the D60 to select shutter speeds as slow as 30 seconds with the flash to help balance a background illuminated with ambient light with your main subject, which will be lit by the electronic flash. Best for shooting pictures at night when the subjects in the foreground are important, and you want to avoid a pitch-black background. I recommend using a tripod in this mode.

- **Red-eye reduction with slow sync.** Another mode that calls for a tripod, this sync setting mode combines slow sync with the D60's red-eye reduction preflash. This is the one to use when your subjects are people who will be facing the camera.

- **Flash off.** Disables the flash in museums, concerts, religious ceremonies, and other situations in which you absolutely do not want it to pop up and fire.

Ghost Images

The difference might not seem like much, but whether you use front-curtain sync (which is the default setting for all sync modes except rear sync) or rear-curtain sync can make a significant difference to your photograph *if the ambient light in your scene also contributes to the image.* At faster shutter speeds, particularly 1/200th second, there isn't much time for the ambient light to register, unless it is very bright. It's likely that the electronic flash will provide almost all the illumination, so first-curtain sync or second-curtain sync isn't very important.

However, at slower shutter speeds, or with very bright ambient light levels, there is a significant difference, particularly if your subject is moving, or the camera isn't steady. In any of those situations, the ambient light will register as a second image accompanying the flash exposure, and if there is movement (camera or subject), that additional image will not be in the same place as the flash exposure. It will show as a ghost image and, if the movement is significant enough, as a blurred ghost image trailing in front of or behind your subject in the direction of the movement.

As I mentioned earlier, when you're using first-curtain sync, the flash goes off the instant the shutter opens, producing an image of the subject on the sensor. Then, the shutter remains open for an additional period (which can be from 30 seconds to 1/200th second). If your subject is moving, say, towards the right side of the frame, the ghost image produced by the ambient light will produce a blur on the right side of the original subject image, making it look as if your sharp (flash-produced) image is chasing the ghost. For those of us who grew up with lightning-fast superheroes that always left a ghost trail *behind them*, that looks unnatural (see Figure 7.7).

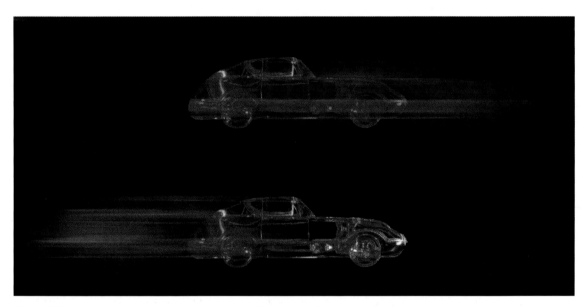

Figure 7.7 Front-curtain sync produces an image that trails in front of the flash exposure (top), while rear-curtain sync creates a more "natural looking" trail behind the flash image (bottom).

So, Nikon provides rear- (second) curtain sync to remedy the situation. In that mode, the shutter opens, as before. The shutter remains open for its designated duration, and the ghost image forms. If your subject moves from the left side of the frame to the right side, the ghost will move from left to right, too. *Then*, about 1.5 milliseconds before the second shutter curtain closes, the flash is triggered, producing a nice, sharp flash image *ahead* of the ghost image. Voilà! We have monsieur *le Flash* outrunning his own trailing image (perhaps to catch up with his streaking auto shown in the figure).

EVERY WHICH WAY, INCLUDING UP

Note that, although I describe the ghost effect in terms of subject matter that is moving left to right in a horizontally oriented composition, it can occur in any orientation, and with the subject moving in *any* direction. (Try photographing a falling rock, if you can, and you'll see the same effect.) Nor are the ghost images affected by the fact that modern shutters travel vertically rather than horizontally. Secondary images are caused between the time the first curtain fully opens, and the second curtain begins to close. The direction of travel of the shutter curtains, or the direction of your subject does not matter.

Working with Nikon Flash Units

If you want to work with dedicated Nikon flash units, at this time you have five choices: the D60's built-in flash, the Nikon SB-800, SB-600, SB-400 on-camera flash units, and the SB-R200 wireless remote flash. These share certain features, which I'll discuss while pointing out differences among them. Nikon may introduce additional flash units during the life of this book, but the current batch and the Nikon Creative Lighting System ushered in with them were significant steps forward, so I don't expect any major changes in the near future.

Nikon D60 Built-in Flash

In automatic mode, the built-in flash has a guide number of 12/39 (meters/feet) at ISO 100, and must be activated by manually flipping it up when not using one of the DVP/Scene modes that feature automatic pop-up. This flash is powerful enough to provide primary direct flash illumination when required, but can't be angled up for diffuse bounce flash off the ceiling. It's useful for balanced fill flash, but, unlike other Nikon cameras you might have used, does *not* operate in Commander mode, which allows the built-in flash to trigger one or more off-camera flash units. You can use manual flash mode and **CSM #14** to dial down the intensity of the built-in flash to 1/32 power.

Because the built-in flash draws its power from the D60's battery, extensive use will reduce the power available to take pictures. For that reason alone, use of an external flash unit can be a good idea when you plan to take a lot of flash pictures.

Nikon SB-800

The Nikon SB-800 (see Figure 7.8) is currently the flagship of the Nikon flash line up, and has a guide number of 38/125 (meters/feet) when the "zooming" flash head (which can be set to adjust the coverage angle of the lens) is set to the 35mm position. It has all the features of the D60's flash unit, but with the addition of Commander mode, repeating flash, modeling light, and selectable power output, along with some extra capabilities.

For example, you can angle the flash and rotate it to provide bounce flash. It includes additional, non-through-the-lens exposure modes, thanks to its built-in light sensor, and can "zoom" and diffuse its coverage angle to illuminate the field of view of lenses from 16mm to 70mm on a D60 (24mm to 105mm on a full-frame camera), plus 14mm with an included diffuser. The SB-800 also has its own powerful focus assist lamp to aid autofocus in dim lighting, and has reduced red-eye effects simply because the unit, when attached to the D60, is mounted in a higher position that tends to eliminate reflections from the eye back to the camera lens.

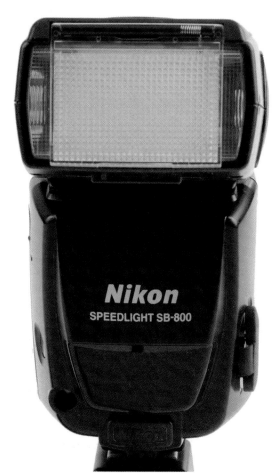

Figure 7.8
The Nikon SB-800 is currently the flagship of the Nikon electronic flash line up.

Nikon SB-600

This lower-cost unit (see Figure 7.9) has a guide number of 30/98 (meters/feet) when set to the 35mm zoom position. It has many of the SB-800's features, including zoomable flash coverage equal to the field of view of a 16-56mm lens on the D60 (24-85mm settings with a full-frame camera), and 14mm with a built-in diffuser panel. It has a built-in modeling flash feature, but lacks repeating flash, accessory filters, and an included flash diffuser dome, which can be purchased separately.

Figure 7.9
The Nikon SB-600 is a popular medium-priced electronic flash with most of the features of the SB-800, except for Commander mode to control remote units.

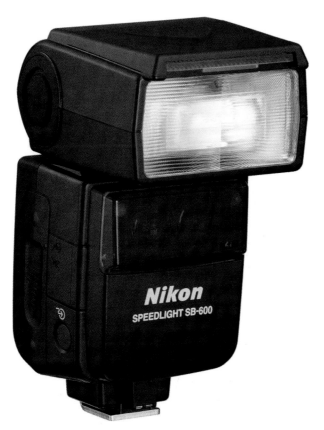

Nikon SB-400

The entry-level SB-400 (see Figure 7.10) is a good choice for most Nikon D60 applications. It's built specifically for entry-level Nikon cameras like the D40 or D60, and has a limited, easy-to-use feature set. It has a limited ISO 100 guide number of 21/68 at the 18mm zoom-head position. It tilts up for bounce flash to 90 degrees, with click detents at the 0, 60, 75, and 90 degree marks. Unless you feel the need for an emergency flash or fill-flash unit that's only slightly more powerful than the D60's built-in flash, for the most flexibility, you might want to consider the SB-600.

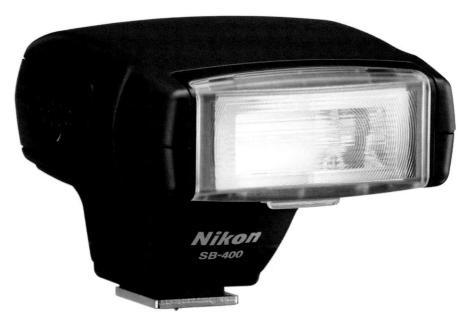

Figure 7.10
The Nikon SB-400 is an entry-level flash best suited for Nikon's entry-level dSLRs.

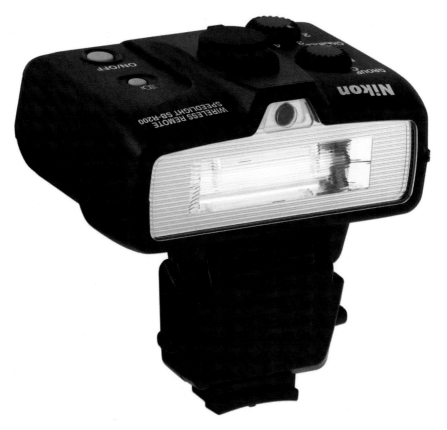

Figure 7.11
The Nikon SB-R200 is a wireless macro-only flash supplied with the Nikon R1 and R1C1 Wireless Close-Up Speedlight systems.

Nikon SB-R200

This is a specialized wireless-only flash (see Figure 7.11) that's especially useful for close-up photography, and is often purchased in pairs for use with the Nikon R1 and R1C1 Wireless Close-Up Speedlight systems. Its output power is low at 10/33 (meters/feet) for ISO 100 as you might expect for a unit used to photograph subjects that are often inches from the camera. It has a fixed coverage angle of 78 degrees horizontal and 60 degrees vertical, but the flash head tilts down to 60 degrees and up to 45 degrees (with detents every 15 degrees in both directions). In this case, "up" and "down" has a different meaning, because the SB-R200 can be mounted on the SX-1 Attachment Ring mounted around the lens, so the pair of flash units are on the sides and titled towards or away from the optical axis. It supports i-TTL, D-TTL, TTL (for film cameras), and Manual modes.

Connecting External Flash

You have three basic choices for linking an external flash unit to your Nikon D60. They are as follows:

- **Mount on the accessory shoe.** Sliding a compatible flash unit into the Nikon D60's accessory shoe provides a direct connection. With a Nikon dedicated flash, all functions of the flash are supported.

- **Connect to the accessory shoe with a cable.** The Nikon SC-28 (see Figure 7.12) and SC-29 TTL coiled remote cords have an accessory shoe on one end of a nine-foot cable to accept a flash, and a foot that slides into the camera accessory shoe on the other end, providing a link that is the same as when the flash is mounted directly on the camera. The SC-29 version also includes a focus assist lamp, like that on the camera and SB-800.

- **Wireless link.** A Nikon electronic flash can be triggered by another Master flash such as the Nikon SB-800 in Commander mode or by the RU-800 infrared unit.

Using Flash Exposure Compensation

If you are using Program, Shutter Priority, Aperture Priority, or Manual exposure modes, you can manually add or subtract exposure to the flash exposure calculated by the D60. Just hold down the Flash button on the camera at the same time as the Exposure Compensation button (just southeast of the shutter release) and rotate the command dial until the amount of exposure compensation you want appears on the Quick Setting screen. You can also use the Quick Setting screen directly, and navigate to the Flash Exposure compensation icon. Finally, flash exposure compensation can also be set from the Custom Setting menu, **CSM #8.**

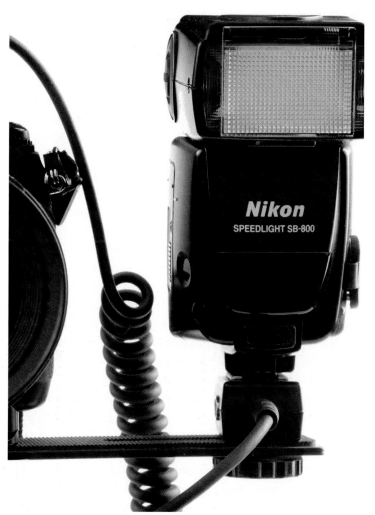

You can make adjustments from –3EV to +1EV in 1/3 EV increments. As with ordinary exposure compensation, the adjustment you make remains in effect until you zero it out by pressing the Flash button and rotating the sub-command dial until 0 appears on the monochrome control panel and in the viewfinder.

More Advanced Lighting Techniques

As you advance in your Nikon D60 photography, you'll want to learn more sophisticated lighting techniques, using more than just straight-on flash, or using just a single flash unit. Entire books have been written on lighting techniques, and I've written multiple chapters on them in books of my own. I'm going to provide a quick introduction to some of the techniques you should be considering.

Diffusing and Softening the Light

Direct light can be harsh and glaring, especially if you're using the flash built into your camera, or an auxiliary flash mounted in the hot shoe and pointed directly at your subject. The first thing you should do is stop using direct light (unless you're looking for a stark, contrasty appearance as a creative effect). There are a number of simple things you can do with both continuous and flash illumination.

■ **Use window light.** Light coming in a window can be soft and flattering, and a good choice for human subjects. Move your subject close enough to the window that its light provides the primary source of illumination. You might want to turn off other lights in the room, particularly to avoid mixing daylight and incandescent light. (See Figure 7.13.)

Figure 7.13
Window light makes the perfect diffuse illumination for informal soft-focus portraits like this one.

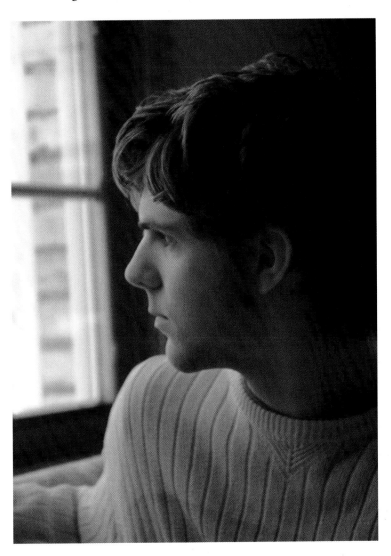

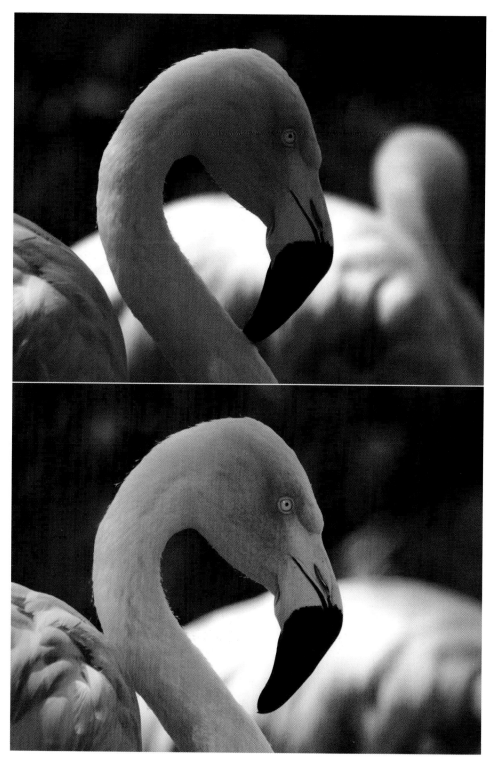

Figure 7.14
The flamingo (top) was in shadow. Fill flash (bottom) brightened up the bird, while adding a little catch light to its eye.

- **Use fill light.** Your D60's built-in flash makes a perfect fill-in light for the shadows, brightening inky depths with a kicker of illumination. (See Figure 7.14.)

- **Bounce the light.** External electronic flash units mounted on the D60 usually have a swivel that allows them to be pointed up at a ceiling for a bounce light effect. You can also bounce the light off a wall. You'll want the ceiling or wall to be white or have a neutral gray color to avoid a color cast.

- **Use reflectors.** Another way to bounce the light is to use reflectors or umbrellas that you can position yourself to provide a greater degree of control over the quantity and direction of the bounced light. Good reflectors can be pieces of foamboard, Mylar, or a reflective disk held in place by a clamp and stand. Although some expensive umbrellas and reflectors are available, spending a lot isn't necessary. A simple piece of white foamboard does the job beautifully. Umbrellas have the advantage of being compact and foldable, while providing a soft, even kind of light. They're relatively cheap, too, with a good 40-inch umbrella available for as little as $20.

- **Use diffusers.** Nikon supplies a Sto-Fen-style diffuser dome with the SB-800 flash. You can purchase a similar diffuser for the SB-600 from Nikon, Sto-Fen, and some other vendors that offer clip-on diffusers. The two examples shown in Figures 7.15 and 7.16 fit over your electronic flash head and provide a soft, flattering light. These add-ons are more portable than umbrellas and other reflectors, yet provide a nice diffuse lighting effect.

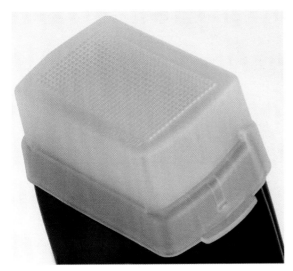

Figure 7.15 This diffuser dome is provided by Nikon with the SB-800, and softens the light of an external flash unit.

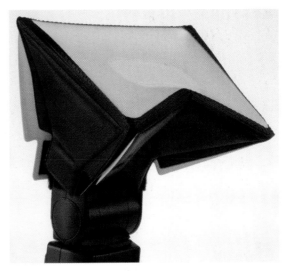

Figure 7.16 Softboxes use Velcro strips to attach them to just about any shoe-mount flash unit.

Using Multiple Light Sources

Once you gain control over the qualities and effects you get with a single light source, you'll want to graduate to using multiple light sources. Using several lights allows you to shape and mold the illumination of your subjects to provide a variety of effects, from backlighting to side lighting to more formal portrait lighting. You can start simply with several incandescent light sources, bounced off umbrellas or reflectors that you construct. Or you can use more flexible multiple electronic flash setups.

Effective lighting is the one element that differentiates great photography from candid or snapshot shooting. Lighting can make a mundane subject look a little more glamorous. Make subjects appear to be soft when you want a soft look, or bright and sparkly when you want a vivid look, or strong and dramatic if that's what you desire. As you might guess, having control over your lighting means that you probably can't use the lights that are already in the room. You'll need separate, discrete lighting fixtures that can be moved, aimed, brightened, and dimmed on command.

Selecting your lighting gear will depend on the type of photography you do, and the budget you have to support it. It's entirely possible for a beginning D60 photographer to create a basic, inexpensive lighting system capable of delivering high-quality results for a few hundred dollars, just as you can spend megabucks ($1,000 and up) for a sophisticated lighting system.

Basic Flash Setups

If you want to use multiple electronic flash units, the Nikon Speedlights described earlier will serve admirably. The higher-end models can be used with Nikon's wireless i-TTL features, which allow you to set up to three separate groups of flash units (several flashes can be included in each group) and trigger them using a master flash and the camera. Just set up one master unit, and arrange the compatible slave units around your subject. You can set the relative power of each unit separately, thereby controlling how much of the scene's illumination comes from the main flash, and how much from the auxiliary flash units, which can be used as fill flash, background lights, or, if you're careful, to illuminate the hair of portrait subjects.

Studio Flash

If you're serious about using multiple flash units, a studio flash setup might be more practical. The traditional studio flash is a multi-part unit, consisting of a flash head that mounts on your light stand, and is tethered to an AC (or sometimes battery) power supply. A single power supply can feed two or more flash heads at a time, with separate control over the output of each head.

When they are operating off AC power, studio flash don't have to be frugal with the juice, and are often powerful enough to illuminate very large subjects or to supply lots and lots of light to smaller subjects. The output of such units is measured in watt seconds (ws), so you could purchase a 200ws, 400ws, or 800ws unit, and a power pack to match.

Their advantages include greater power output, much faster recycling, built-in modeling lamps, multiple power levels, and ruggedness that can stand up to transport, because many photographers pack up these kits and tote them around as location lighting rigs. Studio lighting kits can range in price from a few hundred dollars for a set of lights, stands, and reflectors, to thousands for a high-end lighting system complete with all the necessary accessories.

A more practical choice these days are *monolights* (see Figure 7.17), which are "all-in-one" studio lights that sell for about $200-$400. They have the flash tube, modeling light, and power supply built into a single unit that can be mounted on a light stand. Monolights are available in AC-only and battery-pack versions, although an external battery eliminates some of the advantages of having a flash with everything in one unit. They are very portable, because all you need is a case for the monolight itself, plus the

Figure 7.17
All-in-one "monolights" contain flash, power supply, and a modeling light in one compact package (umbrella not included).

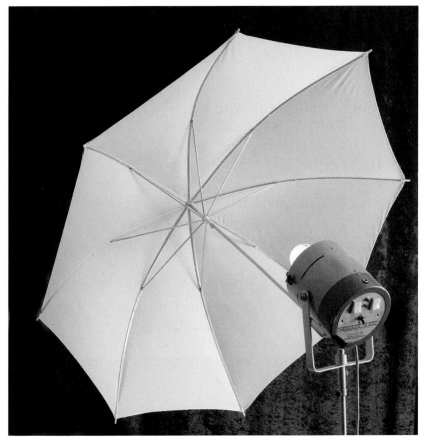

stands and other accessories you want to carry along. Because these units are so popular with photographers who are not full-time professionals, the lower-cost monolights are often designed more for lighter duty than professional studio flash. That doesn't mean they aren't rugged; you'll just need to handle them with a little more care, and, perhaps, not expect them to be used eight hours a day for weeks on end. In most other respects, however, monolights are the equal of traditional studio flash units in terms of fast recycling, built-in modeling lamps, adjustable power, and so forth.

Connecting Multiple Non-Dedicated Units to Your Nikon D60

Non-dedicated electronic flash units can't use the automated i-TTL features of your Nikon D60; you'll need to calculate exposure manually, through test shots evaluated on your camera's LCD, or by using an electronic flash meter. Moreover, you don't have to connect them to the accessory shoe on top of the camera. Instead, you can remove them from the camera and plug in an adaptor like the Nikon AS-15 onto the accessory shoe to provide a PC/X connector for use with an old-style camera sync cord.

You should be aware that older electronic flash units sometimes use a triggering voltage that is too much for your D60 to handle. You can actually damage the camera's electronics if the voltage is too high. You won't need to worry about this if you purchase brand new units from Alien Bees, Adorama, or other vendors. But if you must connect an external flash with an unknown triggering voltage, I recommend using a Wein Safe Sync (see Figure 7.18), which isolates the flash's voltage from the camera triggering circuit.

Finally, some flash units have an optical slave trigger built in, or can be fitted with one, so that they fire automatically when another flash, including your camera's built-in unit, fires.

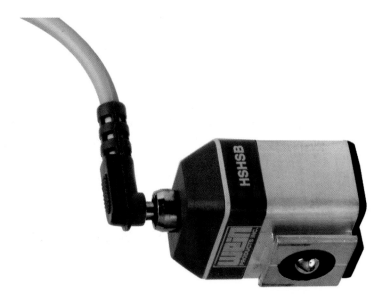

Figure 7.18
A voltage isolator can prevent frying your D60's flash circuits if you use an older electronic flash.

Other Lighting Accessories

Once you start working with light, you'll find there are plenty of useful accessories that can help you. Here are some of the most popular that you might want to consider.

Soft Boxes

Soft boxes are large square or rectangular devices that may resemble a square umbrella with a front cover, and produce a similar lighting effect. They can extend from a few feet square to massive boxes that stand five or six feet tall—virtually a wall of light. With a flash unit or two inside a soft box, you have a very large, semi-directional light source that's very diffuse and very flattering for portraiture and other people photography.

Soft boxes are also handy for photographing shiny objects. They not only provide a soft light, but if the box itself happens to reflect in the subject (say you're photographing a chromium toaster), the box will provide an interesting highlight that's indistinct and not distracting.

You can buy soft boxes or make your own. Some lengths of friction-fit plastic pipe and a lot of muslin cut and sewed just so may be all that you need.

Light Stands

Both electronic flash and incandescent lamps can benefit from light stands. These are lightweight, tripod-like devices (but without a swiveling or tilting head) that can be set on the floor, tabletops, or other elevated surfaces and positioned as needed. Light stands should be strong enough to support an external lighting unit, up to and including a relatively heavy flash with soft box or umbrella reflectors. You want the supports to be capable of raising the lights high enough to be effective. Look for light stands capable of extending six to seven feet high. The nine-foot units usually have larger, steadier bases, and extend high enough that you can use them as background supports. You'll be using these stands for a lifetime, so invest in good ones. I bought the light stand shown in Figure 7.19 when I was in college, and I have been using it for decades.

Backgrounds

Backgrounds can be backdrops of cloth, sheets of muslin you've painted yourself using a sponge dipped in paint, rolls of seamless paper, or any other suitable surface your mind can dream up. Backgrounds provide a complementary and non-distracting area behind subjects (especially portraits) and can be lit separately to provide contrast and separation that outlines the subject, or which helps set a mood.

I like to use plain-colored backgrounds for portraits, and white or gray seamless backgrounds for product photography. You can usually construct these yourself from cheap materials and tape them up on the wall behind your subject, or mount them on a pole stretched between a pair of light stands.

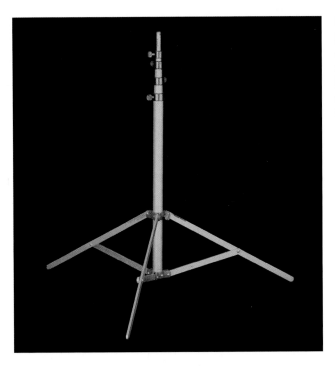

Figure 7.19
Light stands can hold lights, umbrellas, backdrops, and other equipment.

Snoots and Barn Doors

These fit over the flash unit and direct the light at your subject. Snoots are excellent for converting a flash unit into a hair light, while barn doors give you enough control over the illumination by opening and closing their flaps that you can use another flash as a background light, with the capability of feathering the light exactly where you want it on the background. Both are shown in Figure 7.20.

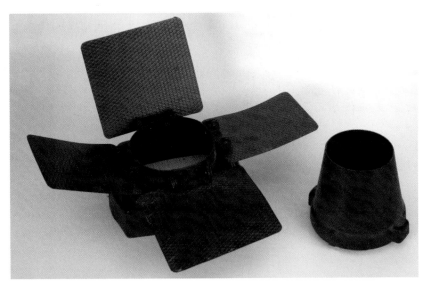

Figure 7.20
Snoots and barn doors allow you to modulate the light from a flash or lamp, and they are especially useful for hair lights and background lights.

8

Useful Software
for the Nikon D60

Unless you only take pictures and then immediately print them directly to a PictBridge-compatible printer, somewhere along the line you're going to need to make use of the broad array of software available for the Nikon D60. The picture-fixing options in the Retouch menu let you make only modest modifications to your carefully crafted photos. If your needs involve more than fixing red-eye, cropping and trimming, and maybe adjusting tonal values with D-lighting, you're definitely going to want to use a utility or editor of some sort to perfect your images. After you've captured some great images and have them safely stored on your Nikon D60's memory card, you'll need to transfer them from your camera and Secure Digital card to your computer, where they can be organized, fine-tuned in an image editor, and prepared for web display, printing, or some other final destination.

Fortunately, there are lots of software utilities and applications to help you do all these things. This chapter will introduce you to a few of them. Please note that this is *not* a "how-to-do-it" software chapter. I'm going to use every available page in this book to offer advice on how to get the most from your D60. There's no space to explain how to use all the features of Nikon Capture NX, nor how to tweak RAW file settings in Adobe Camera Raw. Entire books have been written about both products. This chapter is intended solely to help you get your bearings among the large number of utilities and applications available, to help you better understand what each does, and how you might want to use them. At the very end of the chapter, however, I'm going to make an exception and provide some simple instructions for using Adobe Camera Raw, to help those who have been using Nikon's software exclusively get a feel for what you can do with the Adobe product.

The basic functions found in most of the programs discussed in this chapter include image transfer and management, camera control, and image editing. You'll find that many of the programs overlap several of these capabilities, so it's not always possible to categorize the discussions that follow by function. In fact, I'm going to start off by describing a few of the offerings available from Nikon.

Nikon's Applications and Utilities

If nothing else, Nikon has made sorting through the software for its digital cameras an interesting pursuit. Through the years, we've had various incarnations of programs with names like PictureProject, NikonView, and Nikon Capture. Some have been compatible with both the Nikon dSLR and amateur Coolpix product lines. Many of them have been furnished on disk with the cameras. Others, most notoriously Nikon Capture, have been an extra-cost option, which particularly infuriated those of us who had paid a lot for a Nikon dSLR, and found that we'd need to pay even more to get the software needed for the camera.

Recently, Nikon has begun splitting their software offerings into separate programs that are sort of standalone products, but which integrate with the others. For example, if you bought Nikon Capture NX you found that the program didn't really capture anything, as the previous Nikon Capture 4 did. If you wanted to operate the camera remotely, you needed to buy the off-shoot program, Nikon Camera Control Pro, which costs even *more* money.

If Nikon software wasn't interesting enough already, some years back Nikon began *encrypting* the white balance information in image files, so that third-party utility programmers needed to use Nikon's software development kit or reverse-engineer the encryption to make their utilities work with Nikon NEF files. Even today, each time a new Nikon dSLR is introduced, you must upgrade your copy of most Nikon software products, as well as third-party products like Adobe Camera Raw, to ensure compatibility with the new camera's files. The fact that these upgrades often are not available until months after the camera is introduced is nothing short of frustrating. For example, Version 4.4 of Adobe Camera Raw, the first compatible with the D60, wasn't available until March 14, 2008, almost three full weeks after I had begun shooting NEF photos with my D60. As we used to say back in the days of film cameras, "Bummer!"

The next few sections provide some descriptions of the Nikon software you'll want to use with your D60.

Nikon ViewNX

This latest incarnation of Nikon's basic file viewer is better than ever, making it easy to browse through images, convert RAW files to JPEG or TIFF, and make corrections to white balance and exposure, either on individual files, or on batches of files. It works in tandem with Nikon Transfer and Nikon Capture NX, as you can open files inspected in ViewNX in one of the other programs—or within a third-party application you "register."

First and foremost, Nikon ViewNX is a great file viewer. There are three modes for looking at images: a Thumbnail Grid mode for checking out small previews of your images; an Image Viewer mode (see Figure 8.1) that shows a group of thumbnails along with an enlarged version of a selected image; and Full Screen mode, which allows you to examine an image in maximum detail.

If you like to shoot RAW+JPEG Basic, you can review image pairs as if they were a single image (rather than view the RAW and JPEG versions separately), and work with whichever version you need. The active focus area can be displayed in the image, and there are histogram, highlight, and shadow displays to help you evaluate an image.

Figure 8.1
NikonView NX is a great file viewer.

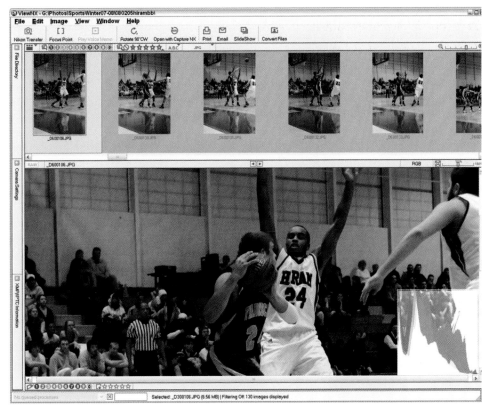

Should you want to organize your images, there are 10 labels available to classify images by criteria such as images printed, images copied, or images sent as e-mail, and you can mark your best shots for easier retrieval with a rating system of one to five stars. ViewNX also allows you to edit embedded XMP/IPTC Information in fields such as Creator, Origin, Image Title, and suitable keywords. The utility can be downloaded from the support/download pages of the Nikon website at www.nikonusa.com.

Nikon Transfer

It seems like everyone offers some sort of image transfer system that automatically recognizes when a memory card is inserted in a reader, or a digital camera like the Nikon D60 is attached to a computer using a USB cable. The most popular operating systems, from Mac OS X to Windows XP and Vista have their own built-in transfer programs, and Adobe Photoshop Elements 6.0 includes one in its suite of utilities.

Nikon Transfer is particularly well-suited for D60 owners, because it integrates easily with other Nikon software products, including ViewNX and Nikon Capture NX. You can download photos to your computer, and then continue to work on them in the Nikon application (or third-party utility) of your choice.

When a memory card is inserted into a card reader, or when the D60 is connected to your computer through a USB cable, Nikon Transfer recognizes the device, searches it for thumbnails, and provides a display like the one shown in Figure 8.2. You can preview the images and mark the ones you want to transfer with checks to create a Transfer Queue.

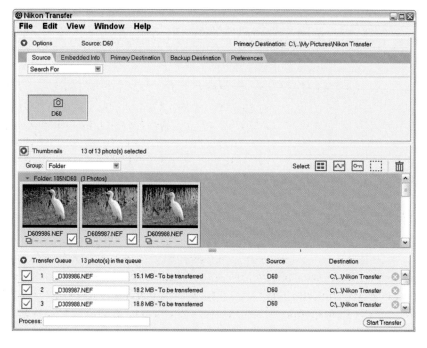

Figure 8.2

After Nikon Transfer displays thumbnails of the images on your memory card or camera, mark the ones you want to transfer.

Then, click on the Primary Destination tab (see Figure 8.3) and choose a location for the photos that will be transferred. Nikon Transfer can create a new folder for each transfer based on a naming convention you set up (click the Edit button next to the box at top center in the figure), or copy to a folder named after the current folder in the D60's memory card. You can keep the current filename as the files are transferred, or assign a new name with a prefix you designate, such as Spain07_ . The program will add a number from 001 to 999 to the filename prefix you specify.

Figure 8.3
Copy files to a destination you specify using an optional file-name template you can define.

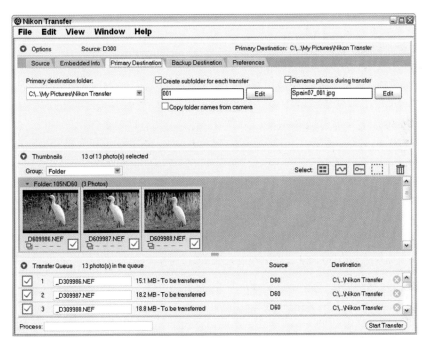

One neat feature is the ability to name a Backup Destination location, so that all transferred pictures can also be copied to a second folder, which can be located on a different hard disk drive or other media. You can embed information such as copyright data, star ratings, and labels in the images as they are transferred. When the file transfer is complete, Nikon Transfer can launch an application of your choice, set with a few clicks in the Preferences tab (see Figure 8.4).

Nikon Capture NX

Capture NX is a pretty hefty chunk of software for the typical entry-level Nikon D60 owner to tackle (and somewhat expensive at about $150), but if you're ambitious and willing to plant your pitons for a steep climb up the learning curve, the program is indeed a powerful image-editing utility. It's designed specifically to process Nikon's NEF-format RAW files (although this new edition has added the ability to manipulate JPEG

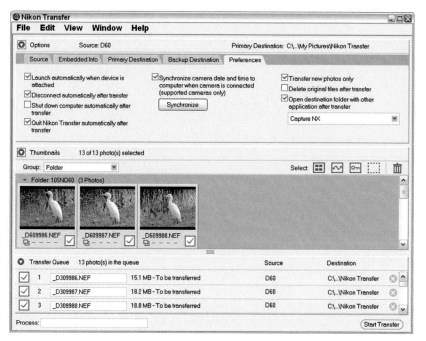

Figure 8.4
You can tell
Nikon Transfer
what to do
after images are
transferred in
the Preferences
tab.

and TIFF images as well). It includes an image browser (with labeling, sorting, and editing) that can be used to make many adjustments directly through the thumbnails. It also has advanced color management tools, impressive noise reduction capabilities, and batch processing features that allow you to apply sets of changes to collections of images. All the tools are arranged in dockable/expandable/collapsible palettes (see Figure 8.5) that tell you everything you need to know about an image, and provide the capabilities to push every pixel in interesting ways.

Photographers tend to love Capture NX or hate it, and it's easy to separate the fans from the furious. Those who are enamored of the program have invested a great deal of time in learning its quirky paradigm and now appreciate just how powerful Capture NX is. The detractors are usually those who are comfortable with another program, such as Photoshop or even Capture 4, this program's predecessor, and are upset that even the simplest functions can be confoundingly difficult for a new user to figure out. Capture NX's murky Help system isn't a lot of help; there's room for a huge book (or two) to explain how to use this program.

For example, instead of masks, Capture NX uses Nik Software's U Point technology, which applies Control Points to select and isolate parts of an image for manipulation. There are Color Control Points, with up to nine different sliders for each selected area. (See Figure 8.6.) There are also Black and White Control points for setting dynamic range, Neutral Control Points for correcting color casts, and a Red-Eye Reduction Control Point that removes crimson glows from pupils.

Figure 8.5
Capture NX's tools are arranged in dockable palettes.

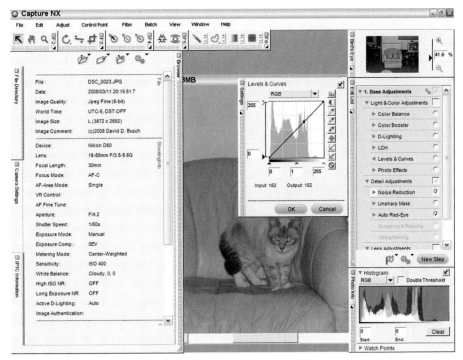

Figure 8.6
Control Points are used to make common adjustments.

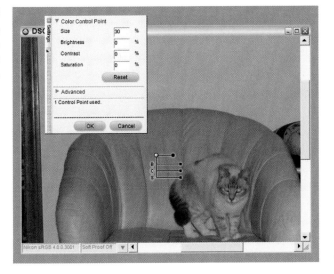

The workflow revolves around an Edit List, which contains a list of enhancements, including Camera Adjustments, RAW Adjustments, Light & Color Adjustments, Detail Adjustments, and Lens Adjustments, which can each be controlled separately. You can add steps of your own, cancel adjustments individually, and store steps in the Edit List as Settings that can be applied to individual images or batches.

There are also Color Aberration Controls, D-Lighting, Image Dust Off, Vignette Control, Fisheye-to-Rectilinear Image Transformation ("de-fishing"), and a Distortion Control to reduce pincushion and barrel distortion.

Nikon Camera Control Pro

Nikon's Camera Control Pro is a versatile utility that allows you to communicate directly with your camera from your computer through a USB cable. Once the two are linked, you can perform a variety of functions:

- **Shoot remotely.** Just about any shooting function you can adjust on the camera can be performed remotely, as you can see from the cluster of tabbed dialog boxes shown at the top and right of Figure 8.7. Set exposure mode, adjust the aperture, add or subtract exposure compensation, choose a focus area, change ISO sensitivity or white balance, all are at your command through the software. You can even change Quality and Size settings, turn on auto bracketing, and change image optimization settings. You can optionally disable the controls on the camera, to prevent having settings you made at the computer changed accidentally.

- **Download directly to your computer.** When doing time-lapse photography, you can use Camera Control Pro to transfer the images you take directly to the computer.

- **Upload comments.** Frustrated by the Nikon D60's text entry screen? Edit your Image Comment and upload it directly to the camera from your computer keyboard (lower left in Figure 8.7).

- **Create and save custom curves.** You can load a sample image and create a special tone compensation custom curve for that image using tools similar to those found in Photoshop.

- **View and change Custom Settings.** This is one of my favorite features. While changing the Custom Settings for any of the Custom Setting options using the D60's menus isn't difficult (particularly after you've absorbed the information in Chapter 3), Camera Control Pro makes playing with these options a joy.

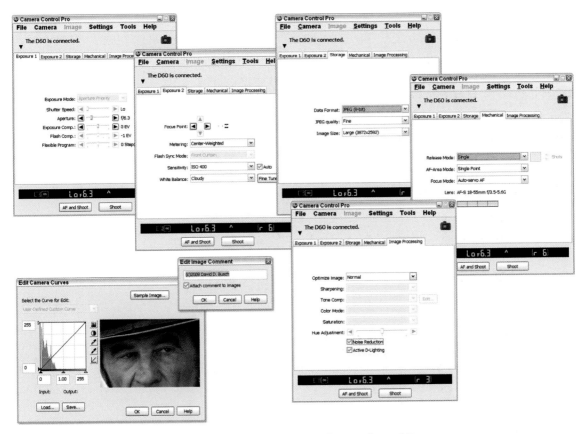

Figure 8.7 You can operate the D60 from your computer using Camera Control Pro.

Other Software

Other useful software for your Nikon D60 falls into several categories. You might want to fine-tune your images, retouch them, change color balance, composite several images together, and perform other tasks we know as image editing, with a program like Adobe Photoshop, Photoshop Elements, or Corel Photo Paint.

You might want to play with the settings in RAW files, too, as you import them into an image editor. There are specialized tools expressly for tweaking RAW files, ranging from Adobe Camera Raw, and PhaseOne's Capture One Pro (C1 Pro). A third type of manipulation is the specialized task of noise reduction, which can be performed within Photoshop, Adobe Camera Raw, or tools like Bibble Professional. There are also specialized tools just for noise reduction, such as Noise Ninja (also included with Bibble) and Neat Image. Some programs, like the incomparable DxO Optics Pro perform magical transformations that you can't achieve any other way.

Each of these utilities and applications deserves a chapter of its own, so I'm simply going to enumerate some of the most popular applications and utilities and tell you a little about what they do.

DxO Optics Pro

DxO Labs (www.DxO.com) offers an incredibly useful program called Optics Pro ($170-$300) that is unique in the range of functions it provides. Ostensibly an image quality enhancement utility that "cures" some of the ails that plague even the best lenses, the latest v5 release also features a new RAW conversion engine that uses a new demosaicing algorithm to translate your NEF files into images with more detail, less noise, and fewer artifacts. These features meld well with the program's original mission: fixing the optical "geometry" of images, using settings custom-tailored for each individual lens. (I'm not kidding: when you "assemble" the program, you specify each and every camera body you want to use with Optics Pro, and designate exactly which lenses are included in your repertoire.)

Once an image has been imported into Optics Pro, it can be manipulated within one of four main sections: Light, Color, Geometry, and Details. It's especially useful for correcting optical flaws, color, exposure, and dynamic range, while adjusting perspective, distortion, and tilting. If you own a fish-eye lens, Optics Pro will "de-fish" your images to produce a passable rectilinear photo from your curved image. A new Dust/Blemish Removal tool operates something like a manual version of the D60's Dust Off Reference Photo. The user creates a dust/blemish template, and the program removes dust from the marked area in multiple images. Figure 8.8 shows you DxO Optics Pro's clean user interface.

Phase One Capture One Pro (C1 Pro)

If there is a Cadillac of RAW converters for Nikon and Canon digital SLR cameras, C1 Pro has to be it. This premium-priced program from Phase One (www.phaseone.com) does everything, does it well, and does it quickly. If you can't justify the price tag of this professional-level software (as much as $500 for the top-of-the-line edition), there are "lite" versions for serious amateurs and cash-challenged professionals for as little as $130.

Aimed at photographers with high-volume needs (that would include school and portrait photographers, as well as busy commercial photographers), C1 Pro is available for both Windows and Mac OS X, and supports a broad range of digital cameras. Phase One is a leading supplier of megabucks digital camera backs for medium and larger format cameras, so they really understand the needs of photographers.

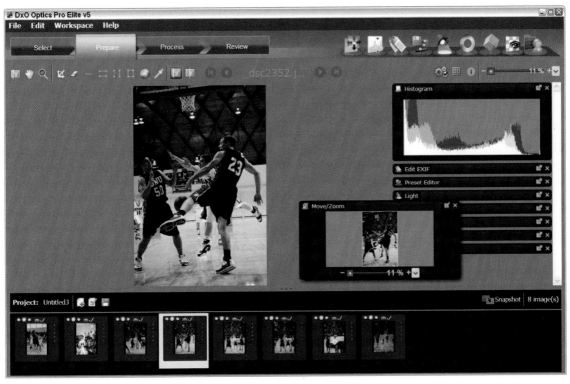

Figure 8.8 DxO Optics Pro fixes lens flaws, and functions as a high-tech RAW converter and noise reduction utility, too.

The latest features include individual noise reduction controls for each image, automatic levels adjustment, a "quick develop" option that allows speedy conversion from RAW to TIFF or JPEG formats, dual-image side-by-side views for comparison purposes, and helpful grids and guides that can be superimposed over an image. Photographers concerned about copyright protection will appreciate the ability to add watermarks to the output images.

Bibble Pro

One of my personal favorites among third-party RAW converters is Bibble Pro. It supports one of the broadest ranges of RAW file formats available (which can be handy if you find yourself with the need to convert a file from a friend or colleague's non-Nikon camera), including NEF files from Nikon cameras dating as far back as the Nikon D1, D1x/h, D2H, and D100. It also supports CRW files from the Canon C30, D60, 10D, and 300D; CR2 files from the Canon 20D and other newer models; ORF files from the Olympus E10, E20, E1, C5050, and C5060; DCR files from the Kodak 720x/760/14n; RAF files from the Fuji S2Pro; PEF files from Pentax ISTD; MRW files from the Minolta Maxxum; and TIF from Canon 1D and 1DS.

The utility supports lots of different platforms, too. It's available for Windows, Mac OS X, and, believe it or not, Linux.

Bibble (www.bibblelabs.com) works fast, which is important when you have to convert many images in a short time (event photographers will know what I am talking about!). Bibble's batch-processing capabilities also let you convert large numbers of files using settings you specify without further intervention. Its customizable interface lets you organize and edit images quickly and then output them in a variety of formats, including 16-bit TIFF and PNG. You can even create a web gallery from within Bibble. I often find myself disliking the generic filenames applied to digital images by cameras, so I really like Bibble's ability to rename batches of files using new names that you specify.

Bibble is fully color managed, which means it can support all the popular color spaces (Adobe sRGB and so forth) and use custom profiles generated by third-party color-management software. There are two editions of Bibble, a Pro version and a Lite version. Because the Pro version is reasonably priced at $129, I don't really see the need to save $60 with the Lite edition, which lacks the top-line's options for tethered shooting, embedding IPTC-compatible captions in images, and can also be used as a Photoshop plug-in (if you prefer not to work with the application in its standalone mode). Bibble Pro now incorporates Noise Ninja technology, so you can get double-duty from this valuable application.

Photoshop/Photoshop Elements

Photoshop is the high-end choice for image editing, and Photoshop Elements is a great alternative for those who need some of the features of Photoshop, but can do without the most sophisticated capabilities, including editing CMYK files. Both editors use the latest version of Adobe's Camera Raw plug-in, which makes it easy to adjust things like image resolution, white balance, exposure, shadows, brightness, sharpness, luminance, and noise reduction. One plus with the Adobe products is that they are available in identical versions for both Windows and Macs (eventually!).

The latest version of Photoshop includes a built-in RAW plug-in that is compatible with the proprietary formats of a growing number of digital cameras, both new and old, and which can perform a limited number of manipulations on JPEG and TIFF files, too. This plug-in also works with Photoshop Elements, but with fewer features. Here's how easy it is to manipulate a RAW file using the Adobe converter:

1. Transfer the RAW images from your camera to your computer's hard drive.

2. In Photoshop, choose Open from the File menu, or use Bridge.

3. Select a RAW image file. The Adobe Camera Raw plug-in will pop up, showing a preview of the image, like the one shown in Figure 8.9.

Figure 8.9
The basic ACR dialog box looks like this when processing a single image.

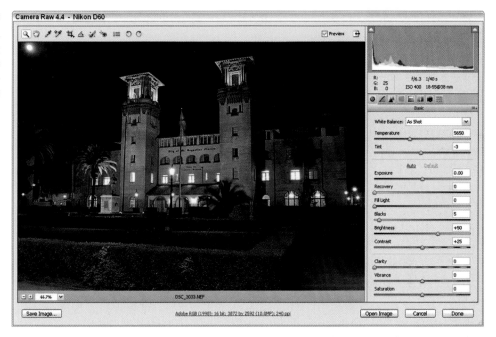

4. If you like, use one of the tools found in the toolbar at the top left of the dialog box. From left to right, they are:

■ **Zoom.** Operates just like the Zoom tool in Photoshop.

■ **Hand.** Use like the Hand tool in Photoshop.

■ **White Balance.** Click an area in the image that should be neutral gray or white to set the white balance quickly.

■ **Color Sampler.** Use to determine the RGB values of areas you click with this eyedropper.

■ **Crop.** Pre-crops the image so that only the portion you specify is imported into Photoshop. This option saves time when you want to work on a section of a large image, and you don't need the entire file.

■ **Straighten.** Drag in the preview image to define what should be a horizontal or vertical line, and ACR will realign the image to straighten it.

■ **Retouch.** Used to heal or clone areas you define.

■ **Red-Eye Removal.** Quickly zap red pupils in your human subjects.

■ **ACR Preferences.** Produces a dialog box of Adobe Camera Raw preferences.

■ **Rotate Counterclockwise.** Rotates counterclockwise in 90-degree increments with a click.

■ **Rotate Clockwise.** Rotates clockwise in 90-degree increments with a click.

5. Using the Basic tab, you can have ACR show you red and blue highlights in the preview that indicate shadow areas that are clipped (too dark to show detail) and light areas that are blown out (too bright). Click the triangles in the upper-left corner of the histogram display (shadow clipping) and upper-right corner (highlight clipping) to toggle these indicators on or off.

6. Also in the Basic tab you can choose white balance, either from the drop-down list or by setting a color temperature and green/magenta color bias (tint) using the sliders.

7. Other sliders are available to control exposure, recovery, fill light, blacks, brightness, contrast, vibrance, and saturation. A checkbox can be marked to convert the image to grayscale.

8. Make other adjustments (described in more detail below).

9. ACR makes automatic adjustments for you . You can click **Default** and make the changes for yourself, or click the **Auto** link (located just above the Exposure slider) to reapply the automatic adjustments after you've made your own modifications.

10. If you've marked more than one image to be opened, the additional images appear in a "filmstrip" at the left side of the screen. You can click on each thumbnail in the filmstrip in turn and apply different settings to each.

11. Click **Open Image/Open image(s)** into Photoshop using the settings you've made.

The Basic tab is displayed by default when the ACR dialog box opens, and it includes most of the sliders and controls you'll need to fine-tune your image as you import it into Photoshop. These include:

- **White Balance.** Leave it **As Shot** or change to a value such as Daylight, Cloudy, Shade, Tungsten, Fluorescent, or Flash. If you like, you can set a custom white balance using the Temperature and Tint sliders.

- **Exposure.** This slider adjusts the overall brightness and darkness of the image.

- **Recovery.** Restores detail in the red, green, and blue color channels.

- **Fill Light.** Reconstructs detail in shadows.

- **Blacks.** Increases the number of tones represented as black in the final image, emphasizing tones in the shadow areas of the image.

- **Brightness.** This slider adjusts the brightness and darkness of an image.

- **Contrast.** Manipulates the contrast of the midtones of your image.

- **Convert to Grayscale.** Mark this box to convert the image to black and white.

- **Vibrance.** Prevents over-saturation when enriching the colors of an image.

- **Saturation.** Manipulates the richness of all colors equally, from zero saturation (gray/black, no color) at the −100 setting to double the usual saturation at the +100 setting.

Additional controls are available on the Tone Curve, Detail, HSL/Grayscale, Split Toning, Lens Corrections, Camera Calibration, and Presets tabs, shown in Figure 8.10.

Figure 8.10
More controls are available within the additional tabbed dialog boxes in Adobe Camera Raw.

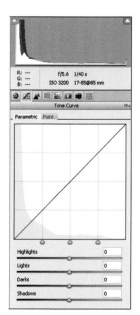
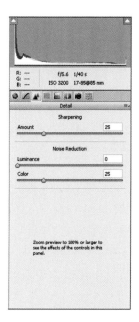
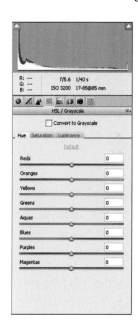
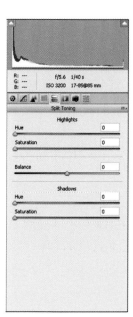
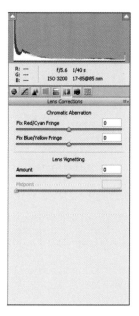
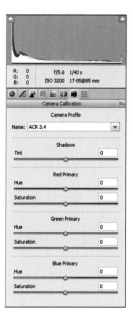

The Tone Curve tab can change the tonal values of your image. The Detail tab lets you adjust sharpness, luminance smoothing, and apply color noise reduction. The HSL/Grayscale tab offers controls for adjusting hue, saturation, and lightness and converting an image to black and white. Split Toning helps you colorize an image with sepia or cyanotype (blue) shades. The Lens Corrections tab has sliders to adjust for chromatic aberrations and vignetting. The Camera Calibration tab provides a way for calibrating the color corrections made in the Camera Raw plug-in. The Presets tab (not shown) is used to load settings you've stored for reuse.

9

Nikon D60: Troubleshooting and Prevention

One of the nice things about modern electronic cameras like the Nikon D60 is that they have fewer mechanical moving parts to fail, so they are less likely to "wear out." No film transport mechanism, no wind lever or motor drive, no complicated mechanical linkages from camera to lens to physically stop down the lens aperture. Instead, tiny, reliable motors are built into each lens (and you lose the use of only that lens should something fail), and one of the few major moving parts in the camera itself is a lightweight mirror (its small size is one of the advantages of the D60's 1.5X crop factor) that flips up and down with each shot.

Of course, the camera also has a moving shutter that can fail, but the shutter is built rugged enough that you can expect it to last 100,000 shutter cycles or more. Unless you're shooting sports in continuous mode day in and day out, the shutter on your D60 is likely to last as long as you expect to use the camera.

The only other things on the camera that move are switches, dials, buttons, the flip-up electronic flash, and the door that slides open to allow you to remove and insert the Secure Digital card. Unless you're extraordinarily clumsy or unlucky and manage to give your built-in flash a good whack while it is in use, there's not a lot that can go wrong mechanically with your Nikon D60.

On the other hand, one of the chief drawbacks of modern electronic cameras is that they are modern *electronic* cameras. Your D60 is fully dependent on two different batteries. Without them, the camera can't be used. There are numerous other electrical and electronic connections in the camera (many connected to those mechanical switches and dials), and components like the color LCD and top-panel status LCD that can potentially fail or suffer damage. The camera also relies on its "operating system," or *firmware*, which can be plagued by bugs that cause unexpected behavior. Luckily, electronic components are generally more reliable and trouble-free, especially when compared to their mechanical counterparts from the pre-electronic film camera days. (Film cameras of the last 10 to 20 years have had almost as many electronic features as digital cameras, but, believe it or not, there were whole generations of film cameras that had *no* electronics or batteries.)

Digital cameras have problems unique to their breed, too; the most troublesome being the need to clean the sensor of dust and grime periodically. This chapter will show you how to diagnose problems, fix some common ills, and, importantly, learn how to avoid them in the future.

Update Your Firmware

As I said, the firmware in your Nikon D60 is the camera's operating system, which handles everything from menu display (including fonts, colors, and the actual entries themselves), what languages are available, and even support for specific devices and features. Upgrading the firmware to a new version makes it possible to add new features while fixing some of the bugs that sneak in.

Firmware upgrades are used most frequently to fix bugs in the software, and much less frequently to add or enhance features. The exact changes made to the firmware are generally spelled out in the firmware release announcement. You can examine the remedies provided and decide if a given firmware patch is important to you. If not, you can usually safely wait a while before going through the bother of upgrading your firmware—at least long enough for the early adopters (such as those who haunt the Digital Photography Review forums at www.dpreview.com) to report whether the bug fixes have introduced new bugs of their own. Each new firmware release incorporates the changes from previous releases, so if you skip a minor upgrade you should have no problems.

How It Works

If you're computer savvy, you might wonder how your Nikon D60 is able to overwrite its own operating system—that is, how can the existing firmware be used to load the new version on top of itself? It's a little like lifting yourself by reaching down and pulling up on your bootstraps. Not ironically, that's almost exactly what happens: At your command (when you start the upgrade process), the D60 shifts into a special mode in which it is no longer operating from its firmware but, rather, from a small piece of software called a *bootstrap loader*, a separate, protected software program that functions only at startup or when upgrading firmware. The loader's function is to look for firmware to launch or, when directed, to copy new firmware from a Secure Digital card to the internal memory space where the old firmware is located. Once the new firmware has replaced the old, you can turn your camera off and then on again, and the updated operating system will be loaded.

Because the loader software is small in size and limited in function, there are some restrictions on what it can do. For one thing, it recognizes only Secure Digital cards that have been formatted using an organizational system called FAT16 (which again, you might be familiar with if you're comfortable with hard disk technology). To ensure that the Secure Digital card is formatted using FAT16, you must upgrade using an SD card at least 8MB in size and no larger than 2GB, and then format the card in your camera. Memory cards that are smaller or larger might be formatted using a different FAT system (FAT12 or FAT32, respectively).

In addition, the loader software isn't set up to go hunting through your Secure Digital card for the firmware file. It looks only in the top or root directory of your card, so that's where you must copy the firmware you download. Once you've determined that a new firmware update is available for your camera and that you want to install it, just follow these steps. (If you chicken out, any Nikon Service Center can install the firmware upgrade for you.)

WARNING

Use a fully charged EN-EL9 charged battery or a Nikon AC adapter to ensure that you'll have enough power to operate the camera for the entire upgrade. Moreover, you should not turn off the camera while your old firmware is being overwritten. Don't open the Secure Digital card door or do anything else that might disrupt operation of the D60 while the firmware is being installed.

Getting Ready

Before you get started, I have to emphasize that at the time this book was written, no new firmware upgrades were available for the Nikon D60, so that I, personally, have never performed this task on my D60. However, I have upgraded the firmware for most of my other Nikon dSLRs, including the very similar D40 model. So, the procedure I am going to describe is the recommended process Nikon has traditionally used. But when it comes time to do an actual firmware upgrade for your D60, you should double check the instructions below against the recommended procedure that Nikon implements at that time. It should be very close to the steps I outline, but there may be some small differences.

The first thing to do is determine whether you need the current firmware update. First, confirm the version number of your Nikon D60's current firmware:

1. Turn on the D60.

2. Press the Menu button and select **Firmware Version** from the Setup menu. The camera's firmware version will be displayed, as in Figure 9.1.

3. Write down the Version number for both Parts A and B.

4. Turn off the D60.

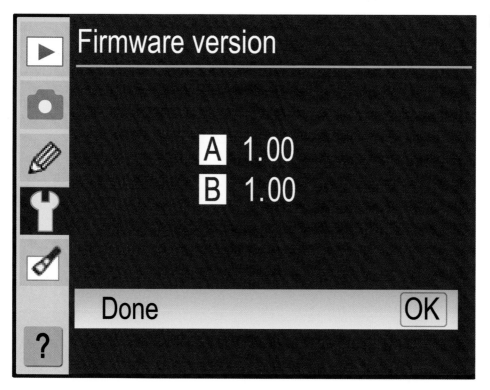

Figure 9.1

Next, go to the Nikon support site, locate, and download the firmware update. In the USA, the place to go is http://support.nikontech.com/, which will offer a list of choices, including one that says **Current Firmware Downloads available for Nikon Products**. Click that link, then click the **DSLR** link on the page displayed next. Scroll down to the D60 row in the table, and review the version number for the current update.

If the version is later than the one you noted in your camera, click the firmware link in either the Windows or Macintosh columns (depending on your computer) to download the file. It will have a name like D60Update.zip (Windows) or D60update.sitx (Macintosh). Extract the file to a folder on your computer using the unzipping or unstuffing software of your choice.

The D60's firmware comes in two parts, A and B, which can be updated individually. The actual update file will be named something like:

A6000101.bin

B6000101.bin

The final preparation you need to make is to decide whether you'd like to upgrade your firmware using a memory card reader, or by transferring the software to the D60 using the UC-E4 USB cable. In either case, you'll need to format an 8MB to 2GB memory card in the D60. Then, perform one of the sets of steps in the sections that follow.

Updating from a Card Reader

To update from a card reader, use a reader connected to your computer with a USB cable. Then, follow these steps:

1. Insert a formatted memory card into the card reader. If you have been using Nikon transfer or the "autoplay" features of your operating system to transfer images from your memory card to the computer, the automated transfer dialog box may appear. Close it.

2. The memory card will appear on your Macintosh desktop, or in the Computer/My Computer folders under Windows Vista/Windows XP.

3. Drag one of the firmware files to the memory card. You can install "A" first or "B" first; it doesn't matter. If your particular upgrade consists of only one of the two files, drag that to the memory card. Remember to copy the firmware to the *root* (top) directory of the memory card. The D60 will be unable to find it if you place it in a folder.

Updating with a USB Connection

You can also copy the firmware to the D60's memory card using a USB connection. Just follow these steps:

1. With the camera turned off, insert the formatted memory card. Then, turn the camera back on.

2. Press the Menu button and navigate to the Setup menu.

3. Choose USB and set the option to Mass Storage, as described in Chapter 3.

4. Turn the D60 off and connect it to your computer using the UC-E4 USB cable.

5. Turn the camera back on. If you have been using Nikon transfer or the "autoplay" features of your operating system to transfer images from your memory card to the computer, the automated transfer dialog box may appear. Close it.

6. The camera will appear on the Macintosh desktop, or in the Computer/My Computer folders under Windows Vista/Windows XP.

7. Drag one of the firmware files to the memory card. It doesn't matter whether you install "A" or "B" first. If your particular upgrade consists of only one .bin file, drag that to the memory card. Remember to copy the firmware to the *root* (top) directory of the memory card. The D60 will be unable to find it if you place it in a folder.

8. Disconnect the camera from the computer.

Starting the Update

To perform the actual update, follow these steps:

1. With the memory card containing the firmware update software in the camera, turn the camera on.

2. Press the **Menu** button and select **Firmware version** in the Setup menu.

3. Select **Version Up** and press the multi-selector button to the right.

4. When the firmware update screen appears, highlight **Yes** and press **OK** to begin the update.

5. The actual process may take a few minutes (from two to five). Be sure not to turn off the camera or perform any other operations while it is underway.

6. When the update is completed, the warning message will no longer be displayed on the screen. You can turn off the camera when the message disappears.

7. Remove the memory card.

8. Turn the D60 back on to load the updated firmware.

9. Press the **Menu** button and select **Firmware version** in the Setup menu to view the current firmware number. If it matches the update, you've successfully upgraded that portion of the firmware.

10. Reformat the memory card.

11. If there is a second part to your firmware upgrade ("A" or "B"), then repeat all the steps for the additional firmware software.

12. If you transferred the firmware files to the memory card using USB transfer, then go back to the Setup menu, choose USB, and set the option to MTP/PTP, as described in Chapter 3.

Protect Your LCD

The large 2.5-inch color LCD on the back of your Nikon D60 almost seems like a target for banging, scratching, and other abuse. The LCD itself is quite rugged, and a few errant knocks are unlikely to shatter the protective cover over the LCD, and scratches won't easily mar its surface. However, if you want to be on the safe side, there are a number of protective products you can purchase to keep your LCD safe—and, in some cases, make it a little easier to view. Here's a quick overview of your options.

■ **Plastic overlays.** The simplest solution (although not always the cheapest) is to apply a plastic overlay sheet or "skin" cut to fit your LCD. These adhere either by static electricity or through a light adhesive coating that's even less clingy than stick-it notes. You can cut down overlays made for PDAs (although these can be pricey at up to $19.95 for a set of several sheets), or purchase overlays sold specifically for digital cameras. Vendors such as Hoodman (www.hoodmanusa.com) offer overlays of this type. These products will do a good job of shielding your D60's LCD screen from scratches and minor impacts, but will not offer much protection from a good whack.

■ **Acrylic shields.** These scratch-resistant acrylic panels, laser cut to fit your camera perfectly, are my choice as the best protection solution, and what I use on my own D60. At about $6 each, they also happen to be the least expensive option as well. I get mine, shown in Figure 9.2, from a company called 'da Products (www.daproducts.com). They attach using strips of sticky adhesive that hold the panel flush and tight, but which allow the acrylic to be pried off and the adhesive removed easily if you want to remove or replace the shield. They don't attenuate your view of the LCD and are non-reflective enough for use under a variety of lighting conditions. The important thing to remember about getting a shield fashioned especially for the D60 is that generic shields may be a smidge too large, and cover up the eye sensor, effectively disabling it.

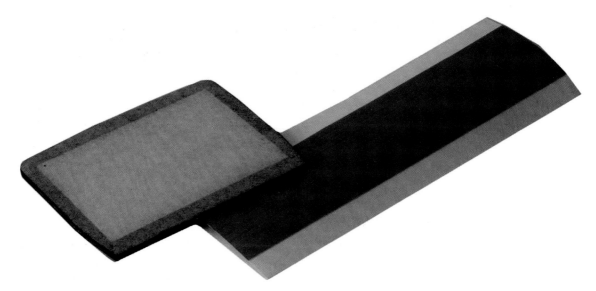

Figure 9.2 A tough acrylic shield, here shown with a piece of plastic containing a set of peel-off sticky strips to help it adhere to the camera, can protect your LCD from scratches.

- **Flip-up hoods.** These protectors slip on using the flanges around your D60's eye-piece, and provide a cover that completely shields the LCD, but unfolds to provide a three-sided hood that allows viewing the LCD while minimizing the extraneous light falling on it and reducing contrast. They're sold for about $40 by Delkin and Hoodman. If you want to completely protect your LCD from hard knocks and need to view the screen outdoors in bright sunlight, there is nothing better. However, I have a couple problems with these devices. First, with the cover closed, you can't peek down after taking a shot to see what your image looks like during picture review. You must open the cap each time you want to look at the LCD. Moreover, with the hood unfolded, it's difficult to look through the viewfinder: Don't count on being able to use the viewfinder *and* the LCD at the same time with one of these hoods in place.

- **Magnifiers.** If you look hard enough, you should be able to find an LCD magnifier that fits over the monitor panel and provides a 2X magnification. These often strap on clumsily, and serve better as a way to get an enlarged view of the LCD than as protection. Hoodman, Photodon (www.photodon.com), and other suppliers offer these specialized devices.

Troubleshooting Memory Cards

Sometimes good memory cards go bad. Sometimes good photographers can treat their memory cards badly. It's possible that a memory card that works fine in one camera won't be recognized when inserted into another. In the worst case, you can have a card full of important photos and find that the card seems to be corrupted and you can't access any of them. Don't panic! If these scenarios sound horrific to you, there are lots of things you can do to prevent them from happening, and a variety of remedies available if they do occur. You'll want to take some time—before disaster strikes—to consider your options.

All Your Eggs in One Basket?

The debate about whether it's better to use one large memory card or several smaller ones has been going on since even before there were memory cards. I can remember when computer users wondered whether it was smarter to install a pair of 200MB (not *gigabyte*) hard drives in their computer, or if they should go for one of those new-fangled 500MB models. By the same token, a few years ago the user groups were full of proponents who insisted that you ought to use 128MB memory cards rather than the huge 512MB versions. Today, most of the arguments involve 8GB cards versus 4GB cards, and I expect that as prices for 16GB SD cards continue to drop, they'll find their way into the debate as well.

Why all the fuss? Are 8GB memory cards more likely to fail than 4GB cards? Are you risking all your photos if you trust your images to a larger card? Isn't it better to use several smaller cards, so that if one fails you lose only half as many photos? Or, isn't it wiser to put all your photos onto one larger card, because the more cards you use, the better your odds of misplacing or damaging one and losing at least some pictures?

In the end, the "eggs in one basket" argument boils down to statistics, and how you happen to use your D60. The rationales can go both ways. If you have multiple smaller cards, you do increase your chances of something happening to one of them, so, arguably, you might be boosting the odds of losing some pictures. If all your images are important, the fact that you've lost 100 rather than 200 pictures isn't very comforting.

Also consider that the eggs/basket scenario assumes that the cards that are lost or damaged are always full. It's actually likely that your 8GB card might suffer a mishap when it's less than half full (indeed, it's more likely that a large card won't be completely filled before it's offloaded to a computer), so you really might not lose any more shots with a single 8GB card than with multiple 4GB or 2GB cards.

If you shoot photojournalist-type pictures, you probably change memory cards when they're less than completely full in order to avoid the need to do so at a crucial moment. (When I shoot sports, my cards rarely reach 80 to 90 percent of capacity before I change them.) Using multiple smaller cards means you have to change them that more often, which can be a real pain when you're taking a lot of photos. As an example, if you use 1GB memory cards with a Nikon D60 and shoot RAW+JPEG Basic, you may get only a few dozen pictures on the card. That's not even twice the capacity of a 36-exposure roll of film (remember those?). In my book, I prefer keeping all my eggs in one basket, and then making very sure that nothing happens to that basket.

There are only two really good reasons to justify limiting yourself to smaller memory cards when larger ones can be purchased at the same cost per-gigabyte. One of them applies only to owners of older cameras that don't accept memory cards larger than 2GB. That rationale doesn't apply to you, because the D60 is not limited to cards of 2GB or smaller (it's actually good to go up to 32GB).

The other reason comes into play when every single picture is precious to you and the loss of any of them would be a disaster. If you were a wedding photographer, for example, and unlikely to be able to restage the nuptials if a memory card goes bad, you'll probably want to shoot no more pictures than you can afford to lose on a single card, and have an assistant ready to copy each card removed from the camera onto a backup hard drive or DVD onsite.

If none of these options are available to you, consider *interleaving* your shots. Say you don't shoot weddings with a Nikon D60, but you do go on vacation from time to time. Take 50 or so pictures on one card, or whatever number of images might fill about 25 percent of its capacity. Then, replace it with a different card and shoot about 25 percent of that card's available space. Repeat these steps with diligence (you'd have to be determined to go through this inconvenience), and, if you use four or more memory cards you'll find your pictures from each location scattered among the different Secure Digital cards. If you lose or damage one, you'll still have *some* pictures from all the various stops on your trip on the other cards. That's more work than I like to do (I usually tote around a portable hard disk and copy the files to the drive as I go), but it's an option.

What Can Go Wrong?

There are lots of things that can go wrong with your memory card, but the ones that aren't caused by human stupidity are statistically very rare. Yes, a Secure Digital card's internal bit bin or controller can suddenly fail due to a manufacturing error or some inexplicable event caused by old age. However, if your SD card works for the first week or two that you own it, it should work forever. There's really not a lot that can wear out.

The typical Secure Digital card is rated for a Mean Time Between Failures of 1,000,000 hours of use. That's constant use 24/7 for more than 100 years! According to the manufacturers, they are good for 10,000 insertions in your camera, and should be able to retain their data (and that's without an external power source) for something on the order of 11 years. Of course, with the millions of SD cards in use, there are bound to be a few lemons here or there.

Given the reliability of solid-state memory compared to magnetic memory, though, it's more likely that your Secure Digital problems will stem from something that you do. SD cards are small and easy to misplace if you're not careful. For that reason, it's a good idea to keep them in their original cases or a "card safe" offered by Gepe (www.gepecard-safe.com), Pelican (www.pelican.com), and others. Always placing your memory card in a case can provide protection from the second-most common mishap that befalls Secure Digital cards: the common household laundry. If you slip a memory card in a pocket, rather than a case or your camera bag often enough, sooner or later it's going to end up in the washing machine and probably the clothes dryer, too. There are plenty of reports of relieved digital camera owners who've laundered their memory cards and found they still worked fine, but it's not uncommon for such mistreatment to do some damage.

Memory cards can also be stomped on, accidentally bent, dropped into the ocean, chewed by pets, and otherwise rendered unusable in myriad ways. Or, if the card is formatted in your computer with a memory card reader, your D60 may fail to recognize it. Occasionally, I've found that a memory card used in one camera would fail if used in a different camera (until I reformatted it in Windows, and then again in the camera). Every once in awhile, a card goes completely bad and—seemingly—can't be salvaged.

Another way to lose images is to do commonplace things with your SD card at an inopportune time. If you remove the card from the D60 while the camera is writing images to the card, you'll lose any photos in the buffer and may damage the file structure of the card, making it difficult or impossible to retrieve the other pictures you've taken. The same thing can happen if you remove the SD card from your computer's card reader while the computer is writing to the card (say, to erase files you've already moved to your computer). You can avoid this by *not* using your computer to erase files on a Secure Digital card but, instead, always reformatting the card in your D60 before you use it again.

What Can You Do?

Pay attention: If you're having problems, the *first* thing you should do is *stop* using that memory card. Don't take any more pictures. Don't do anything with the card until you've figured out what's wrong. Your second line of defense (your first line is to be sufficiently careful with your cards that you avoid problems in the first place) is to *do no harm* that hasn't already been done. Read the rest of this section and then, if necessary, decide on a course of action (such as using a data recovery service or software described later) before you risk damaging the data on your card further.

Now that you've calmed down, the first thing to check is whether you've actually inserted a card in the camera. If you've set the camera in the Custom Setting so that the **No memory card?** option has been set to allow taking pictures without a card, it's entirely possible (although not particularly plausible) that you've been snapping away with no memory card to store the pictures to, which can lead to massive disappointment later on. You can avoid all this by setting the **No Memory Card? (CSM #6)** feature to **Release locked**, and leaving it there.

Things get more exciting when the card itself is put in jeopardy. If you lose a card, there's not a lot you can do other than take a picture of a similar card and print up some Have You Seen This Lost Flash Memory? flyers to post on utility poles all around town.

If all you care about is reusing the card, and have resigned yourself to losing the pictures, try reformatting the card in your camera. You may find that reformatting removes the corrupted data and restores your card to health. Sometimes I've had success reformatting a card in my computer using a memory card reader (this is normally a no-no because your operating system doesn't understand the needs of your D60), and *then* reformatting again in the camera.

If your Secure Digital card is not behaving properly, and you *do* want to recover your images, things get a little more complicated. If your pictures are very valuable, either to you or to others (for example, a wedding), you can always turn to professional data recovery firms. Be prepared to pay hundreds of dollars to get your pictures back, but these pros often do an amazing job. You wouldn't want them working on your memory card on behalf of the police if you'd tried to erase some incriminating pictures. There are many firms of this type, and I've never used them myself, so I can't offer a recommendation. Use a Google search to turn up a ton of them.

THE ULTIMATE IRONY

I recently purchased an 8GB Kingston memory card that was furnished with some nifty OnTrack data recovery software. The first thing I did was format the card to make sure it was OK. Then I hunted around for the free software, only to discover it was preloaded onto the memory card. I was supposed to copy the software to my computer before using the memory card for the first time.

Fortunately, I had the OnTrack software that would reverse my dumb move, so I could retrieve the software. No, wait. I *didn't* have the software I needed to recover the software I erased. I'd reformatted it to oblivion. Chalk this one up as either the ultimate irony or Stupid Photographer Trick #523.

A more reasonable approach is to try special data recovery software you can install on your computer and use to attempt to resurrect your "lost" images yourself. They may not actually be gone completely. Perhaps your SD card's "table of contents" is jumbled, or only a few pictures are damaged in such a way that your camera and computer can't read some or any of the pictures on the card. Some of the available software was written specifically to reconstruct lost pictures, while other utilities are more general-purpose applications that can be used with any media, including floppy disks and hard disk drives. They have names like OnTrack, Photo Rescue 2, Digital Image Recovery, MediaRecover, Image Recall, and the aptly named Recover My Photos. You'll find a comprehensive list and links, as well as some picture-recovery tips at www.ultimateslr.com/memory-card-recovery.php.

DIMINISHING RETURNS

Usually, once you've recovered any images on a Secure Digital card, reformatted it, and returned it to service, it will function reliably for the rest of its useful life. However, if you find a particular card going bad more than once, you'll almost certainly want to stop using it forever. See if you can get it replaced by the manufacturer if you can, but, in the case of SD card failures, the third time is never the charm.

Clean Your Sensor

Yes, the Nikon D60 has a two-pronged sensor dust prevention scheme: an innovative air control system that keeps dust away from the sensor in the first place, and a sensor-shaking cleaning mechanism. But no dust-busting technology is 100-percent effective.

Indeed, there's no avoiding dust. No matter how careful you are, some of it is going to settle on your camera and on the mounts of your lenses, eventually making its way inside your camera to settle in the mirror chamber. As you take photos, the mirror flipping up and down causes the dust to become airborne and eventually make its way past the shutter curtain to come to rest on the anti-aliasing filter atop your sensor. There, dust and particles can show up in every single picture you take at a small enough aperture to bring the foreign matter into sharp focus. No matter how careful you are and how cleanly you work, eventually you will get some of this dust on your camera's sensor.

But as I mentioned, one of the Nikon D60's most useful new features is the automatic sensor cleaning system that reduces or eliminates the need to clean your camera's sensor manually. The sensor vibrates ultrasonically each time the D60 is powered either on or off (or both, at your option), shaking loose any dust.

Although the automatic sensor cleaning feature operates when you power the camera up or turn it off (depending on the behavior you specify in the Setup menu), you can activate it manually at any time. Choose **Clean image sensor** from the Setup menu, and select **Clean now**. If you'd rather specify when automatic cleaning occurs, choose **On** (clean at power up), **Off** (clean when the camera is switched off), **On/Off** (clean at both power up and power down), or **Cleaning off** (no automatic sensor cleaning will take place).

If some dust does collect on your sensor, you can often map it out of your images (making it invisible) using software techniques with the Dust off ref photo feature in the Shooting menu. Operation of this feature is described in Chapter 3.

Of course, even with the Nikon D60's automatic sensor cleaning/dust resistance features, you may still be required to manually clean your sensor from time to time. This section explains the phenomenon and provides some tips on minimizing dust and eliminating it when it begins to affect your shots. I also cover this subject in my book, *Digital SLR Pro Secrets*, with complete instructions for constructing your own sensor cleaning tools. However, I'll provide a condensed version here of some of the information in that book, because sensor dust and sensor cleaning are two of the most contentious subjects Nikon D60 owners have to deal with.

Dust the FAQs, Ma'am.

Here are some of the most frequently asked questions about sensor dust issues.

Q. I see tiny specks in my viewfinder. Do I have dust on my sensor?

A. If you see sharp, well-defined specks, they are clinging to the underside of your focus screen and not on your sensor. They have absolutely no effect on your photographs, and are merely annoying or distracting.

Q. I can see dust on my mirror. How can I remove it?

A. Like focus-screen dust, any artifacts that have settled on your mirror won't affect your photos. You can often remove dust on the mirror or focus screen with a bulb air blower, which will loosen it and whisk it away. Stubborn dust on the focus screen can sometimes be gently flicked away with a soft brush designed for cleaning lenses. I don't recommend brushing the mirror or touching it in any way. The mirror is a special front-surface-silvered optical device (unlike conventional mirrors, which are silvered on the back side of a piece of glass or plastic) and can be easily scratched. If you can't blow mirror dust off, it's best to just forget about it. You can't see it in the viewfinder, anyway.

Q. I see a bright spot in the same place in all of my photos. Is that sensor dust?

A. You've probably got either a "hot" pixel or one that is permanently "stuck" due to a defect in the sensor. A hot pixel is one that shows up as a bright spot only during long exposures as the sensor warms. A pixel stuck in the "on" position always appears in the image. Both show up as bright red, green, or blue pixels, usually surrounded by a small cluster of other improperly illuminated pixels, caused by the camera's interpolating the hot or stuck pixel into its surroundings, as shown in Figure 9.3. A stuck pixel can also be permanently dark. Either kind is likely to show up when they contrast with plain, evenly colored areas of your image.

Finding one or two hot or stuck pixels in your sensor is unfortunately fairly common. They can be "removed" by telling the D60 to ignore them through a simple process called *pixel mapping*. If the bad pixels become bothersome, Nikon can remap your sensor's pixels with a quick trip to a service center.

Bad pixels can also show up on your camera's color LCD panel, but, unless they are abundant, the wisest course is to just ignore them.

Q. I see an irregular out-of-focus blob in the same place in my photos. Is that sensor dust?

A. Yes. Sensor contaminants can take the form of tiny spots, larger blobs, or even curvy lines if they are caused by minuscule fibers that have settled on the sensor. They'll appear out of focus because they aren't actually on the sensor surface but, rather, a fraction of a millimeter above it on the filter that covers the sensor. The smaller the f/stop used, the more in-focus the dust becomes. At large apertures, it may not be visible at all.

Figure 9.3
A stuck pixel is surrounded by improperly interpolated pixels created by the D60's demosaicing algorithm.

Q. I never see any dust on my sensor. What's all the fuss about?

A. Those who never have dust problems with their Nikon D60 fall into one of four categories: those for whom the camera's automatic dust removal features are working well; those who seldom change their lenses and have clean working habits that minimize the amount of dust that invades their cameras in the first place; those who simply don't notice the dust (often because they don't shoot many macro photos or other pictures using the small f/stops that makes dust evident in their images); and those who are very, very lucky.

Identifying and Dealing with Dust

Sensor dust is less of a problem than it might be because it shows up only under certain circumstances. Indeed, you might have dust on your sensor right now and not be aware of it. The dust doesn't actually settle on the sensor itself, but, rather, on a protective filter a very tiny distance above the sensor, subjecting it to the phenomenon of *depth-of-focus*. Depth-of-focus is the distance the focal plane can be moved and still render an object in sharp focus. At f/2.8 to f/5.6 or even smaller, sensor dust, particularly if small, is likely to be outside the range of depth-of-focus and blur into an unnoticeable dot.

However, if you're shooting at f/16 to f/22 or smaller, those dust motes suddenly pop into focus. Forget about trying to spot them by peering directly at your sensor with the shutter open and the lens removed. The period at the end of this sentence, about .33mm in diameter, could block a group of pixels measuring 40 × 40 pixels (160 pixels in all!). Dust spots that are even smaller than that can easily show up in your images if you're shooting large, empty areas that are light colored. Dust motes are most likely to show up in the sky, as in Figure 9.4, or in white backgrounds of your seamless product shots and are less likely to be a problem in images that contain lots of dark areas and detail.

To see if you have dust on your sensor, take a few test shots of a plain, blank surface (such as a piece of paper or a cloudless sky) at small f/stops, such as f/22, and a few wide open. Open Photoshop or another image editor, copy several shots into a single document in separate layers, then flip back and forth between layers to see if any spots you see are present in all layers. You may have to boost contrast and sharpness to make the dust easier to spot.

Avoiding Dust

Of course, the easiest way to protect your sensor from dust is to prevent it from settling on the sensor in the first place. Here are my stock tips for eliminating the problem before it begins.

- **Clean environment.** Avoid working in dusty areas if you can do so. Hah! Serious photographers will take this one with a grain of salt, because it usually makes sense to go where the pictures are. Only a few of us are so paranoid about sensor dust

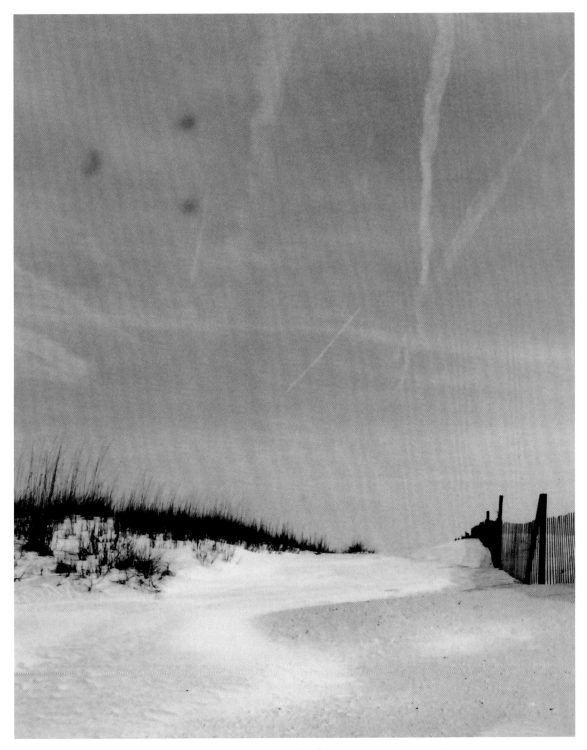

Figure 9.4 Only the dust spots in the sky are apparent in this shot.

(considering that it is so easily removed) that we'll avoid moderately grimy locations just to protect something that is, when you get down to it, just a tool. If you find a great picture opportunity at a raging fire, during a sandstorm, or while surrounded by dust clouds, you might hesitate to take the picture, but, with a little caution (don't remove your lens in these situations, and clean the camera afterwards!) you can still shoot. However, it still makes sense to store your camera in a clean environment. One place cameras and lenses pick up a lot of dust is inside a camera bag. Clean your bag from time to time, and you can avoid problems.

- **Clean lenses.** There are a few paranoid types that avoid swapping lenses in order to minimize the chance of dust getting inside their cameras. It makes more sense just to use a blower or brush to dust off the rear lens mount of the replacement lens first, so you won't be introducing dust into your camera simply by attaching a new, dusty lens. Do this before you remove the current lens from your camera, and then avoid stirring up dust before making the exchange.

- **Work fast.** Minimize the time your camera is lens-less and exposed to dust. That means having your replacement lens ready and dusted off, and a place to set down the old lens as soon as it is removed, so you can quickly attach the new lens.

- **Let gravity help you.** Face the camera downward when the lens is detached so any dust in the mirror box will tend to fall away from the sensor. Turn your back to any breezes, indoor forced air vents, fans, or other sources of dust to minimize infiltration.

- **Protect the lens you just removed.** Once you've attached the new lens, quickly put the end cap on the one you just removed to reduce the dust that might fall on it.

- **Clean out the vestibule.** From time to time, remove the lens while in a relatively dust-free environment and use a blower bulb like the one shown in Figure 9.5 (*not* compressed air or a vacuum hose) to clean out the mirror box area. A blower bulb is generally safer than a can of compressed air, or a strong positive/negative airflow, which can tend to drive dust further into nooks and crannies.

- **Be prepared.** If you're embarking on an important shooting session, it's a good idea to clean your sensor *now*, rather than come home with hundreds or thousands of images with dust spots caused by flecks that were sitting on your sensor before you even started. Before I left on my recent trip to Spain, I put both cameras I was taking through a rigid cleaning regimen, figuring they could remain dust-free for a measly 10 days. I even left my bulky blower bulb at home, and took along a new, smaller version for emergencies.

Figure 9.5
Use a robust air
bulb like the
Giottos Rocket
for cleaning
your sensor.

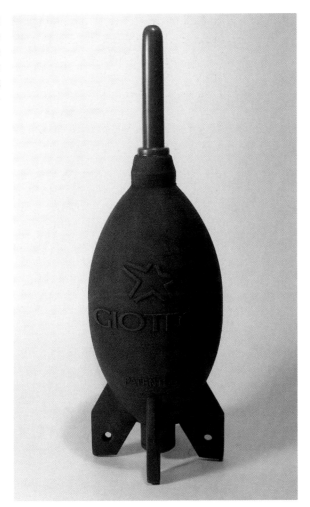

■ **Clone out existing spots in your image editor.** Photoshop and other editors have a clone tool or healing brush you can use to copy pixels from surrounding areas over the dust spot or dead pixel. This process can be tedious, especially if you have lots of dust spots and/or lots of images to be corrected. The advantage is that this sort of manual fix-it probably will do the least damage to the rest of your photo. Only the damaged pixels will be affected.

■ **Use filtration in your image editor.** A semi-smart filter like Photoshop's Dust & Scratches filter can remove dust and other artifacts by selectively blurring areas that the plug-in decides represent dust spots. This method can work well if you have many dust spots, because you won't need to patch them manually. However, any automated method like this has the possibility of blurring areas of your image that you didn't intend to soften.

Sensor Cleaning

Those new to the concept of sensor dust actually hesitate before deciding to clean their camera themselves. Isn't it a better idea to pack up your D60 and send it to a Nikon service center so their crack technical staff can do the job for you? Or, at the very least, shouldn't you let the friendly folks at your local camera store do it?

Of course, if you choose to let someone else clean your sensor, they will be using methods that are more or less identical to the techniques you would use yourself. None of these techniques are difficult, and the only difference between their cleaning and your cleaning is that they might have done it dozens or hundreds of times. If you're careful, you can do just as good a job.

Of course vendors like Nikon won't tell you this, but it's not because they don't trust you. It's not that difficult for a real goofball to mess up their camera by hurrying or taking a shortcut. Perhaps the person uses the "bulb" method of holding the shutter open and a finger slips, allowing the shutter curtain to close on top of a sensor cleaning brush. Or, someone tries to clean the sensor using masking tape, and ends up with goo all over its surface. If Nikon recommended *any* method that's mildly risky, someone would do it wrong, and then the company would face lawsuits from those who'd contend they did it exactly in the way the vendor suggested, so the ruined camera is not their fault.

You can see that vendors like Nikon tend to be conservative in their recommendations, and, in doing so, make it seem as if sensor cleaning is more daunting and dangerous than it really is. Some vendors recommend only dust-off cleaning, through the use of reasonably gentle blasts of air, while condemning more serious scrubbing with swabs and cleaning fluids. However, these cleaning kits for the exact types of cleaning they recommended against are for sale in Japan only, where, apparently, your average photographer is more dexterous than those of us in the rest of the world. These kits are similar to those used by official repair staff to clean your sensor if you decide to send your camera in for a dust-up.

As I noted, sensors can be affected by dust particles that are much smaller than you might be able to spot visually on the surface of your lens. The filters that cover sensors tend to be fairly hard compared to optical glass. Cleaning the 23.6mm × 15.8mm sensor in your Nikon D60 within the tight confines of the mirror box can call for a steady hand and careful touch. If your sensor's filter becomes scratched through inept cleaning, you can't simply remove it yourself and replace it with a new one.

There are four basic kinds of cleaning processes that can be used to remove dusty and sticky stuff that settles on your dSLR's sensor. All of these must be performed with the shutter locked open. I'll describe these methods and provide instructions for locking the shutter later in this section.

- **Air cleaning.** This process involves squirting blasts of air inside your camera with the shutter locked open. This works well for dust that's not clinging stubbornly to your sensor.

- **Brushing.** A soft, very fine brush is passed across the surface of the sensor's filter, dislodging mildly persistent dust particles and sweeping them off the imager.

- **Liquid cleaning.** A soft swab dipped in a cleaning solution such as ethanol is used to wipe the sensor filter, removing more obstinate particles.

- **Tape cleaning.** There are some who get good results by applying a special form of tape to the surface of their sensor. When the tape is peeled off, all the dust goes with it. Supposedly. I'd be remiss if I didn't point out right now that this form of cleaning is somewhat controversial; the other three methods are much more widely accepted.

Placing the Mirror/Shutter in the Locked and Fully Upright Position for Landing

Make sure you're using a fully charged battery or a Nikon AC adapter. Fortunately, the Nikon D60 is smart enough that it won't let you try to clean the sensor manually unless the battery has a sufficient charge.

1. Remove the lens from the camera and then turn the camera on.

2. You'll find the **Mirror lock-up** menu choice in the Setup menu. Select it.

3. Choose **On**. The mirror will flip up when you press the shutter release button, and the shutter will open.

4. Remove the lens from the camera.

5. Use one of the methods described below to remove dust and grime from your sensor. Be careful not to accidentally switch the power off or open the Secure Digital card or battery compartment doors as you work. If that happens, the shutter may be damaged if it closes onto your cleaning tool.

6. When you're finished, turn the power off, replace your lens, and switch your camera back on.

Air Cleaning

Your first attempts at cleaning your sensor should always involve gentle blasts of air. Many times, you'll be able to dislodge dust spots, which will fall off the sensor and, with luck, out of the mirror box. Attempt one of the other methods only when you've already tried air cleaning and it didn't remove all the dust.

Here are some tips for doing air cleaning:

- **Use a clean, powerful air bulb.** Your best bet is bulb cleaners designed for the job, like the Giottos Rocket shown in Figure 9.5. Smaller bulbs, like those air bulbs with a brush attached sometimes sold for lens cleaning or weak nasal aspirators may not provide sufficient air or a strong enough blast to do much good.

- **Hold the Nikon D60 upside down.** Then look up into the mirror box as you squirt your air blasts, increasing the odds that gravity will help pull the expelled dust downward, away from the sensor. You may have to use some imagination in positioning yourself.

- **Never use air canisters.** The propellant inside these cans can permanently coat your sensor if you tilt the can while spraying. It's not worth taking a chance.

- **Avoid air compressors.** Super-strong blasts of air are likely to force dust under the sensor filter and possibly damage some internal parts.

Brush Cleaning

If your dust is a little more stubborn and can't be dislodged by air alone, you may want to try a brush, charged with static electricity, which can pick off dust spots by electrical attraction. One good, but expensive, option is the Sensor Brush sold at www.visible-dust.com. A cheaper version can be purchased at www.copperhillimages.com. You need a 16mm version, like the one shown in Figure 9.6, which can be stroked across the short dimension of your D60's sensor.

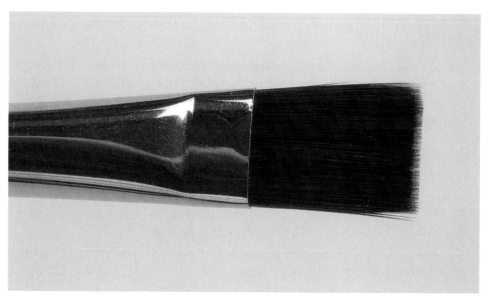

Figure 9.6
A proper brush, such as this 16mm wide utensil, is required for dusting off your sensor.

Ordinary artist's brushes are much too coarse and stiff and have fibers that are tangled or can come loose and settle on your sensor. A good sensor brush's fibers are resilient and described as "thinner than a human hair." Moreover, the brush has a wooden handle that reduces the risk of static sparks. Check out my *Digital SLR Pro Secrets* book if you want to make a sensor brush (or sensor swabs) yourself.

Brush cleaning is done with a dry brush by gently swiping the surface of the sensor filter with the tip. The dust particles are attracted to the brush particles and cling to them. You should clean the brush with compressed air before and after each use, and store it in an appropriate air-tight container between applications to keep it clean and dust-free. Although these special brushes are expensive, one should last you a long time.

Liquid Cleaning

Unfortunately, you'll often encounter really stubborn dust spots that can't be removed with a blast of air or flick of a brush. These spots may be combined with some grease or a liquid that causes them to stick to the sensor filter's surface. In such cases, liquid cleaning with a swab may be necessary. During my first clumsy attempts to clean my own sensor, I accidentally got my blower bulb tip too close to the sensor, and some sort of deposit from the tip of the bulb ended up on the sensor. I panicked until I discovered that liquid cleaning did a good job of removing whatever it was that took up residence on my sensor.

You can make your own swabs out of pieces of plastic (some use fast food restaurant knives, with the tip cut at an angle to the proper size) covered with a soft cloth or Pec-Pad, as shown in Figures 9.7 and 9.8. However, if you've got the bucks to spend, you can't go wrong with good-quality commercial sensor cleaning swabs, such as those sold by Photographic Solutions, Inc. (www.photosol.com/swabproduct.htm).

You want a sturdy swab that won't bend or break so you can apply gentle pressure to the swab as you wipe the sensor surface. Use the swab with methanol (as pure as you can get it, particularly medical grade; other ingredients can leave a residue), or the Eclipse 2 solution also sold by Photographic Solutions. Eclipse 2 (see Figure 9.9) is actually quite a bit purer than even medical-grade methanol. A couple drops of solution should be enough, unless you have a spot that's extremely difficult to remove. In that case, you may need to use extra solution on the swab to help "soak" the dirt off. Note: the E2 version of Eclipse is now recommended for cleaning what are termed "tin oxide" sensors, similar to the Nikon D60. If you have some of the older Eclipse solution, it's great for cleaning lenses! Buy the new stuff to be safe.

Once you overcome your nervousness at touching your D60's sensor, the process is easy. You'll wipe continuously with the swab in one direction, then flip it over and wipe in the other direction. You need to completely wipe the entire surface; otherwise, you may end up depositing the dust you collect at the far end of your stroke. Wipe; don't rub.

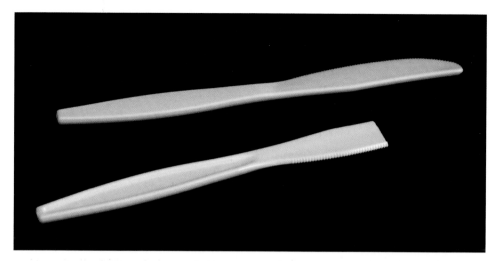

Figure 9.7
You can make your own sensor swab from a plastic knife that's been truncated.

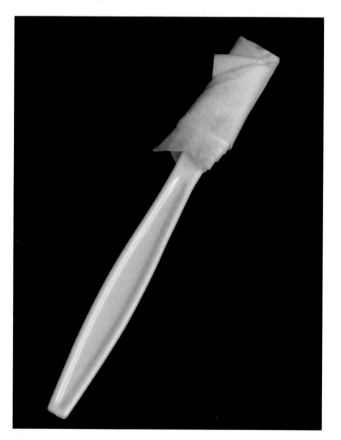

Figure 9.8 Carefully wrap a Pec-Pad around the swab.

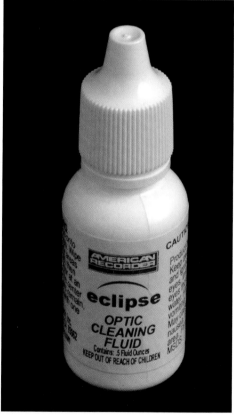

Figure 9.9 Pure Eclipse solution makes the best sensor cleaning liquid.

Tape Cleaning

There are people who absolutely swear by the tape method of sensor cleaning. The concept seems totally wacky, and I have never tried it personally, so I can't say with certainty that it either does or does not work. In the interest of completeness, I'm including it here. I can't give you a recommendation, so if you have problems, please don't blame me. The Nikon D60 is still too new to have generated any reports of users accidentally damaging the anti-dust coating on the sensor filter using this method.

Tape cleaning works by applying a layer of Scotch Brand Magic Tape to the sensor. This is a minimally sticky tape that some of the tape cleaning proponents claim contains no adhesive. I did check this out with 3M, and can say that Magic Tape certainly *does* contain an adhesive. The question is whether the adhesive comes off when you peel back the tape, taking any dust spots on your sensor with it. The folks who love this method claim there is no residue. There have been reports from those who don't like the method that residue is left behind. This is all anecdotal evidence, so you're pretty much on your own in making the decision whether to try out the tape cleaning method.

Glossary

It's always handy to have a single resource where you can look up various terms you'll encounter while working with your digital camera. Here is the latest update of a glossary I've compiled over the years, with some new additions specifically for the Nikon D60.

AE-L/AF-L A button on the D60 that allows locking exposure and/or focus point prior to taking a photo.

ambient lighting Diffuse, non-directional lighting that doesn't appear to come from a specific source but, rather, bounces off walls, ceilings, and other objects in the scene when a picture is taken.

analog/digital converter The module in a camera that electronically converts the analog information captured by the D60's sensor into digital bits that can be stored as an image.

angle of view The area of a scene that a lens can capture, determined by the focal length of the lens. Lenses with a shorter focal length have a wider angle of view than lenses with a longer focal length.

anti-alias A process that smoothes the look of rough edges in images (called *jaggies* or *staircasing*) by adding partially transparent pixels along the boundaries of diagonal lines that are merged into a smoother line by our eyes. *See also* jaggies.

aperture The size of the opening in the iris or diaphragm of a lens, relative to the lens's focal length. Also called an *f/stop*. For example, with a lens having a focal length of 100mm, an f/stop with a diameter of 12.5mm would produce an aperture value of f/8.

aperture priority A camera setting that allows you to specify the lens opening or f/stop that you want to use, with the camera selecting the required shutter speed automatically based on its light-meter reading. *See also* shutter priority.

artifact A type of noise in an image, or an unintentional image component produced in error by a digital camera during processing, usually caused by the JPEG compression process in digital cameras, or, in some cases, by dust settling on the sensor.

aspect ratio The proportions of an image as printed, displayed on a monitor, or captured by a digital camera.

autofocus A camera setting that allows the Nikon D60 to choose the correct focus distance for you, based on the contrast of an image (the image will be at maximum contrast when in sharp focus). The camera can be set for *Single-Servo Autofocus (AF-S)*, in which the lens is not focused until the shutter release is partially depressed, *Continuous-Servo Autofocus (AF-C)*, in which the lens refocuses constantly as you frame and reframe the image, and *Automatic Autofocus (AF-A)* in which the D60 focuses using AF-S mode, but switches to AF-C mode if the subject starts to move while the picture is framing. The D60 can also be set for *Manual* focus.

backlighting A lighting effect produced when the main light source is located behind the subject. Backlighting can be used to create a silhouette effect, or to illuminate translucent objects. *See also* front lighting *and* sidelighting.

barrel distortion A lens defect that causes straight lines at the top or side edges of an image to bow outward into a barrel shape. *See also* pincushion distortion.

blooming An image distortion caused when a photosite in an image sensor has absorbed all the photons it can handle so that additional photons reaching that pixel overflow to affect surrounding pixels, producing unwanted brightness and overexposure around the edges of objects.

blur To soften an image or part of an image by throwing it out of focus, or by allowing it to become soft due to subject or camera motion. Blur can also be applied creatively in an image-editing program.

bokeh A term derived from the Japanese word for blur, which describes the aesthetic qualities of the out-of-focus parts of an image. Some lenses produce "good" bokeh and others offer "bad" bokeh. Some lenses produce uniformly illuminated out-of-focus discs. Others produce a disc that has a bright edge and a dark center, producing a "doughnut" effect, which is the worst from a bokeh standpoint. Lenses that generate a bright center that fades to a darker edge are favored, because their bokeh allows the circle of confusion to blend more smoothly with the surroundings. The bokeh characteristics of a lens are most important when you're using selective focus (say, when shooting a portrait) to deemphasize the background, or when shallow depth-of-field is a given because you're working with a macro lens, with a long telephoto, or with a wide-open aperture. *See also* circle of confusion.

bounce lighting Light bounced off a reflector, including ceiling and walls, to provide a soft, natural-looking light.

buffer The digital camera's internal memory where an image is stored immediately after it is taken until it can be written to the camera's non-volatile (semi-permanent) memory card.

burst mode The digital camera's equivalent of the film camera's motor drive, used to take multiple shots within a short period of time, each stored in a memory buffer temporarily before writing them to the media.

calibration A process used to correct for the differences in the output of a printer or monitor when compared to the original image. Once you've calibrated your scanner, monitor, and/or your image editor, the images you see on the screen more closely represent what you'll get from your printer, even though calibration is never perfect.

Camera Raw A plug-in included with Photoshop and Photoshop Elements that can manipulate the unprocessed images captured by digital cameras, such as the Nikon D60's .NEF files. The latest versions of this module can also work with JPEG and TIFF images.

camera shake Movement of the camera, aggravated by slower shutter speeds, which produces a blurred image.

center-weighted meter A light-measuring device that emphasizes the area in the middle of the frame when calculating the correct exposure for an image. *See also* spot meter.

channel In an electronic flash, a channel is a protocol used to communicate between a master flash unit and the remote units slaved to that main flash. The ability to change channels allows several master flash units to operate in the same environment without interfering with each other.

chromatic aberration An image defect, often seen as green or purple fringing around the edges of an object, caused by a lens failing to focus all colors of a light source at the same point. *See also* fringing.

circle of confusion A term applied to the fuzzy discs produced when a point of light is out of focus. The circle of confusion is not a fixed size. The viewing distance and amount of enlargement of the image determine whether we see a particular spot on the image as a point or as a disc. *See also* bokeh.

close-up lens A lens add-on that allows you to take pictures at a distance that is less than the closest-focusing distance of the lens alone.

color correction Changing the relative amounts of color in an image to produce a desired effect, typically a more accurate representation of those colors. Color correction can fix faulty color balance in the original image, or compensate for the deficiencies of the inks used to reproduce the image.

compression Reducing the size of a file by encoding using fewer bits of information to represent the original. Some compression schemes, such as JPEG, operate by discarding some image information, while others, such as RAW, preserve all the detail in the original, discarding only redundant data.

continuous-servo autofocus An automatic focusing setting (AF-C) in which the camera constantly refocuses the image as you frame the picture. This setting is often the best choice for moving subjects. *See also* single-servo autofocus.

contrast The range between the lightest and darkest tones in an image. A high-contrast image is one in which the shades fall at the extremes of the range between white and black. In a low-contrast image, the tones are closer together.

Creative Lighting System (CLS) Nikon's electronic flash system used to coordinate exposure, camera information, and timing between a camera's built-in flash (if present) and external flash units, which can be linked through direct electrical connections or wirelessly.

Custom Settings A group of different settings you can make to specify how the Nikon D60 behaves, such as the function of certain controls, electronic flash features, and other customizable attributes.

dedicated flash An electronic flash unit, such as the Nikon SB-600 Speedlight, designed to work with the automatic exposure features of a specific camera.

depth-of-field A distance range in a photograph in which all included portions of an image are at least acceptably sharp.

diaphragm An adjustable component, similar to the iris in the human eye, which can open and close to provide specific-sized lens openings, or f/stops and thus control the amount of light reaching the sensor or film.

diffuse lighting Soft, low-contrast lighting.

digital processing chip A solid-state device found in digital cameras that's in charge of applying the image algorithms to the raw picture data prior to storage on the memory card.

diopter A value used to represent the magnification power of a lens, calculated as the reciprocal of a lens's focal length (in meters). Diopters are most often used to represent the optical correction used in a viewfinder to adjust for limitations of the photographer's eyesight, and to describe the magnification of a close-up lens attachment.

equivalent focal length A digital camera's focal length translated into the corresponding values for a 35mm film camera. This value can be calculated for lenses used with the Nikon D60 by multiplying by 1.5.

exchangeable image file format (Exif) Developed to standardize the exchange of image data between hardware devices and software. A variation on JPEG, Exif is used by most digital cameras, and includes information such as the date and time a photo was taken, the camera settings, resolution, amount of compression, and other data.

Exif *See* exchangeable image file format (Exif).

exposure The amount of light allowed to reach the film or sensor, determined by the intensity of the light, the amount admitted by the iris of the lens, the length of time determined by the shutter speed, and the sensitivity of the sensor or film to light.

exposure compensation Exposure compensation, which uses exposure value (EV) settings, is a way of adding or decreasing exposure without the need to reference f/stops or shutter speeds. For example, if you tell your camera to add +1EV, it will provide twice as much exposure, either by using a larger f/stop, slower shutter speed, or both. The D60 offers both conventional exposure compensation and flash exposure compensation.

fill lighting In photography, lighting used to illuminate shadows. Reflectors or additional incandescent lighting or electronic flash can be used to brighten shadows. One common technique outdoors is to use the camera's flash as a fill in sunlit situations.

filter In photography, a device that fits over the lens, changing the light in some way. In image editing, a feature that changes the pixels in an image to produce blurring, sharpening, and other special effects. Photoshop includes several interesting filter effects, including Lens Blur and Photo Filters.

flash sync The timing mechanism that insures that an internal or external electronic flash fires at the correct time during the exposure cycle. A digital SLR's flash sync speed is the highest shutter speed that can be used with flash, ordinarily 1/200th of a second with the Nikon D60. *See also* front-curtain sync *and* rear-curtain sync.

focal plane An imaginary line, perpendicular to the optical axis, which passes through the focal point forming a plane of sharp focus when the lens is set at infinity. A focal plane indicator is etched into the Nikon D60 on the top panel.

focal length The distance between the film and the optical center of the lens when the lens is focused on infinity, usually measured in millimeters.

focus tracking The ability of the automatic focus feature of a camera to change focus as the distance between the subject and the camera changes. One type of focus tracking is *predictive,* in which the mechanism anticipates the motion of the object being focused on, and adjusts the focus to suit.

format To erase a memory card and prepare it to accept files.

fringing A chromatic aberration that produces fringes of color around the edges of subjects, caused by a lens's inability to focus the various wavelengths of light onto the same spot. Purple fringing is especially troublesome with backlit images.

front-curtain sync (first-curtain sync) The default kind of electronic flash synchronization technique, originally associated with focal plane shutters, which consists of a traveling set of curtains, including a *front curtain*, which opens to reveal the film or sensor, and a *rear curtain*, which follows at a distance determined by shutter speed to conceal the film or sensor at the conclusion of the exposure. For a flash picture to be taken, the entire sensor must be exposed at one time to the brief flash exposure, so the image is exposed after the front curtain has reached the other side of the focal plane, but before the rear curtain begins to move. Front-curtain sync causes the flash to fire at the beginning of this period when the shutter is completely open, in the instant that the first curtain of the focal plane shutter finishes its movement across the film or sensor plane. With slow shutter speeds, this feature can create a blur effect from the ambient light, showing as patterns that follow a moving subject with the subject shown sharply frozen at the beginning of the blur trail. *See also* rear-curtain sync.

front lighting Illumination that comes from the direction of the camera. *See also* backlighting *and* sidelighting.

f/stop The relative size of the lens aperture, which helps determine both exposure and depth-of-field. The larger the f/stop number, the smaller the f/stop itself.

graduated filter A lens attachment with variable density or color from one edge to another. A graduated neutral density filter, for example, can be oriented so the neutral density portion is concentrated at the top of the lens's view with the less dense or clear portion at the bottom, thus reducing the amount of light from a very bright sky while not interfering with the exposure of the landscape in the foreground. Graduated filters can also be split into several color sections to provide a color gradient between portions of the image.

gray card A piece of cardboard or other material with a standardized 18-percent reflectance. Gray cards can be used as a reference for determining correct exposure or for setting white balance.

group A way of bundling more than one wireless flash unit into a single cluster that all share the same flash output setting, as controlled by the master flash unit.

high contrast A wide range of density in a print, negative, or other image.

highlights The brightest parts of an image containing detail.

histogram A kind of chart showing the relationship of tones in an image using a series of 256 vertical bars, one for each brightness level. A histogram chart, such as the one the Nikon D60 can display during picture review, typically looks like a curve with one or more slopes and peaks, depending on how many highlight, midtone, and shadow tones are present in the image.

hot shoe A mount on top of a camera used to hold an electronic flash, while providing an electrical connection between the flash and the camera. Also called an accessory shoe.

hyperfocal distance A point of focus where everything from half that distance to infinity appears to be acceptably sharp. For example, if your lens has a hyperfocal distance of four feet, everything from two feet to infinity would be sharp. The hyperfocal distance varies by the lens and the aperture in use. If you know you'll be making a grab shot without warning, sometimes it is useful to turn off your camera's automatic focus, and set the lens to infinity, or, better yet, the hyperfocal distance. Then, you can snap off a quick picture without having to wait for the lag that occurs with most digital cameras as their autofocus locks in.

image rotation A feature that senses whether a picture was taken in horizontal or vertical orientation. That information is embedded in the picture file so that the camera and compatible software applications can automatically display the image in the correct orientation.

image stabilization A technology that compensates for camera shake, usually by adjusting the position of the camera sensor or (with Nikon technology) by rearranging the position of certain lens elements in response to movements of the camera.

incident light Light falling on a surface.

International Organization for Standardization (ISO) A governing body that provides standards used to represent film speed, or the equivalent sensitivity of a digital camera's sensor. Digital camera sensitivity is expressed in ISO settings.

interpolation A technique digital cameras, scanners, and image editors use to create new pixels required whenever you resize or change the resolution of an image based on the values of surrounding pixels. Devices such as scanners and digital cameras can also use interpolation to create pixels in addition to those actually captured, thereby increasing the apparent resolution or color information in an image.

ISO *See* International Organization for Standardization (ISO).

i-TTL Nikon's intelligent through the lens flash metering system, which uses preflashes to calculate exposure and to communicate between flash units, using the camera's 420-sensor viewfinder exposure meter.

jaggies Staircasing effect of lines that are not perfectly horizontal or vertical, caused by pixels that are too large to represent the line accurately. *See also* anti-alias.

JPEG A file "lossy" format (short for Joint Photographic Experts Group) that supports 24-bit color and reduces file sizes by selectively discarding image data. Digital cameras generally use JPEG compression to pack more images onto memory cards. You can select how much compression is used (and, therefore, how much information is thrown away) by selecting from among the Standard, Fine, Super Fine, or other quality settings offered by your camera. *See also* RAW.

Kelvin (K) A unit of measure based on the absolute temperature scale in which absolute zero is zero; it's used to describe the color of continuous-spectrum light sources and applied when setting white balance. For example, daylight has a color temperature of about 5,500K, and a tungsten lamp has a temperature of about 3,400K.

lag time The interval between when the shutter is pressed and when the picture is actually taken. During that span, the camera may be automatically focusing and calculating exposure. With digital SLRs like the Nikon D60, lag time is generally very short; with non-dSLRs, the elapsed time easily can be one second or more under certain conditions.

latitude The degree by which exposure can be varied and still produce an acceptable photo.

lens flare A feature of conventional photography that is both a bane and a creative outlet. It is an effect produced by the reflection of light internally among elements of an optical lens. Bright light sources within or just outside the field of view cause lens flare. Flare can be reduced by the use of coatings on the lens elements or with the use of lens hoods. Photographers sometimes use the effect as a creative technique, and Photoshop includes a filter that lets you add lens flare at your whim.

lighting ratio The proportional relationship between the amount of light falling on the subject from the main light and other lights, expressed in a ratio, such as 3:1.

lossless compression An image-compression scheme, such as TIFF, that preserves all image detail. When the image is decompressed, it is identical to the original version.

lossy compression An image-compression scheme, such as JPEG, that creates smaller files by discarding image information, which can affect image quality.

macro lens A lens that provides continuous focusing from infinity to extreme close-ups, often to a reproduction ratio of 1:2 (half life-size) or 1:1 (life-size).

matrix metering A system of exposure calculation that looks at many different segments of an image to determine the brightest and darkest portions, and bases f/stop and shutter speed on settings derived from a database of images.

maximum burst   The number of frames that can be exposed at the current settings until the buffer fills.

midtones   Parts of an image with tones of an intermediate value, usually in the 25 to 75 percent brightness range. Many image-editing features allow you to manipulate midtones independently from the highlights and shadows.

mirror lock-up   The ability of the D60 to retract its mirror to allow access to the sensor for cleaning.

neutral color   A color in which red, green, and blue are present in equal amounts, producing a gray.

neutral density filter   A gray camera filter that reduces the amount of light entering the camera without affecting the colors.

noise   In an image, pixels with randomly distributed color values. Noise in digital photographs tends to be the product of low-light conditions and long exposures, particularly when you've set your camera to a higher ISO rating than normal.

noise reduction   A technology used to cut down on the amount of random information in a digital picture, usually caused by long exposures at increased sensitivity ratings.

normal lens   A lens that makes the image in a photograph appear in a perspective that is like that of the original scene, typically with a field of view of roughly 45 degrees.

overexposure   A condition in which too much light reaches the film or sensor, producing a dense negative or a very bright/light print, slide, or digital image.

pincushion distortion   A type of lens distortion in which lines at the top and side edges of an image are bent inward, producing an effect that looks like a pincushion. *See also* barrel distortion.

polarizing filter   A filter that forces light, which normally vibrates in all directions, to vibrate only in a single plane, reducing or removing the specular reflections from the surface of objects.

RAW   An image file format, such as the NEF format in the Nikon D60, which includes all the unprocessed information captured by the camera after conversion to digital form. RAW files are very large compared to JPEG files and must be processed by a special program such as Nikon Capture NX or Adobe's Camera RAW filter after being downloaded from the camera.

rear-curtain sync (second-curtain sync) An optional kind of electronic flash synchronization technique, originally associated with focal plane shutters, which consists of a traveling set of curtains, including a *front (first) curtain* (which opens to reveal the film or sensor) and a *rear (second) curtain* (which follows at a distance determined by shutter speed to conceal the film or sensor at the conclusion of the exposure). For a flash picture to be taken, the entire sensor must be exposed at one time to the brief flash exposure, so the image is exposed after the front curtain has reached the other side of the focal plane, but before the rear curtain begins to move. Rear-curtain sync causes the flash to fire at the end of the exposure, an instant before the second or rear curtain of the focal plane shutter begins to move. With slow shutter speeds, this feature can create a blur effect from the ambient light, showing as patterns that follow a moving subject with the subject shown sharply frozen at the end of the blur trail. If you were shooting a photo of The Flash, the superhero would appear sharp, with a ghostly trail behind him. *See also* front-curtain sync (first-curtain sync).

red-eye An effect from flash photography that appears to make a person's eyes glow red, or an animal's yellow or green. It's caused by light bouncing from the retina of the eye and is most pronounced in dim illumination (when the irises are wide open) and when the electronic flash is close to the lens and, therefore, prone to reflect directly back. Image editors can fix red-eye through cloning other pixels over the offending red or orange ones.

RGB color A color model that represents the three colors--red, green, and blue--used by devices such as scanners or monitors to reproduce color. Photoshop works in RGB mode by default, and even displays CMYK images by converting them to RGB.

saturation The purity of color; the amount by which a pure color is diluted with white or gray.

selective focus Choosing a lens opening that produces a shallow depth-of-field. Usually this is used to isolate a subject in portraits, close-ups, and other types of images, by causing most other elements in the scene to be blurred.

self-timer A mechanism that delays the opening of the shutter for some seconds after the release has been operated.

sensitivity A measure of the degree of response of a film or sensor to light, measured using the ISO setting.

shadow The darkest part of an image, represented on a digital image by pixels with low numeric values.

sharpening Increasing the apparent sharpness of an image by boosting the contrast between adjacent pixels that form an edge.

shutter In a conventional film camera, the shutter is a mechanism consisting of blades, a curtain, a plate, or some other movable cover that controls the time during which light reaches the film. Digital cameras can use both a mechanical shutter and an electronic shutter for higher effective speeds.

shutter priority An exposure mode in which you set the shutter speed and the camera determines the appropriate f/stop. *See also* aperture priority.

sidelighting Applying illumination from the left or right sides of the camera. *See also* backlighting *and* front lighting.

slave unit An accessory flash unit that supplements the main flash, usually triggered electronically when the slave senses the light output by the main unit, or through radio waves.

slow sync An electronic flash synchronizing method that uses a slow shutter speed so that ambient light is recorded by the camera in addition to the electronic flash illumination. This allows the background to receive more exposure for a more realistic effect.

specular highlight Bright spots in an image caused by reflection of light sources.

spot meter An exposure system that concentrates on a small area in the image. *See also* center-weighted meter.

time exposure A picture taken by leaving the shutter open for a long period, usually more than one second. The camera is generally locked down with a tripod to prevent blur during the long exposure.

through the lens (TTL) A system of providing viewing and exposure calculation through the actual lens taking the picture.

tungsten light Light from ordinary room lamps and ceiling fixtures, as opposed to fluorescent illumination.

underexposure A condition in which too little light reaches the film or sensor, producing a thin negative, a dark slide, a muddy-looking print, or a dark digital image.

unsharp masking The process for increasing the contrast between adjacent pixels in an image, increasing sharpness, especially around edges.

vignetting Dark corners of an image, often produced by using a lens hood that is too small for the field of view, a lens that does not completely fill the image frame, or generated artificially using image-editing techniques.

white balance The adjustment of a digital camera to the color temperature of the light source. Interior illumination is relatively red; outdoor light is relatively blue. Digital cameras like the Nikon D60 set correct white balance automatically or let you do it through menus. Image editors can often do some color correction of images that were exposed using the wrong white balance setting, especially when working with RAW files that contain the information originally captured by the camera before white balance was applied.

zoom head The capability of an electronic flash to change the area of its coverage to more closely match the focal length setting of a prime or zoom lens.

Index

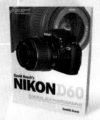
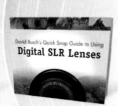
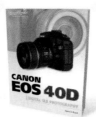
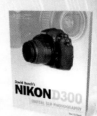
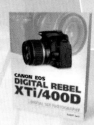
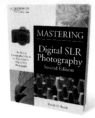
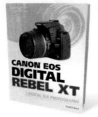
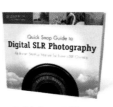
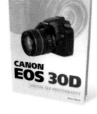
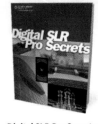

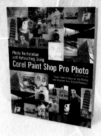
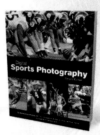
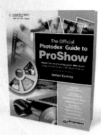
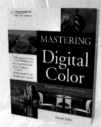
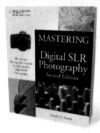
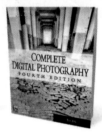
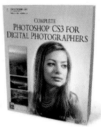
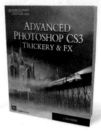
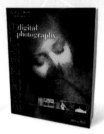
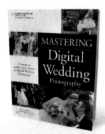
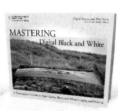
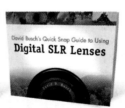
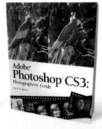
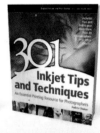